THE CONSTITUTION

OF THE

PRESBYTERIAN CHURCH (U.S.A.)

PART II

BOOK OF ORDER

2013–2015

THE CONSTITUTION

OF THE

PRESBYTERIAN CHURCH (U.S.A.)

PART II

BOOK OF ORDER
2013–2015

PUBLISHED BY
THE OFFICE OF THE GENERAL ASSEMBLY

100 Witherspoon Street
Louisville, KY 40202-1396

Library of Congress Cataloging-in-Publication Data

ISBN 978-0-9837536-2-9

Printed in the United States of America

Additional copies available from Presbyterian Distribution Services (PDS)
100 Witherspoon Street, Louisville, KY 40202-1396, by calling 1-800-524-2612 (PDS)

Please specify PDS order #OGA-13-001—Standard Print Version

PREFACE

The Constitution of the Presbyterian Church (U.S.A.), as defined in F-3.04, consists of the *Book of Confessions* (Part I) and the *Book of Order* (Part II).

The *Book of Confessions* contains the Nicene Creed, the Apostles' Creed, the Scots Confession, the Heidelberg Catechism, the Second Helvetic Confession, the Westminster Confession of Faith, the Shorter Catechism, the Larger Catechism, the Theological Declaration of Barmen, the Confession of 1967, and A Brief Statement of Faith—Presbyterian Church (U.S.A.).

The *Book of Order* contains the Foundations of Presbyterian Polity, the Form of Government, the Directory for Worship, and the Rules of Discipline.

In this *Book of Order*

(1) SHALL and IS TO BE/ARE TO BE signify practice that is mandated,

(2) SHOULD signifies practice that is strongly recommended,

(3) IS APPROPRIATE signifies practice that is commended as suitable,

(4) MAY signifies practice that is permissible but not required.

(5) ADVISORY HANDBOOK signifies a handbook produced by agencies of the General Assembly to guide synods and presbyteries in procedures related to the oversight of ministry. Such handbooks suggest procedures that are commended, but not required.

The 219th General Assembly (2010) took action to replace the Form of Government with a new Foundations of Presbyterian Polity and a new Form of Government. In light of the addition of the Foundations of Presbyterian Polity and the revision of the Form of Government (2011), the following terms in use in the Directory for Worship and in the Rules of Discipline have been replaced with terms employed in the new and revised documents: "minister" or "minister of the Word and Sacrament" with "teaching elder"; "elder" with "ruling elder"; "governing body" with "council"; "commissioned lay pastor" with "ruling elder commissioned to particular pastoral service" or "ruling elder commissioned to pastoral service"; "office" or "ordained office" with "ordered ministry"; and "officer/s," "church officer/s," or "ordained officer/s" with "[person/those in] ordered ministry."

The amendments to the Form of Government, Directory for Worship, and Rules of Discipline, proposed to the presbyteries by the 220th General Assembly (2012) and approved by a majority of the presbyteries, are included in this volume. Words that have been stricken are omitted from the text. New wording appears in boldface within the appropriate paragraph. These amendments take effect on July 7, 2013. Amendments have been made in the following places:

Book of Order	Minutes, 2012	Book of Order	Minutes, 2012
G-1.0503	26, 27, 591–92	D-3.0101b(2)	26, 28, 612
G-3.0104	26, 28, 614	D-5.0101	20, 23, 342
G-3.0109a	20, 23, 341	D-5.0106	20, 23, 342
G-3.0109b(6)	20, 23, 341–42	D-5.0203	20, 23, 342
G-3.0301	26, 578	D-5.0206	20, 23, 342–43
G-3.0302d	72–73, 241	D-6.0101	20, 23, 343
G-3.0305	26, 28, 614	D-6.0202a(6)	20, 23, 343
G-3.0404	20, 23, 342	D-10.0106	26, 27, 590
W-4.4002	12, 13, 1496–1497	D-10.0202	26, 572–73

June 2013

Gradye Parsons
Stated Clerk of the General Assembly
Presbyterian Church (U.S.A.)

EXPLANATION OF THE
REFERENCE NUMBER SYSTEM
OF THE
BOOK OF ORDER

The four parts of the *Book of Order* are abbreviated by the use of capital letters:

F — The Foundations of Presbyterian Polity

G — Form of Government

W — Directory for Worship

D — Rules of Discipline

Each reference in the text begins with the appropriate letter. The numeral appearing after the letter, and to the left of the decimal, indicates the chapter number. There are four numerals to the right of the decimal. The first two indicate the number of a section. The second two indicate the number of the subsection.

Each page is noted in numerals preceded by the proper letter to identify the material that appears on it. For example, in the Foundations of Presbyterian Polity, the first page of Chapter One bears the notation:

F-1.01–F-1.02
F-1.0201–1.0202

This indicates that Chapter One of the Foundations of Presbyterian Polity begins here and the page includes sections 1.01 and 1.02 with two titled subsections: 1.0201 and 1.0202.

The chapters and sections of the *Book of Order* are so notated that it is possible for chapters and sections to be added by amendment without changing any of the present notations.

This notation makes it possible for citations to the *Book of Order* in minutes, reports, and correspondence to remain the same from year to year in English, Korean, Spanish, and Braille editions.

CONTENTS

THE FOUNDATIONS OF PRESBYTERIAN POLITY

Chapter One: The Mission of the Church

God's Mission...F-1.01

Jesus Christ Is Head of the Church...................................F-1.02
    The Authority of Christ...F-1.0201
    Christ Calls and Equips the Church..........................F-1.0202
    Christ Gives the Church Its Life...............................F-1.0203
    Christ Is the Church's Hope......................................F-1.0204
    Christ Is the Foundation of the Church......................F-1.0205

The Calling of the Church...F-1.03
    The Church Is the Body of Christ..............................F-1.0301
    The Marks of the Church...F-1.0302
    The Notes of the Reformed Church............................F-1.0303
    The Great Ends of the Church...................................F-1.0304

Openness to the Guidance of the Holy Spirit......................F-1.04
    Continuity and Change...F-1.0401
    Ecumenicity..F-1.0402
    Unity in Diversity...F-1.0403
    Openness..F-1.0404

Chapter Two: The Church and Its Confessions

The Purpose of Confessional Statements............................F-2.01

The Confessions as Subordinate Standards F-2.02

The Confessions as Statements of the Faith of the
    Church Catholic F-2.03

The Confessions as Statements of the Faith of the
    Protestant Reformation F-2.04

The Confessions as Statements of the Faith of the
    Reformed Tradition...F-2.05

Chapter Three: Principles of Order and Government

Historic Principles of Church Order F-3.01
    God Is Lord of the Conscience.................................F-3.0101
    Corporate Judgment F-3.0102

Officers F-3.0103
Truth and Goodness F-3.0104
Mutual Forbearance F-3.0105
Election by the People F-3.0106
Church Power F-3.0107
The Value of Ecclesiastical Discipline F-3.0108

Principles of Presbyterian Government F-3.02
One Church F-3.0201
Governed by Presbyters F-3.0202
Gathered in Councils F-3.0203
Seek and Represent the Will of Christ F-3.0204
Decision by Majority Vote F-3.0205
Review and Control F-3.0206
Ordination by Council F-3.0207
Shared Power, Exercised Jointly F-3.0208
General Authority of Councils F-3.0209

Foundational Statements F-3.03

The Constitution of the Presbyterian
Church (U.S.A) Defined F-3.04

THE FORM OF GOVERNMENT

Chapter One: Congregations and Their Membership

The Congregation G-1.01
The Mission of the Congregation G-1.0101
The Fellowship of the Congregation G-1.0102
Governed by the Constitution of the Presbyterian
Church (U.S.A.) G-1.0103

The Organizing of a Congregation G-1.02
Organizing Covenant G-1.0201

The Membership of a Congregation G-1.03
The Meaning of Membership and Baptism G-1.0301
Welcome and Openness G-1.0302
Entry into Membership G-1.0303
The Ministry of Members G-1.0304

Categories of Membership G-1.04
Baptized Member G-1.0401
Active Member G-1.0402

Affiliate Member.. G-1.0403
Other Participants G-1.0404

Meetings of the Congregation.. G-1.05
Annual and Special Meetings G-1.0501
Calling a Congregational Meeting................................ G-1.0502
Business Proper to Congregational Meetings............. G-1.0503
Moderator G-1.0504
Secretary and Minutes G-1.0505

Chapter Two: Ordered Ministry, Commissioning, and Certification

Ordered Ministries of the Church G-2.01
Christ's Ministry.. G-2.0101
Ordered Ministries... G-2.0102
Call to Ordered Ministry G-2.0103
Gifts and Qualifications... G-2.0104
Freedom of Conscience G-2.0105

Deacons: The Ministry of Compassion and Service......... G-2.02
Deacon Defined.. G-2.0201
Under Authority of the Session G-2.0202

Ruling Elders: The Ministry of Discernment
and Governance.. G-2.03
Ruling Elder Defined.. G-2.0301

General Provisions for Ruling Elders and Deacons.......... G-2.04
Election of Ruling Elders and Deacons....................... G-2.0401
Preparation for Ministry as a Ruling Elder
or Deacon... G-2.0402
Service of Ordination and Installation......................... G-2.0403
Terms of Service G-2.0404
Dissolution of Relationship G-2.0405
Release from Ministry as a Ruling Elder
or Deacon... G-2.0406
Renunciation of Jurisdiction.. G-2.0407

Teaching Elders: The Ministry of the Word
and Sacrament.. G-2.05
Teaching Elder Defined.. G-2.0501
Presbytery and the Teaching Elder.............................. G-2.0502
Categories of Membership G-2.0503
Pastoral Relationships G-2.0504

Transfer of Ministers of Other Denominations G-2.0505
Temporary Membership in Presbytery for a
    Period of Service G-2.0506
Release from Ministry as a Teaching Elder................ G-2.0507
Failure to Engage in Validated Ministry G-2.0508
Renunciation of Jurisdiction....................................... G-2.0509

Preparation for Ministry.. G-2.06
Nature and Purpose of Preparation............................ G-2.0601
Time Requirements G-2.0602
Purpose of Inquiry.. G-2.0603
Purpose of Candidacy... G-2.0604
Oversight G-2.0605
Service in Covenant Relationship G-2.0606
Final Assessment and Negotiation for Service.......... G-2.0607
Transfer of Relationship... G-2.0608
Removal from Relationship... G-2.0609
Exceptions G-2.0610

Ordination G-2.07
Ordination.. G-2.0701
Place of Ordination... G-2.0702
Service of Ordination G-2.0703
Record of Ordination... G-2.0704

Call and Installation G-2.08
Pastoral Vacancy G-2.0801
Election of a Pastor Nominating Committee.............. G-2.0802
Call Process G-2.0803
Terms of Call... G-2.0804
Installation Service G-2.0805

Dissolution of Pastoral Relationships G-2.09
Congregational Meeting.. G-2.0901
Pastor, Co-Pastor or Associate Pastor Requests......... G-2.0902
Congregation Requests.. G-2.0903
Presbytery Action... G-2.0904
Officiate by Invitation Only G-2.0905

Commissioning Ruling Elders to Particular
Pastoral Service.. G-2.10
Functions G-2.1001
Training, Examination and Commissioning............... G-2.1002

    Commissioning Service.. G-2.1003
    Supervision.. G-2.1004

  Certified Church Service... G-2.11
    Forms of Certified Church Service............................. G-2.1101
    Presbytery and Certified Church Service G-2.1102
    Christian Educators G-2.1103

Chapter Three: Councils of the Church

  General Principles of Councils G-3.01
    Councils as an Expression of Unity of the Church..... G-3.0101
    Ecclesiastical Jurisdiction.. G-3.0102
    Participation and Representation................................. G-3.0103
    Officers.. G-3.0104
    Meetings G-3.0105
    Administration of Mission.. G-3.0106
    Records.. G-3.0107
    Administrative Review... G-3.0108
    Committees and Commissions G-3.0109
    Administrative Staff G-3.0110
    Nominating Process.. G-3.0111
    Insurance G-3.0112
    Finances... G-3.0113

  The Session G-3.02
    Composition and Responsibilities G-3.0201
    Relations with Other Councils.................................... G-3.0202
    Meetings G-3.0203
    Minutes and Records.. G-3.0204
    Finances... G-3.0205

  The Presbytery G-3.03
    Composition and Responsibilities G-3.0301
    Relations with Synod and General Assembly G-3.0302
    Relations with Sessions... G-3.0303
    Meetings and Quorum.. G-3.0304
    Minutes and Records.. G-3.0305
    Membership of Presbytery G-3.0306
    Pastor, Counselor, and Advisor to Teaching
      Elders and Congregations...................................... G-3.0307

  The Synod.. G-3.04
    Composition and Responsibilities G-3.0401

Relations with General Assembly G-3.0402
Relations with Presbyteries G-3.0403
Reduced Function G-3.0404
Meetings and Quorum G-3.0405
Minutes and Records G-3.0406

The General Assembly G-3.05
Composition and Responsibilities G-3.0501
Relations with Other Councils G-3.0502
Meetings and Quorum G-3.0503

Chapter Four: The Church and Civil Authority

Incorporation and Trustees G-4.01
Incorporation and Power G-4.0101
Members of the Corporation G-4.0102

Church Property G-4.02
Property as a Tool for Mission G-4.0201
Decisions Concerning Property G-4.0202
Church Property Held in Trust G-4.0203
Property Used Contrary to the Constitution G-4.0204
Property of a Dissolved or Extinct Congregation G-4.0205
Selling, Encumbering, or Leasing
        Church Property G-4.0206
Property of Congregation in Schism G-4.0207
Exceptions G-4.0208

Confidence And Privilege G-4.03
Trust and Confidentiality G-4.0301
Mandatory Reporting G-4.0302

Chapter Five: Ecumenicity and Union

Ecumenical Commitment G-5.01
Ecumenicity G-5.0101
Interfaith Relations G-5.0102
Secular Organizations G-5.0103

Relations with Other Denominations G-5.02
Correspondence G-5.0201
Full Communion G-5.0202
Ecumenical Statements G-5.0203

Full Organic Union G-5.03

Union Presbyteries.. G-5.04
    Constitutional Authority... G-5.0401
    Plan of Union.. G-5.0402

Joint Congregational Witness G-5.05

Chapter Six: Interpreting and Amending the Constitution

Reform G-6.01

Interpreting the Constitution G-6.02

Amending *The Book of Confessions* G-6.03

Amending the *Book of Order* G-6.04

Exceptions.. G-6.05

Amendments to Special Provisions.................................... G-6.06

DIRECTORY FOR WORSHIP

Preface

CHAPTER I   THE DYNAMICS OF CHRISTIAN WORSHIP W-1.0000

1. Christian Worship: An Introduction.................................... W-1.1000
2. The Language of Worship... W-1.2000
3. Time, Space, and Matter.. W-1.3000
4. Responsibility and Accountability for Worship W-1.4000

CHAPTER II   THE ELEMENTS OF CHRISTIAN WORSHIP W-2.0000

1. Prayer.. W-2.1000
2. Scripture Read and Proclaimed W-2.2000
3. Baptism... W-2.3000
4. The Lord's Supper.. W-2.4000
5. Self-Offering W-2.5000
6. Relating to Each Other and the World W-2.6000

CHAPTER III ORDERING OF CHRISTIAN WORSHIP W-3.0000

1. Principles and Sources of Ordering.................................... W-3.1000
2. Days and Seasons W-3.2000
3. Service for the Lord's Day W-3.3000
4. Service of Daily Prayer W-3.4000
5. Other Regularly Scheduled Services of Worship.................. W-3.5000
6. Special Gatherings... W-3.6000

CHAPTER IV ORDERING WORSHIP FOR
              SPECIAL PURPOSES W-4.0000

1. Special Occasions and Recognitions.................................. W-4.1000
2. Services of Welcome and Reception.................................. W-4.2000
3. Commissioning for Specific Acts of Discipleship W-4.3000
4. Ordination, Installation, and Commissioning...................... W-4.4000
5. Transitions in Ministry W-4.5000
6. Censure and Restoration.. W-4.6000
7. Recognition of Service to the Community W-4.7000
8. Services of Acceptance and Reconciliation......................... W-4.8000
9. Marriage W-4.9000
10. Services on the Occasion of Death.................................... W-4.10000

CHAPTER V WORSHIP AND PERSONAL DISCIPLESHIP........ W-5.0000

1. Personal Worship, Discipleship, and
   the Community of Faith W-5.1000
2. The Discipline of Daily Personal Worship........................... W-5.2000
3. Scripture in Personal Worship.. W-5.3000
4. Prayer in Personal Worship.. W-5.4000
5. Other Disciplines in Personal Worship
   and Discipleship W-5.5000
6. Christian Vocation.. W-5.6000
7. Worship in Families and Households.................................. W-5.7000

CHAPTER VI WORSHIP AND MINISTRY WITHIN
              THE COMMUNITY OF FAITH W-6.0000

1. Mutual Ministries in the Church....................................... W-6.1000
2. Christian Nurture... W-6.2000
3. Pastoral Care... W-6.3000

CHAPTER VII WORSHIP AND THE MINISTRY OF
THE CHURCH IN THE WORLD W-7.0000
1. Worship and Mission... W-7.1000
2. Proclamation and Evangelism W-7.2000
3. Compassion W-7.3000
4. Reconciliation: Justice and Peace........................ W-7.4000
5. Caring for Creation and Life W-7.5000
6. The Church and the Reign of God......................... W-7.6000
7. Worship as Praise W-7.7000

RULES OF DISCIPLINE

CHAPTER I   PRINCIPLES OF CHURCH DISCIPLINE D-1.0000

(Preamble)

Church Discipline D-1.0101
Power Vested in Christ's Church................................. D-1.0102
Conciliate and Mediate D-1.0103

CHAPTER II   JUDICIAL PROCESS DEFINED D-2.0000
1. Judicial Process D-2.0100
   Church Discipline... D-2.0101
      a.   Prevention and Correction of
           Irregularities and Delinquencies.................... D-2.0101a
      b.   Correction of Offenses D-2.0101b
   Councils of the Church.. D-2.0102
   Alternative Forms of Resolution D-2.0103

2. Types of Cases.. D-2.0200
   Remedial or Disciplinary..................................... D-2.0201
   Remedial... D-2.0202
      a.   Irregularity.. D-2.0202a
      b.   Delinquency D-2.0202b
   Disciplinary D-2.0203
      a.   Persons in Ordered Ministries D-2.0203a
      b.   Offense D-2.0203b

CHAPTER III   JURISDICTION IN JUDICIAL PROCESS D-3.0000

   Jurisdiction D-3.0101
      a.   Session D-3.0101a
      b.   Presbytery D-3.0101b
      c.   Presbytery, Synod, General Assembly D-3.0101c
      d.   Church Is Dissolved D-3.0101d
   No Further Judicial Action D-3.0102
   Lower Council Fails to Act D-3.0103
   Jurisdiction Over Transferred Teaching Elders D-3.0104
   Enforce and Recognize Judgments and Decisions D-3.0105
   When Jurisdiction Ends D-3.0106

CHAPTER IV   REFERENCE D-4.0000

   1.   Reference D-4.0100
        Definition D-4.0101
        Proper Subject D-4.0102
        Duty of Lower Council D-4.0103

   2.   Action on Reference D-4.0200
        Duty of Higher Council D-4.0201
        Acceptance D-4.0202
        Refusal D-4.0203

CHAPTER V   PERMANENT JUDICIAL COMMISSIONS D-5.0000

   1.   Service on Permanent Judicial Commissions D-5.0100
        Election D-5.0101
        Term D-5.0102
        Classes D-5.0103
        Vacancy D-5.0104
        Eligibility D-5.0105
        Commission Expenses D-5.0106

   2.   Meetings D-5.0200
        Officers D-5.0201
        Bases of Power D-5.0202
        Meetings D-5.0203

Quorum..D-5.0204

Who Shall Not Participate......................................D-5.0205

Lack of Quorum..D-5.0206
    a.   Inability to Reach a Quorum D-5.0206a
    b.   Roster of Former Members D-5.0206b
    c.   Participant Expense D-5.0206c

CHAPTER VI REMEDIAL CASES D-6.0000

1. Initiating a Remedial Case and
    Obtaining a Stay of Enforcement D-6.0100

    Method of Initiation...D-6.0101

    Definition of Complaint D-6.0102

    Stay of Enforcement..D-6.0103
        a.   Time Limit to File a Request for a Stay D-6.0103a
        b.   Request Given to Moderator and Clerk..............D-6.0103b
        c.   Time Line for Preliminary Questions..................D-6.0103c
        d.   Time Line for Entering a Stay of Enforcement D-6.0103d
        e.   Distribution of Stay D-6.0103e
        f.   Effective Time.......................................D-6.0103f
        g.   Objection to Stay of Enforcement..........D-6.0103g

2. Filing a Complaint in a Remedial Case...................D-6.0200

    Parties...D-6.0201

    Who May File Complaint......................................D-6.0202
        a.   Against Presbytery, Synod, or
            Council at Same Level D-6.0202a
        b.   Against Session or Presbyterian Mission
            Agency or Entity D-6.0202b

3. Pretrial Procedures D-6.0300

    Statements in Complaint D-6.0301

    Committee of Counsel..D-6.0302
        a.   Provide by Rule.....................................D-6.0302a
        b.   Shall Not Serve.....................................D-6.0302b

    Answer to Complaint..D-6.0303

    Procedure Prior to Trial..D-6.0304

    Examination of Papers..D-6.0305

    Preliminary Questions Determined D-6.0306

Duty of Respondent Clerk of Session or Stated Clerk D-6.0307

Procedures for Records D-6.0308

Trial Briefs D-6.0309

Pretrial Conference..D-6.0310

CHAPTER VII TRIAL IN A REMEDIAL CASE...............................D-7.0000

1. Conduct of Trial D-7.0100

   Trial—Remedial...D-7.0101

   Conducted Formally...D-7.0102

2. Citations and Testimony...D-7.0200

   Citation of Parties and Witnesses.........................D-7.0201
      a. Members Cited...D-7.0201a
      b. Others Requested......................................D-7.0201b
      c. Witnesses from Another Council D-7.0201c
      d. Expenses...D-7.0201d

   Service of Citation...D-7.0202

   Second Citation D-7.0203

   Refusal of Witness to Testify D-7.0204

   Deposition D-7.0205

3. Procedures in Trial D-7.0300
   Counsel..D-7.0301

   Circulation of Materials..D-7.0302

   Control Conduct of Trial D-7.0303
      a. Questions as to Procedure D-7.0303a
      b. Absences...D-7.0303b

   Loss of Quorum..D-7.0304

4. Trial..D-7.0400

   Procedure in a Remedial Case...............................D-7.0401
      a. Announcement by the Moderator............D-7.0401a
      b. Eligibility of Commission Members D-7.0401b
         (1) Disqualification..............................D-7.0401b(1)
         (2) Challenges.....................................D-7.0401b(2)
      c. Procedural Objections D-7.0401c

    d.   Amend Complaint D-7.0401d

    e.   Opening Statements... D-7.0401e

    f.   Rules of Evidence... D-7.0401f

    g.   Evidence D-7.0401g

    h.   Final Statements D-7.0401h

   Decision... D-7.0402

    a.   Deliberation... D-7.0402a

    b.   Decision.. D-7.0402b

    c.   Written Decision... D-7.0402c

    d.   Filed Promptly... D-7.0402d

    e.   Further Publicity.. D-7.0402e

5.   Provisions for Appeal... D-7.0500

    Appeal Time D-7.0501

    Appeals.. D-7.0502

6.   Record of Proceedings.. D-7.0600

    Record of Proceedings.. D-7.0601

    a.   Verbatim Recording D-7.0601a

    b.   Exhibits.. D-7.0601b

    c.   Minutes.. D-7.0601c

    d.   Record D-7.0601d

    e.   Preservation... D-7.0601e

    f.   Transcript D-7.0601f

    Additions to the Record.. D-7.0602

7.   Duty of Stated Clerk... D-7.0700

    Reporting the Decision D-7.0701

CHAPTER VIII   APPEAL IN A REMEDIAL CASE D-8.0000

1.   Initiation of an Appeal... D-8.0100

    Definition.. D-8.0101

    Initiation of Appeal D-8.0102

    Effect of Appeal D-8.0103

    Withdrawal of Appeal D-8.0104

    Grounds for Appeal D-8.0105

2. Filings in Appeal Process D-8.0200
    Time for Filing Written Notice of Appeal D-8.0201
    Content of Written Notice of Appeal D-8.0202
    Transmittal of Notice of Appeal to Officers D-8.0203

3. Prehearing Proceedings D-8.0300
    Examination of Papers D-8.0301
    Preliminary Questions Determined D-8.0302
    Record on Appeal D-8.0303
        a. List of Record D-8.0303a
        b. Additional Records D-8.0303b
        c. Filing of Record on Appeal D-8.0303c
        d. Correction of the Record D-8.0303d
        e. Notice of Date of Reception D-8.0303e
        f. Copy Furnished at Cost D-8.0303f
        g. Extension D-8.0303g

    Filing of Appellant's Brief D-8.0304
        a. Copy to Other Party D-8.0304a
        b. Extension D-8.0304b
        c. Failure to File Brief D-8.0304c

    Filing of Appellee's Brief D-8.0305
        a. Copy to Other Party D-8.0305a
        b. Extension D-8.0305b
        c. Failure to File Brief D-8.0305c

    Transmittal of Records and Briefs D-8.0306
    Prehearing Conference D-8.0307

4. Hearing of Appeal D-8.0400
    Notice of Hearing D-8.0401
    Failure to Appear D-8.0402
    Hearing D-8.0403
        a. New Evidence D-8.0403a
        b. Hearing D-8.0403b

    Decision of Permanent Judicial Commission D-8.0404
        a. If No Errors Are Found D-8.0404a
        b. If Errors Are Found D-8.0404b
        c. Written Decision D-8.0404c

    d.   Determination of Each Error D-8.0404d

    e.   Filed Promptly D-8.0404e

    f.   Further Publicity D-8.0404f

CHAPTER IX REQUEST FOR VINDICATION D-9.0000

   Request for Vindication D-9.0101

    a.   Review by Council D-9.0101a

    b.   Investigating Committee D-9.0101b

   Conclusion of the Matter D-9.0102

CHAPTER X DISCIPLINARY CASES D-10.0000

1. Procedure Preliminary to a Disciplinary Case D-10.0100

   Initiation of Preliminary Procedures D-10.0101

   Statement of Offense D-10.0102

    a.   Accusation D-10.0102a

    b.   Council D-10.0102b

    c.   Self-Accusation D-10.0102c

   Referral to Investigating Committee D-10.0103

   Accusation from Other Council D-10.0104

   Transfer Prohibited D-10.0105

   Administrative Leave D-10.0106

2. Investigation D-10.0200

   Investigating Committee D-10.0201

    a.   Membership D-10.0201a

    b.   Appointment by Rule D-10.0201b

    c.   Expenses D-10.0201c

   Investigating Committee Responsibilities D-10.0202a-l

   Rights of the Persons D-10.0203

    a.   Rights of the Accuser D-10.0203a

    b.   Rights of the Person Alleging Harm D-10.0203b

    c.   Rights of the Person Alleged Against D-10.0203c

   Petition Commission to Review Procedures D-10.0204

3. Communicate Determination D-10.0300

   Investigating Committee May Utilize
   Alternate Dispute Resolution D-10.0301

If Charges Are to Be Filed..D-10.0302

Petition for Review if No Charges Filed.............................D-10.0303

Disposition of Records D-10.0304

4.   Charges..D-10.0400

Time Limit..D-10.0401

Prosecution of Case D-10.0402
   a.   Parties..D-10.0402a
   b.   Only Two Parties..D-10.0402b

Form of Charge D-10.0403
   a.   Several Together...D-10.0403a
   b.   Details of the Charge....................................D-10.0403b
   c.   Tried Together..D-10.0403c

Filing of Charge..D-10.0404
   a.   Session...D-10.0404a
   b.   Presbytery..D-10.0404b

Pretrial Conference..D-10.0405
   a.   Time and Place...D-10.0405a
   b.   Those Present D-10.0405b
   c.   Nothing More D-10.0405c

Witnesses Disclosed D-10.0406

CHAPTER XI TRIAL IN A DISCIPLINARY CASE D-11.0000

1.   Conduct of Trial D-11.0100

Trial—Disciplinary D-11.0101

Conducted Formally...D-11.0102

2.   Citations and Testimony...D-11.0200

Citation of Parties and Witnesses...................................D-11.0201
   a.   Members Cited D-11.0201a
   b.   Others Requested..D-11.0201b
   c.   Witnesses from Another Council D-11.0201c
   d.   Expenses..D-11.0201d

Service of Citation...D-11.0202
   a.   Second Citation D-11.0202a

      b.   Accused Does Not Appear D-11.0202b

    Refusal of Witness to Testify D-11.0203

    Deposition D-11.0204

3.   Procedures in Trial D-11.0300

    Counsel D-11.0301

    Unable to Secure Counsel D-11.0302

    Circulation of Materials D-11.0303

    Control Conduct of Trial D-11.0304

          a.   Questions as to Procedure D-11.0304a

          b.   Absences D-11.0304b

    Loss of Quorum D-11.0305

    Closed Proceedings D-11.0306

4.   Trial D-11.0400

    Presumption of Innocence D-11.0401

    Procedure in a Disciplinary Case D-11.0402

          a.   Announcement by the Moderator D-11.0402a

          b.   Eligibility of Commission Members D-11.0402b

              (1) Disqualification ....D-11.0402b(1)

              (2) Challenges ....D-11.0402b(2)

          c.   Preliminary Objections D-11.0402c

          d.   Plea D-11.0402d

          e.   Opening Statements D-11.0402e

          f.   Rules of Evidence D-11.0402f

          g.   Prosecution D-11.0402g

          h.   Defense D-11.0402h

          i.   Rebuttal D-11.0402i

          j.   Final Statements D-11.0402j

    Decision D-11.0403

          a.   Beyond a Reasonable Doubt D-11.0403a

          b.   Judgment of Guilt by 2/3 Vote D-11.0403b

          c.   Written Decisions D-11.0403c

          d.   Announcements in Open Meeting D-11.0403d

          e.   Degree of Censure D-11.0403e

	f.	Filed Promptly	D-11.0403f
	g.	Notification of Parties	D-11.0403g
	h.	Further Publicity	D-11.0403h

5. Provisions for Appeal ... D-11.0500
   Appeal Time ... D-11.0501
       Appeals ... D-11.0502

6. Record of Proceedings ... D-11.0600
   Record of Proceedings ... D-11.0601
       a. Verbatim Recordings ... D-11.0601a
       b. Exhibits ... D-11.0601b
       c. Minutes ... D-11.0601c
       d. Record ... D-11.0601d
       e. Preservation of the Record ... D-11.0601e
       f. Transcript ... D-11.0601f
   Additions to the Record ... D-11.0602

7. Duty of Stated Clerk ... D-11.0700
   Reporting the Decision ... D-11.0701

8. Enforcement ... D-11.0800
   Enforcement by Council ... D-11.0801

CHAPTER XII CENSURE AND RESTORATION IN A
    DISCIPLINARY CASE ... D-12.0000

1. Censures ... D-12.0100
   Degrees of Church Censure ... D-12.0101
   Rebuke Followed by Prayer ... D-12.0102
   Rebuke with Supervised Rehabilitation ... D-12.0103
       a. Prayer ... D-12.0103a
       b. Communicate Goals of Rehabilitation ... D-12.0103b
       c. Statement of Evaluation and Rehabilitation ... D-12.0103c
       d. Voluntary Acts of Repentance if Involving
          Sexual Abuse of Another Person ... D-12.0103d
   Temporary Exclusion ... D-12.0104
       a. Prayer ... D-12.0104a

   b.   Supervised Rehabilitation.....................................D-12.0104b
   c.   Voluntary Act of Repentance if Involving
        Sexual Abuse of Another Person..........................D-12.0104c
   d.   Refrain from Exercise of Ordered Ministry.........D-12.0104d
   e.   Cannot Vote or Hold Office.................................D-12.0104e
   f.   Effect of Temporary Exclusion of a Pastor..........D-12.0104f
   g.   Notice of Temporary Exclusion..........................D-12.0104g
   h.   Termination of Censure of
        Temporary Exclusion..D-12.0104h
   i.   Early Restoration...D-12.0104i

Removal from Ordered Ministry or Membership.............D-12.0105
   a.   Removal from Ordered Ministry..........................D-12.0105a
   b.   Removal from Membership...................................D-12.0105b
   c.   Prayer...D-12.0105c
   d.   Consequences of Removal from
        Ordered Ministry..D-12.0105d
   e.   Notice of Removal...D-12.0105e

2. Restoration..D-12.0200

Decision of Council..D-12.0201

Form of Restoration to Ordered Ministry After Removal...D-12.0202
   a.   Form..D-12.0202a
   b.   Restored to Roll..D-12.0202b

Form of Restoration to Membership After Removal...........D-12.0203
   a.   Form..D-12.0203a
   b.   Restored to Roll..D-12.0203b
   c.   Restored to Ordered Ministry..............................D-12.0203c

CHAPTER XIII   APPEAL IN A DISCIPLINARY CASE.................D-13.0000

1. Initiation of Appeal...D-13.0100

Definition...D-13.0101

Initiation of Appeal...D-13.0102

Appeal of Appellate Decision...D-13.0103

Effect of Appeal..D-13.0104

Withdrawal of Appeal..D-13.0105

Grounds for Appeal...D-13.0106

2. Filings in Appeal Process...D-13.0200

   Time for Filing Written Notice of Appeal............................D-13.0201

   Content of Written Notice of Appeal D-13.0202

   Transmittal of Notice of Appeal to Officers.......................D-13.0203

3. Prehearing Proceedings D-13.0300

   Examination of Papers..D-13.0301

   Preliminary Questions Determined D-13.0302

   Record on Appeal...D-13.0303

     a. List of Record..D-13.0303a

     b. Additional Records...D-13.0303b

     c. Filing of Record on Appeal D-13.0303c

     d. Correction of the Record D-13.0303d

     e. Notice of Date of Reception...............................D-13.0303e

     f. Copy Furnished at Cost......................................D-13.0303f

     g. Extension...D-13.0303g

   Filing of Appellant's Brief..D-13.0304

     a. Copy to Other Party...D-13.0304a

     b. Extension...D-13.0304b

     c. Failure to File Brief...D-13.0304c

   Filing of Appellee's Brief...D-13.0305

     a. Copy to Other Party...D-13.0305a

     b. Extension...D-13.0305b

     c. Failure to File Brief...D-13.0305c

   Transmittal of Records and Briefs.......................................D-13.0306

   Prehearing Conference D-13.0307

4. Hearing of Appeal D-13.0400

   Notice of Hearing...D-13.0401

   Failure to Appear...D-13.0402

   Hearing...D-13.0403

     a. New Evidence..D-13.0403a

     b. Hearing..D-13.0403b

   Decision of Permanent Judicial Commission......................D-13.0404

     a. If No Errors Are Found D-13.0404a

     b. If Errors Are Found D-13.0404b

     c. Written Decision..D-13.0404c

     d. Determination of Each Error D-13.0404d

    e. Filed Promptly...D-13.0404e

    f.   Further Publicity..D-13.0404f

  Effect of Reversal on Appeal in Disciplinary Case.............D-13.0405

CHAPTER XIV EVIDENCE IN REMEDIAL OR
              DISCIPLINARY CASES D-14.0000

1. Evidence D-14.0100

    Evidence Defined D-14.0101

2. Witnesses...D-14.0200

    Challenge...D-14.0201

    Husband or Wife D-14.0202

    Counselor...D-14.0203

    Counsel for Parties D-14.0204

    Credibility of Witnesses D-14.0205

3. Testimony..D-14.0300

    Separate Examination...D-14.0301

    Examination of Witnesses D-14.0302

        a. Oath D-14.0302a

        b. Affirmation..D-14.0302b

    Record of Testimony D-14.0303

    Testimony Taken by Deposition D-14.0304

        a. Person from Another Council............................D-14.0304a

        b. Taking of Testimony D-14.0304b

        c. Offered as Evidence D-14.0304c

        d. Questions of Admissibility...............................D-14.0304d

    Member as Witness D-14.0305

4. Records as Evidence..D-14.0400

    Admissibility of Records..D-14.0401

    Admissibility of Testimony Taken by
    Another Council D-14.0402

5. New Evidence...D-14.0500

    Application for New Trial D-14.0501

    Consideration in Appeal...D-14.0502

APPENDIXES

Appendix A: Articles of Agreement.. A-1–A-16

Appendix B: A Formula of Agreement...B-1–B-9

Appendix C: Covenant Relationship Between the Korean
Presbyterian Church in America and the Presbyterian
Church (U.S.A.)...C-1–C-4

Appendix D: Polity and Church Law Resources....................................D-1–D-2

INDEXES

Scriptural Allusion Index

Index

THE FOUNDATIONS OF PRESBYTERIAN POLITY

[TEXT]

For comparison charts with the former 2009-2011 Form of Government, go to the following Web sites:

- For a comparison chart of the former Form of Government to the new Foundations and Form of Government: http://www.pcusa.org/resource/comparison-chart-former-form-government-new-founda/

- For a comparison chart of the new Foundations and Form of Government to the former Form of Government: http://www.pcusa.org/resource/comparison-chart-new-foundations-and-form-governme/

THE FOUNDATIONS OF PRESBYTERIAN POLITY

CHAPTER ONE

THE MISSION OF THE CHURCH[1]

F-1.01 GOD'S MISSION

The good news of the Gospel is that the triune God—Father, Son, and Holy Spirit—creates, redeems, sustains, rules, and transforms all things and all people. This one living God, the Scriptures say, liberated the people of Israel from oppression and covenanted to be their God. By the power of the Spirit, this one living God is incarnate in Jesus Christ, who came to live in the world, die for the world, and be raised again to new life. The Gospel of Jesus Christ announces the nearness of God's kingdom, bringing good news to all who are impoverished, sight to all who are blind, freedom to all who are oppressed, and proclaiming the Lord's favor upon all creation.

The mission of God in Christ gives shape and substance to the life and work of the Church. In Christ, the Church participates in God's mission for the transformation of creation and humanity by proclaiming to all people the good news of God's love, offering to all people the grace of God at font and table, and calling all people to discipleship in Christ. Human beings have no higher goal in life than to glorify and enjoy God now and forever, living in covenant fellowship with God and participating in God's mission.

F-1.02 JESUS CHRIST IS HEAD OF THE CHURCH

F-1.0201 The Authority of Christ

Almighty God, who raised Jesus Christ from the dead and set him above all rule and authority, has given to him all power in heaven and on earth, not only in this age but also in the age to come.[a] God has put all things under the Lordship of Jesus Christ and has made Christ Head of the Church, which is his body.[b] The Church's life and mission are a joyful participation in Christ's ongoing life and work.

F-1.0202 Christ Calls and Equips the Church

Christ calls the Church into being, giving it all that is necessary for its mission in the world, for its sanctification, and for its service to God. Christ is present with the Church in both Spirit and Word. Christ alone rules, calls, teaches, and uses the Church as he wills.

---

[1] Throughout this document and the Form of Government, the capitalized term "Church" refers to the Church Universal, the Church as it is called to be in Christ; except as part of a title (i.e. Presbyterian Church (U.S.A.).

F-1.0203   *Christ Gives the Church Its Life*

Christ gives to the Church its faith and life, its unity and mission, its order and discipline. Scripture teaches us of Christ's will for the Church, which is to be obeyed. In the worship and service of God and the government of the church, matters are to be ordered according to the Word by reason and sound judgment, under the guidance of the Holy Spirit.

F-1.0204   *Christ Is the Church's Hope*

In affirming with the earliest Christians that Jesus is Lord, the Church confesses that he is its hope, and that the Church, as Christ's body, is bound to his authority and thus free to live in the lively, joyous reality of the grace of God.

F-1.0205   *Christ Is the Foundation of the Church*

In Christ all the fullness of God was pleased to dwell, and through Christ God reconciles all things, whether on earth or in heaven, making peace by the blood of the cross (Col. 1:19–20). In Christ's name, therefore, the Church is sent out to bear witness to the good news of reconciliation with God, with others, and with all creation. In Christ the Church receives its truth and appeal, its holiness, and its unity.

F-1.03   THE CALLING OF THE CHURCH

F-1.0301   *The Church Is the Body of Christ*

The Church is the body of Christ[c]. Christ gives to the Church all the gifts necessary to be his body. The Church strives to demonstrate these gifts in its life as a community in the world (1 Cor. 12:27–28):

> The Church is to be a community of faith, entrusting itself to God alone, even at the risk of losing its life.

> The Church is to be a community of hope, rejoicing in the sure and certain knowledge that, in Christ, God is making a new creation. This new creation is a new beginning for human life and for all things. The Church lives in the present on the strength of that promised new creation.

> The Church is to be a community of love, where sin is forgiven, reconciliation is accomplished, and the dividing walls of hostility are torn down.

> The Church is to be a community of witness, pointing beyond itself through word and work to the good news of God's transforming grace in Christ Jesus its Lord.

F-1.0302   *The Marks of the Church*[2]

With all Christians of the Church catholic, we affirm that the Church is "one, holy, catholic, and apostolic."

---

[2] See "The Nicene Creed," *The Book of Confessions,* 1.3.

a. The Unity of the Church

Unity is God's gift to the Church in Jesus Christ. Just as God is one God and Jesus Christ is our one Savior, so the Church is one because it belongs to its one Lord, Jesus Christ. The Church seeks to include all people and is never content to enjoy the benefits of Christian community for itself alone. There is one Church, for there is one Spirit, one hope, "one Lord, one faith, one baptism, one God and Father of all, who is above all and through all and in all" (Eph. 4:5–6).

Because in Christ the Church is one, it strives to be one. To be one with Christ is to be joined with all those whom Christ calls into relationship with him. To be thus joined with one another is to become priests for one another, praying for the world and for one another and sharing the various gifts God has given to each Christian for the benefit of the whole community. Division into different denominations obscures but does not destroy unity in Christ. The Presbyterian Church (U.S.A.), affirming its historical continuity with the whole Church of Jesus Christ, is committed to the reduction of that obscurity, and is willing to seek and to deepen communion with all other churches within the one, holy, catholic, and apostolic Church[d].

b. The Holiness of the Church

Holiness is God's gift to the Church in Jesus Christ. Through the love of Christ, by the power of the Spirit, God takes away the sin of the world. The holiness of the Church comes from Christ who sets it apart to bear witness to his love, and not from the purity of its doctrine or the righteousness of its actions.

Because in Christ the Church is holy, the Church, its members, and those in its ordered ministries strive to lead lives worthy of the Gospel we proclaim. In gratitude for Christ's work of redemption, we rely upon the work of God's Spirit through Scripture and the means of grace (W-5.5001) to form every believer and every community for this holy living. We confess the persistence of sin in our corporate and individual lives. At the same time, we also confess that we are forgiven by Christ and called again and yet again to strive for the purity, righteousness, and truth revealed to us in Jesus Christ and promised to all people in God's new creation.

c. The Catholicity of the Church

Catholicity is God's gift to the Church in Jesus Christ. In the life, death, and resurrection of Christ, by the power of the Spirit, God overcomes our alienation and repairs our division.

Because in Christ the Church is catholic, it strives everywhere to testify to Christ's embrace of men, women, and children of all times, places, races, nations, ages, conditions, and stations in life. The catholicity of the Church summons the Church to a deeper faith, a larger hope, and a more complete love as it bears witness to God's grace.

d. The Apostolicity of the Church

Apostolicity is God's gift to the Church in Jesus Christ. In Christ, by the power of the Spirit, God sends the Church into the world to share the gospel of God's redemption of all things and people.

Because in Christ the Church is apostolic, it strives to proclaim this gospel faithfully. The Church receives the good news of salvation in Jesus Christ through the testimony of those whom Christ sent, both those whom we call apostles and those whom Christ has called throughout the long history of the Church. The Church has been and is even now sent into the world by Jesus Christ to bear that testimony to others. The Church bears witness in word and work that in Christ the new creation has begun, and that God who creates life also frees those in bondage, forgives sin, reconciles brokenness, makes all things new, and is still at work in the world. To be members of the body of Christ is to be sent out to pursue the mission of God and to participate in God's new creation, God's kingdom drawing the present into itself. The Presbyterian Church (U.S.A.) affirms the Gospel of Jesus Christ as received from the prophets and apostles, and stands in continuity with God's mission through the ages.

The Church strives to be faithful to the good news it has received and accountable to the standards of the confessions. The Church seeks to present the claims of Jesus Christ, leading persons to repentance, acceptance of Christ alone as Savior and Lord, and new life as his disciples.

The Church is sent to be Christ's faithful evangelist:

> making disciples of all nations in the name of the Father, the Son, and the Holy Spirit;

> sharing with others a deep life of worship, prayer, fellowship, and service; and

> participating in God's mission to care for the needs of the sick, poor, and lonely; to free people from sin, suffering, and oppression; and to establish Christ's just, loving, and peaceable rule in the world.

F-1.0303   The Notes of the Reformed Church[3]

Where Christ is, there is the true Church. Since the earliest days of the Reformation, Reformed Christians have marked the presence of the true Church wherever:

> the Word of God is truly preached and heard,

> the Sacraments are rightly administered, and

> ecclesiastical discipline is uprightly ministered.

---

[3] See The Scots Confession, Ch. XVIII (*The Book of Confessions*, 3.18)

In our own time, we affirm that, in the power of the Spirit, the Church is faithful to the mission of Christ as it:

> *Proclaims and hears the Word of God,*
> responding to the promise of God's new creation in Christ, and
> inviting all people to participate in that new creation;

> *Administers and receives the Sacraments,*
> welcoming those who are being engrafted into Christ,
> bearing witness to Christ's saving death and resurrection,
> anticipating the heavenly banquet that is to come, and
> committing itself in the present to solidarity with the marginalized and the hungry; and

> *Nurtures a covenant community of disciples of Christ,*
> living in the strength of God's promise and
> giving itself in service to God's mission.

F-1.0304   The Great Ends of the Church

The great ends of the Church are:

the proclamation of the gospel for the salvation of humankind;

the shelter, nurture, and spiritual fellowship of the children of God;

the maintenance of divine worship;

the preservation of the truth;

the promotion of social righteousness; and

the exhibition of the Kingdom of Heaven to the world.[4]

F-1.04   OPENNESS TO THE GUIDANCE OF THE HOLY SPIRIT

F-1.0401   Continuity and Change

The presbyterian form of government set forth in the Constitution of the Presbyterian Church (U.S.A.) is grounded in Scripture and built around the marks of the true Church. It is in all things subject to the Lord of the Church. In the power of the Spirit, Jesus Christ draws worshiping communities and individual believers into the sovereign activity of the triune God at all times and places. As the Church seeks reform and fresh direction, it

---

[4]This statement of the Great Ends of the Church, slightly edited here, came from the United Presbyterian Church of North America, which united with the Presbyterian Church in the United States of America in 1958. The statement was then made a part of the Constitution of The United Presbyterian Church in the United States of America, as the united body was called. This now classic statement was adopted by the United Presbyterian Church of North America in 1910, following various actions between 1904 and 1910 looking forward to the revision of the church's Constitution.

looks to Jesus Christ who goes ahead of us and calls us to follow him. United with Christ in the power of the Spirit, the Church seeks "not [to] be conformed to this world, but [to] be transformed by the renewing of [our] minds, so that [we] may discern what is the will of God—what is good and acceptable and perfect" (Rom. 12:2).

F-1.0402   Ecumenicity

The presbyterian system of government in the Constitution of the Presbyterian Church (U.S.A.) is established in light of Scripture[e] but is not regarded as essential for the existence of the Christian Church nor required of all Christians.

F-1.0403   Unity in Diversity

"As many of you as were baptized into Christ have clothed yourselves with Christ. There is no longer Jew or Greek, there is no longer slave or free, there is no longer male and female; for all of you are one in Christ Jesus. And if you belong to Christ, then you are Abraham's offspring, heirs according to the promise" (Gal. 3:27–29).

The unity of believers in Christ is reflected in the rich diversity of the Church's membership. In Christ, by the power of the Spirit, God unites persons through baptism regardless of race, ethnicity, age, sex, disability, geography, or theological conviction. There is therefore no place in the life of the Church for discrimination against any person. The Presbyterian Church (U.S.A.) shall guarantee full participation and representation in its worship, governance, and emerging life to all persons or groups within its membership. No member shall be denied participation or representation for any reason other than those stated in this Constitution.

F-1.0404   Openness

In Jesus Christ, who is Lord of all creation, the Church seeks a new openness to God's mission in the world. In Christ, the triune God tends the least among us, suffers the curse of human sinfulness, raises up a new humanity, and promises a new future for all creation. In Christ, Church members share with all humanity the realities of creatureliness, sinfulness, brokenness, and suffering, as well as the future toward which God is drawing them. The mission of God pertains not only to the Church but also to people everywhere and to all creation. As it participates in God's mission, the Presbyterian Church (U.S.A) seeks:

> a new openness to the sovereign activity of God in the Church and in the world, to a more radical obedience to Christ, and to a more joyous celebration in worship and work;

> a new openness in its own membership, becoming in fact as well as in faith a community of women and men of all ages, races, ethnicities, and worldly conditions, made one in Christ by the power of the Spirit, as a visible sign of the new humanity;

a new openness to see both the possibilities and perils of its institutional forms in order to ensure the faithfulness and usefulness of these forms to God's activity in the world; and

a new openness to God's continuing reformation of the Church ecumenical, that it might be more effective in its mission.

CHAPTER TWO
THE CHURCH AND ITS CONFESSIONS

F-2.01 THE PURPOSE OF CONFESSIONAL STATEMENTS

The Presbyterian Church (U.S.A.) states its faith and bears witness to God's grace in Jesus Christ in the creeds and confessions in *The Book of Confessions*. In these statements the church declares to its members and to the world who and what it is, what it believes, and what it resolves to do. These statements identify the church as a community of people known by its convictions as well as by its actions. They guide the church in its study and interpretation of the Scriptures; they summarize the essence of Reformed Christian tradition; they direct the church in maintaining sound doctrines; they equip the church for its work of proclamation. They serve to strengthen personal commitment and the life and witness of the community of believers.

The creeds and confessions of this church arose in response to particular circumstances within the history of God's people. They claim the truth of the Gospel at those points where their authors perceived that truth to be at risk. They are the result of prayer, thought, and experience within a living tradition. They appeal to the universal truth of the Gospel while expressing that truth within the social and cultural assumptions of their time. They affirm a common faith tradition, while also from time to time standing in tension with each other.

F-2.02 THE CONFESSIONS AS SUBORDINATE STANDARDS

These confessional statements are subordinate standards in the church,[a] subject to the authority of Jesus Christ, the Word of God, as the Scriptures bear witness to him. While confessional standards are subordinate to the Scriptures, they are, nonetheless, standards. They are not lightly drawn up or subscribed to, nor may they be ignored or dismissed. The church is prepared to instruct, counsel with, or even to discipline one ordained who seriously rejects the faith expressed in the confessions. Moreover, the process for changing the confessions of the church is deliberately demanding, requiring a high degree of consensus across the church. Yet the church, in obedience to Jesus Christ, is open to the reform of its standards of doctrine as well as of governance. The church affirms *Ecclesia reformata, semper reformanda secundum verbum Dei*, that is, "The church reformed, always to be reformed according to the Word of God" in the power of the Spirit.

F-2.03 THE CONFESSIONS AS STATEMENTS OF THE FAITH OF THE CHURCH CATHOLIC

In its confessions, the Presbyterian Church (U.S.A.) witnesses to the faith of the Church catholic. The confessions express the faith of the one, holy, catholic, and apostolic Church[b] in the recognition of canonical Scriptures and the formulation and adoption of the ecumenical creeds, notably the Nicene and Apostles' Creeds with their definitions of the mystery of the triune God and of the incarnation of the eternal Word of God in Jesus Christ.

F-2.04   THE CONFESSIONS AS STATEMENTS OF THE FAITH OF THE PROTESTANT REFORMATION

In its confessions, the Presbyterian Church (U.S.A.) upholds the affirmations of the Protestant Reformation. The focus of these affirmations is God's grace in Jesus Christ as revealed in the Scriptures. The Protestant watchwords—grace alone,[c] faith alone,[d] Scripture alone[e]—embody principles of understanding that continue to guide and motivate the people of God in the life of faith.

F-2.05   THE CONFESSIONS AS STATEMENTS OF THE FAITH OF THE REFORMED TRADITION

In its confessions, the Presbyterian Church (U.S.A.) expresses the faith of the Reformed tradition. Central to this tradition is the affirmation of the majesty,[f] holiness,[g] and providence of God[h] who in Christ and by the power of the Spirit creates,[i] sustains,[j] rules,[k] and redeems[l] the world in the freedom of sovereign righteousness and love.[m] Related to this central affirmation of God's sovereignty are other great themes of the Reformed tradition:

The election[n] of the people of God for service as well as for salvation[o];

Covenant life marked by a disciplined concern for order in the church according to the Word of God;

A faithful stewardship that shuns ostentation and seeks proper use of the gifts of God's creation; and

The recognition of the human tendency to idolatry[p] and tyranny,[q] which calls the people of God to work for the transformation of society by seeking justice and living in obedience to the Word of God.

Chapter Three
Principles of Order and Government

F-3.01   Historic Principles of Church Order[1]

In setting forth this *Book of Order*, the Presbyterian Church (U.S.A.) reaffirms the historic principles of church order, which have been a part of our common heritage and which are basic to our Presbyterian concept and system of church government, namely:

F-3.0101   *God Is Lord of the Conscience*

a.   That "God alone is Lord of the conscience, and hath left it free from the doctrines and commandments of men[2] which are in anything contrary to his Word, or beside it, in matters of faith or worship."[3]

b.   Therefore we consider the rights of private judgment, in all matters that respect religion, as universal and unalienable: We do not even wish to see any religious constitution aided by the civil power, further than may be necessary for protection and security, and at the same time, be equal and common to all others.

F-3.0102   *Corporate Judgment*

That, in perfect consistency with the above principle of common right, every Christian Church, or union or association of particular churches, is entitled to declare the terms of admission into its communion, and the qualifications of its ministers and members, as well as the whole system of its internal government which Christ hath appointed; that in the exercise of this right they may, notwithstanding, err, in making the terms of communion either too lax or too narrow; yet, even in this case, they do not infringe upon the liberty or the rights of others, but only make an improper use of their own.

F-3.0103   *Officers*

That our blessed Savior, for the edification of the visible Church, which is his body, hath appointed officers,[4] not only to preach the gospel and administer the Sacraments, but

---

[1]This section, with the exception of the first paragraph, was first drawn up by the Synod of New York and Philadelphia, and prefixed to the Form of Government as published by that body in 1788. In that year, the synod was divided into four synods and gave place to the General Assembly of the Presbyterian Church in the United States of America, which held its first meeting the following year. The four synods formed were the Synod of New York and New Jersey, the Synod of Philadelphia, the Synod of Virginia, and the Synod of the Carolinas. The presbyteries of these four synods were represented in the first General Assembly, which met in Philadelphia on May 21, 1789. The general plan drawn up in 1788 became that by which the Presbyterian Church in the United States and The United Presbyterian Church in the United States of America were subsequently governed.

[2] The words "men" and "man's" throughout this quotation from the eighteenth century should be understood as applying to all persons.

[3] See the Westminster Confession of Faith (*The Book of Confessions*, 6.109).

[4] The terms "officers" and "office" are preserved here as part of the historic language of the Principles. Elsewhere in the Form of Government the terms "ordered minister" and "ordered ministry" are used in place of "officer" and "office."

also to exercise discipline, for the preservation of both truth and duty; and that it is incumbent upon these officers, and upon the whole Church, in whose name they act, to censure or cast out the erroneous and scandalous, observing, in all cases, the rules contained in the Word of God.

F-3.0104   Truth and Goodness

That truth is in order to goodness; and the great touchstone of truth, its tendency to promote holiness, according to our Savior's rule, "By their fruits ye shall know them." And that no opinion can either be more pernicious or more absurd than that which brings truth and falsehood upon a level, and represents it as of no consequence what a man's opinions are. On the contrary, we are persuaded that there is an inseparable connection between faith and practice, truth and duty. Otherwise it would be of no consequence either to discover truth or to embrace it.

F-3.0105   Mutual Forbearance

That, while under the conviction of the above principle we think it necessary to make effectual provision that all who are admitted as teachers be sound in the faith, we also believe that there are truths and forms with respect to which men of good characters and principles may differ. And in all these we think it the duty both of private Christians and societies to exercise mutual forbearance toward each other.

F-3.0106   Election by the People

That though the character, qualifications, and authority of Church officers are laid down in the Holy Scriptures, as well as the proper method of their investiture and institution, yet the election of the persons to the exercise of this authority, in any particular society, is in that society.

F-3.0107   Church Power

That all Church power, whether exercised by the body in general or in the way of representation by delegated authority, is only ministerial and declarative[a]; that is to say, that the Holy Scriptures are the only rule of faith and manners; that no Church judicatory[5] ought to pretend to make laws to bind the conscience in virtue of their own authority; and that all their decisions should be founded upon the revealed will of God. Now though it will easily be admitted that all synods and councils may err, through the frailty inseparable from humanity, yet there is much greater danger from the usurped claim of making laws than from the right of judging upon laws already made, and common to all who profess the gospel, although this right, as necessity requires in the present state, be lodged with fallible men.

---

[5] The term "judicatory," employed here as part of the historical language of the Principles, is elsewhere in the Form of Government replaced with "council."

F-3.0108   The Value of Ecclesiastical Discipline

Lastly, that if the preceding scriptural and rational principles be steadfastly adhered to, the vigor and strictness of its discipline will contribute to the glory and happiness of any church. Since ecclesiastical discipline must be purely moral or spiritual in its object,[b] and not attended with any civil effects, it can derive no force whatever but from its own justice, the approbation of an impartial public, and the countenance and blessing of the great Head of the Church universal.

F-3.02   Principles of Presbyterian Government[6]

The Presbyterian Church (U.S.A.) reaffirms, within the context of its commitment to the Church universal, a special commitment to basic principles of Presbyterian polity:

F-3.0201   One Church

The particular congregations of the Presbyterian Church (U.S.A.) wherever they are, taken collectively, constitute one church, called the church.

F-3.0202   Governed by Presbyters

This church shall be governed by presbyters, that is, ruling elders and teaching elders. Ruling elders are so named not because they "lord it over" the congregation (Matt. 20:25), but because they are chosen by the congregation to discern and measure its fidelity to the Word of God, and to strengthen and nurture its faith and life. Teaching elders shall be committed in all their work to equipping the people of God for their ministry and witness.

F-3.0203   Gathered in Councils

These presbyters shall come together in councils in regular gradation. These councils are sessions, presbyteries, synods, and the General Assembly. All councils of the church are united by the nature of the church and share with one another responsibilities, rights, and powers as provided in this Constitution. The councils are distinct, but have such mutual relations that the act of one of them is the act of the whole church performed by it

---

[6] This provision is derived from and intended to restate the Historic Principles of Church Government, which were adopted in 1797 by the General Assembly of the Presbyterian Church in the United States of America, and the Principles of Presbyterian Government. In this quotation, the word "radical" is used in its primary meaning of "fundamental and basic," and the word "appeals" is used in a general sense rather than with reference to a case involved in judicial process: "The radical[c] principles of Presbyterian church government and discipline are: 'That the several different congregations of believers, taken collectively, constitute one Church of Christ, called emphatically the Church; that a larger part of the Church, or a representation of it, should govern a smaller, or determine matters of controversy which arise therein; that, in like manner, a representation of the whole should govern and determine in regard to every part, and to all the parts united: that is, that a majority shall govern; and consequently that appeals may be carried from lower to higher governing bodies [councils], till they be finally decided by the collected wisdom and united voice of the whole Church. For these principles and this procedure, the example of the apostles and the practice of the primitive Church are considered as authority.'"

through the appropriate council. The larger part of the church, or a representation thereof, shall govern the smaller.

F-3.0204   Seek and Represent the Will of Christ

Presbyters are not simply to reflect the will of the people, but rather to seek together to find and represent the will of Christ.

F-3.0205   Decision by Majority Vote

Decisions shall be reached in councils by vote, following opportunity for discussion and discernment, and a majority shall govern.

F-3.0206   Review and Control

A higher council shall have the right of review and control over a lower one and shall have power to determine matters of controversy upon reference, complaint, or appeal.

F-3.0207   Ordination by Council

Presbyters (ruling elders and teaching elders) and deacons are ordained only by the authority of a council.

F-3.0208   Shared Power, Exercised Jointly

Ecclesiastical jurisdiction is a shared power, to be exercised jointly by presbyters gathered in councils.

F-3.0209   General Authority of Councils

Councils possess whatever administrative authority is necessary to give effect to duties and powers assigned by the Constitution of the church. The jurisdiction of each council is limited by the express provisions of the Constitution, with powers not mentioned being reserved to the presbyteries.

F-3.03   FOUNDATIONAL STATEMENTS

The statements contained in this section, "The Foundations of Presbyterian Polity," describe the ecclesiological and historical commitments on which the polity of the Presbyterian Church (U.S.A.) rests. Provisions of any part of this Constitution are to be interpreted in light of the whole Constitution. No provision of the *Book of Order* can of itself invalidate any other. Where there are tensions and ambiguities between provisions, it is the task of councils and judicial commissions to resolve them in such a way as to give effect to all provisions.

F-3.04   THE CONSTITUTION OF THE PRESBYTERIAN CHURCH (U.S.A) DEFINED

The Constitution of the Presbyterian Church (U.S.A.) consists of *The Book of Confessions* and the *Book of Order.*

The Book of Confessions includes:

The Nicene Creed

The Apostles' Creed

The Scots Confession

The Heidelberg Catechism

The Second Helvetic Confession

The Westminster Confession of Faith

The Westminster Shorter Catechism

The Westminster Larger Catechism

The Theological Declaration of Barmen

The Confession of 1967

A Brief Statement of Faith—Presbyterian Church (U.S.A.)

The *Book of Order* includes:

The Foundations of Presbyterian Polity

The Form of Government

The Directory for Worship

The Rules of Discipline

THE
FORM OF GOVERNMENT
[TEXT]

For comparison charts with the former 2009-2011 Form of Government, go to the following Web sites:

- For a comparison chart of the former Form of Government to the new Foundations and Form of Government: http://www.pcusa.org/resource/comparison-chart-former-form-government-new-founda/

- For a comparison chart of the new Foundations and Form of Government to the former Form of Government: http://www.pcusa.org/resource/comparison-chart-new-foundations-and-form-governme/

The Form of Government

Chapter One
Congregations and Their Membership

G-1.01 The Congregation

G-1.0101 The Mission of the Congregation

The congregation is the church engaged in the mission of God in its particular context. The triune God gives to the congregation all the gifts of the gospel necessary to being the Church. The congregation is the basic form of the church, but it is not of itself a sufficient form of the church. Thus congregations are bound together in communion with one another, united in relationships of accountability and responsibility, contributing their strengths to the benefit of the whole, and are called, collectively, the church.

Through the congregation God's people carry out the ministries of proclamation, sharing the Sacraments[a], and living in covenant life with God and each other. In the life of the congregation, individual believers are equipped for the ministry of witness to the love and grace of God in and for the world. The congregation reaches out to people, communities, and the world to share the good news of Jesus Christ, to gather for worship, to offer care and nurture to God's children, to speak for social justice and righteousness, to bear witness to the truth and to the reign of God that is coming into the world.

G-1.0102 The Fellowship of the Congregation

The polity of the Presbyterian Church (U.S.A.) presupposes the fellowship of women, men, and children united in covenant relationship with one another and with God through Jesus Christ. The organization rests on the fellowship and is not designed to work without trust and love.

G-1.0103 Governed by the Constitution of the Presbyterian Church (U.S.A.)

A "congregation," as used in this Form of Government, refers to a formally organized community chartered and recognized by a presbytery as provided in this Constitution. Each congregation of the Presbyterian Church (U.S.A.) shall be governed by this Constitution. The members of a congregation put themselves under the leadership of the session and the higher councils (presbytery, synod, and General Assembly[b,c]). The session is responsible to guide and govern the life of the congregation. The session leads the congregation in fulfilling its responsibilities for the service of all people, for the upbuilding of the whole church, and for the glory of God.

Other forms of corporate witness established by the presbytery shall also be governed by this Constitution and shall be subject to the authority of the presbytery.

G-1.02 The Organizing of a Congregation

A congregation in the Presbyterian Church (U.S.A.) can be organized only by the authority of a presbytery and shall function under the provisions of this Constitution.

G-1.0201   *Organizing Covenant*

In organizing a congregation, presbytery shall receive applications for membership from persons wishing to unite in forming a new congregation. These persons shall covenant together as follows:

> "We, the undersigned, in response to the grace of God, desire to be constituted and organized as a congregation of the Presbyterian Church (U.S.A.), to be known as _____. We promise and covenant to live together in unity and to work together in ministry as disciples of Jesus Christ, bound to him and to one another as a part of the body of Christ in this place according to the principles of faith, mission, and order of the Presbyterian Church (U.S.A.).

> "(Signatures)"

At its sole discretion the presbytery may then declare them an organized congregation of the presbytery. The congregation shall then proceed to the election of ruling elders and, if they so decide, deacons. The presbytery shall prepare, examine, ordain, and install these newly elected persons. Presbytery shall continue to work closely with the congregation in securing pastoral leadership, in plans for the service and witness of the congregation, in coordinating its work with other congregations, in counseling concerning incorporation and bylaws for the congregation conforming to the Constitution of the Presbyterian Church (U.S.A.), and in giving other forms of support and encouragement that will strengthen the mission of the congregation in the larger life of the denomination.

G-1.03   The Membership of a Congregation

G-1.0301   *The Meaning of Membership and Baptism*

In Jesus Christ, God calls people to faith and to membership in the Church, the body of Christ. Baptism is the visible sign of that call and claim on a human life and of entrance into the membership of the church. The baptism of children witnesses to the truth that God's love claims people before they are able to respond in faith. The baptism of those who enter the covenant of membership upon their own profession of faith in Jesus Christ as Lord and Savior witnesses to the truth that God's gift of grace calls forth a response of faithfulness. Thus, the triune God, incarnate in the life, death, and resurrection of Jesus Christ, gives to the Church not only its mission but also its understanding of membership.

G-1.0302   *Welcome and Openness*

A congregation shall welcome all persons who trust in God's grace in Jesus Christ and desire to become part of the fellowship and ministry of his Church (F-1.0403). No person shall be denied membership for any reason not related to profession of faith. The Gospel leads members to extend the fellowship of Christ to all persons. Failure to do so constitutes a rejection of Christ himself and causes a scandal to the Gospel.

G-1.0303   Entry into Membership

Persons may enter into active church membership in the following ways:

a.   Public profession of faith, made after careful examination by the session in the meaning and responsibilities of membership; if not already baptized, the person making profession of faith shall be baptized;

b.   Certificate of transfer, when a person is a member of another Christian church at the time of transfer;

c.   Reaffirmation of faith, for persons previously baptized in the name of the triune God and having publicly professed their faith.

G-1.0304   The Ministry of Members

Membership in the Church of Jesus Christ is a joy and a privilege. It is also a commitment to participate in Christ's mission. A faithful member bears witness to God's love and grace and promises to be involved responsibly in the ministry of Christ's Church. Such involvement includes:

proclaiming the good news in word and deed,

taking part in the common life and worship of a congregation,

lifting one another up in prayer, mutual concern, and active support,

studying Scripture and the issues of Christian faith and life,

supporting the ministry of the church through the giving of money, time, and talents,

demonstrating a new quality of life within and through the church,

responding to God's activity in the world through service to others,

living responsibly in the personal, family, vocational, political, cultural, and social relationships of life,

working in the world for peace, justice, freedom, and human fulfillment,

participating in the governing responsibilities of the church, and

reviewing and evaluating regularly the integrity of one's membership, and considering ways in which one's participation in the worship and service of the church may be increased and made more meaningful.

G-1.04 CATEGORIES OF MEMBERSHIP

The membership of a congregation of the Presbyterian Church (U.S.A.) includes baptized members, active members, and affiliate members.

G-1.0401 Baptized Member

A baptized member is a person who has received the Sacrament of Baptism, whether in this congregation or elsewhere, and who has been enrolled as a baptized member by the session but who has not made a profession of faith in Jesus Christ as Lord and Savior. Such baptized members receive the pastoral care and instruction of the church, and may participate in the Sacrament of the Lord's Supper.

G-1.0402 Active Member

An active member is a person who has made a profession of faith in Christ, has been baptized, has been received into membership of the church, has voluntarily submitted to the government[d] of this church, and participates in the church's work and worship. In addition, active members participate in the governance of the church and may be elected to ordered ministry (see G-2.0102). Active members shall regularly, after prayerful consideration, recommit themselves to the disciplines and responsibilities of membership outlined in G-1.0304. The session shall have responsibility for preparing those who would become active members of the congregation.

G-1.0403 Affiliate Member

An affiliate member is a member of another congregation of this denomination or of another denomination or Christian body, who has temporarily moved from the community where the congregation of membership is situated, has presented a certificate of good standing from the appropriate council or governing body of that congregation, and has been received by the session as an affiliate member. An affiliate member may participate in the life of the congregation in the same manner as an active member except that an affiliate member may not vote in congregational meetings or be elected to ordered ministry or other office in the congregation.

G-1.0404 Other Participants

Persons who are not members of, or who may have ceased active participation in, the Presbyterian Church (U.S.A.) are welcome and may participate in the life and worship of this church and receive its pastoral care and instruction. The invitation to the Lord's Supper is extended to all who have been baptized, remembering that access to the table is not a right conferred upon the worthy, but a privilege given to the undeserving who come in faith, repentance, and love (W-2.4011). Confessing members of other Christian churches may present children for baptism, in conformity with W-2.3014.

G-1.05 MEETINGS OF THE CONGREGATION

G-1.0501   Annual and Special Meetings

The congregation shall hold an annual meeting and may hold special meetings as necessary, for any or all of the purposes appropriate for congregational consideration. The business to be transacted at special meetings shall be limited to items specifically listed in the call for the meeting.

All active members of the congregation present at either annual or special meetings are entitled to vote. Congregations shall provide by rule the quorum necessary to conduct business.

G-1.0502   Calling a Congregational Meeting

Meetings of the congregation shall be called by the session, by the presbytery, or by the session when requested in writing by one fourth of the active members on the roll of the congregation. Adequate public notice of all congregational meetings shall be given. Congregations shall provide by their own rule for minimum notification requirements and give notice at regular services of worship prior to the meeting.

G-1.0503   Business Proper to Congregational Meetings

Business to be transacted at meetings of the congregation shall be limited to matters related to the following:

    a.   electing ruling elders, deacons, and trustees;

    b.   calling a pastor, co-pastor, or associate pastor;

    c.   changing existing pastoral relationships, by such means as reviewing the adequacy of and approving changes to the terms of call of the pastor or pastors, or requesting, consenting to, or declining to consent to dissolution;

    d.   buying, mortgaging, or selling real property;

    e.   requesting the presbytery to grant an exemption as permitted in this Constitution (G-2.0404).

    f.   approving a plan for the creation of a joint congregational witness, or amending or dissolving the joint congregational witness (G-5.05).

Whenever permitted by civil law, both ecclesiastical and corporate business may be conducted at the same congregational meeting.

G-1.0504   Moderator

The installed pastor shall ordinarily moderate all meetings of the congregation. If it is impractical for the pastor to preside, he or she shall invite another teaching elder who is a member of the presbytery or a person authorized by the presbytery to serve as moderator. If there is no installed pastor, or the installed pastor is unable to moderate and/or to name another moderator, the presbytery shall make provision for a moderator.

G-1.0505   Secretary and Minutes

The clerk of session shall serve as secretary for all meetings of the congregation. If the clerk of session is unable to serve, the congregation shall elect a secretary for that meeting. The secretary shall record the actions of the congregation in minutes of the meeting.

CHAPTER TWO

ORDERED MINISTRY, COMMISSIONING, AND CERTIFICATION

G-2.01   ORDERED MINISTRIES OF THE CHURCH

G-2.0101   *Christ's Ministry*

The Church's ministry is a gift from Jesus Christ to the whole Church. Christ alone rules, calls, teaches, and uses the Church as he wills, exercising his authority by the ministry of women and men for the establishment and extension of God's new creation. Christ's ministry is the foundation and standard for all ministry, the pattern of the one who came "not to be served but to serve" (Matt. 20:28). The basic form of ministry is the ministry of the whole people of God, from whose midst some are called to ordered ministries, to fulfill particular functions. Members and those in ordered ministries serve together under the mandate of Christ.

G-2.0102   *Ordered Ministries*

The Church's ordered ministries described in the New Testament and maintained by this church are deacons[a] and presbyters (teaching elders[b] and ruling elders[c]). Ordered ministries are gifts to the church to order its life so that the ministry of the whole people of God may flourish. The existence of these ordered ministries in no way diminishes the importance of the commitment of all members to the total ministry of the church.

The government of this church is representative[d], and the right of God's people to elect presbyters and deacons is inalienable. Therefore, no person can be placed in any ordered ministry in a congregation or council of the church except by election of that body.

Ordination to the ministry of teaching elder, ruling elder, or deacon is unique to that order of ministry.

G-2.0103   *Call to Ordered Ministry*

The call to ordered ministry in the Church is the act of the triune God. This call is evidenced by the movement of the Holy Spirit in the individual conscience, the approval of a community of God's people, and the concurring judgment of a council of the Church.

G-2.0104   *Gifts and Qualifications*

a.   To those called to exercise special functions in the church—deacons, ruling elders, and teaching elders—God gives suitable gifts for their various duties. In addition to possessing the necessary gifts and abilities, those who undertake particular ministries should be persons of strong faith, dedicated discipleship, and love of Jesus Christ as Savior and Lord. Their manner of life should be a demonstration of the Christian gospel in the church and in the world. They must have the approval of God's people and the concurring judgment of a council of the church.

b.   Standards for ordained service reflect the church's desire to submit joyfully to the Lordship of Jesus Christ in all aspects of life (F-1.02). The council responsible for ordination and/or installation (G.2.0402; G-2.0607; G-3.0306) shall examine each candidate's calling, gifts, preparation, and suitability for the responsibilities of ordered ministry. The examination shall include, but not be limited to, a determination of the candidate's ability and commitment to fulfill all requirements as expressed in the constitutional questions for ordination and installation (W-4.4003). Councils shall be guided by Scripture and the confessions in applying standards to individual candidates.

G-2.0105   Freedom of Conscience

It is necessary to the integrity and health of the church that the persons who serve it in ordered ministries shall adhere to the essentials of the Reformed faith and polity as expressed in this Constitution. So far as may be possible without serious departure from these standards, without infringing on the rights and views of others, and without obstructing the constitutional governance of the church, freedom of conscience with respect to the interpretation of Scripture is to be maintained. It is to be recognized, however, that in entering the ordered ministries of the Presbyterian Church (U.S.A.), one chooses to exercise freedom of conscience within certain bounds. His or her conscience is captive to the Word of God as interpreted in the standards of the church so long as he or she continues to seek, or serve in, ordered ministry. The decision as to whether a person has departed from essentials of Reformed faith and polity is made initially by the individual concerned but ultimately becomes the responsibility of the council in which he or she is a member.[1]

G-2.02   DEACONS: THE MINISTRY OF COMPASSION AND SERVICE

G-2.0201   Deacon Defined

The ministry of deacon as set forth in Scripture[e] is one of compassion, witness, and service, sharing in the redeeming love of Jesus Christ for the poor, the hungry, the sick, the lost, the friendless, the oppressed, those burdened by unjust policies or structures, or anyone in distress[f]. Persons of spiritual character, honest repute, exemplary lives, brotherly and sisterly love, sincere compassion, and sound judgment should be chosen for this ministry.

---

[1] Very early in the history of the Presbyterian Church in the United States of America, even before the General Assembly was established, the plan of reunion of the Synod of New York and Philadelphia contained the following sentences: 'That when any matter is determined by a majority vote, every member shall either actively concur with or passively submit to such determination; or if his conscience permit him to do neither, he shall, after sufficient liberty modestly to reason and remonstrate, peaceably withdraw from our communion without attempting to make any schism. Provided always that this shall be understood to extend only to such determination as the body shall judge indispensable in doctrine or Presbyterian government.' (Hist. Dig. (P) p. 1310.) (Plan of Union of 1758, par. II.)

G-2.0202   *Under Authority of the Session*

Deacons may be individually commissioned or organized as a board of deacons. In either case, their ministry is under the supervision and authority of the session. Deacons may also be given special assignments in the congregation, such as caring for members in need, handling educational tasks, cultivating liberality in giving, collecting and disbursing monies to specific persons or causes, or overseeing the buildings and property of the congregation. Deacons shall assume other duties as may be delegated to them by the session, including assisting with the Lord's Supper. (W-3.3616). A congregation by a majority vote may choose not to utilize the ordered ministry of deacons. If the congregation has neither a board of deacons nor individually commissioned deacons, the function of this ordered ministry shall be the responsibility of the ruling elders and the session.

G-2.03   RULING ELDERS: THE MINISTRY OF DISCERNMENT AND GOVERNANCE

G-2.0301 *Ruling Elder Defined*

As there were in Old Testament times elders for the government of the people, so the New Testament church provided persons with particular gifts to share[g] in discernment of God's Spirit and governance of God's people. Accordingly, congregations should elect persons of wisdom and maturity of faith, having demonstrated skills in leadership and being compassionate in spirit. Ruling elders are so named not because they "lord it over" the congregation (Matt. 20:25), but because they are chosen by the congregation to discern and measure its fidelity to the Word of God, and to strengthen and nurture its faith and life. Ruling elders, together with teaching elders, exercise leadership, government, spiritual discernment, and discipline[h] and have responsibilities for the life of a congregation as well as the whole church, including ecumenical relationships. When elected by the congregation, they shall serve faithfully as members of the session. When elected as commissioners to higher councils, ruling elders participate and vote with the same authority as teaching elders, and they are eligible for any office.

G-2.04   GENERAL PROVISIONS FOR RULING ELDERS AND DEACONS

G-2.0401   *Election of Ruling Elders and Deacons*

Ruling elders and deacons are men and women elected by the congregation from among its members. The nomination and election of ruling elders and deacons shall express the rich diversity of the congregation's membership and shall guarantee participation and inclusiveness (F-1.0403). Ruling elders and deacons shall be nominated by a committee elected by the congregation, drawn from and representative of its membership. Congregations may provide by their own rule for a congregational nominating committee, provided that the committee shall consist of at least three active members of the congregation, and shall include at least one ruling elder who is currently serving on the session. The pastor shall serve ex officio and without vote. When elections are held, full opportunity shall always be given to the congregation for nomination from the floor of the congregational meeting by any active member of the congregation. A majority of all the active members present and voting shall be required to elect.

G-2.0402   *Preparation for Ministry as a Ruling Elder or Deacon*

When persons have been elected to the ordered ministry of ruling elder or deacon, the session shall provide a period of study and preparation, after which the session shall examine them as to their personal faith; knowledge of the doctrine, government, and discipline contained in the Constitution of the church; and the duties of the ministry. The session shall also confer with them as to their willingness to undertake the ministry appropriate to the order. If the examination is approved, the session shall appoint a day for the service of ordination and installation.

G-2.0403   *Service of Ordination and Installation*

The service of ordination and installation shall focus upon Christ and the joy and responsibility of serving him through the mission and ministry of the church, and shall include a sermon appropriate to the occasion. The moderator of session or person authorized to preside shall state briefly the nature of the ministry of ruling elder and deacon. The act of ordination and installation takes place in the context of worship. The order for that service of worship in the Directory for Worship (W-4.4000) shall be followed.

G-2.0404   *Terms of Service*

Ruling elders and deacons shall be elected to serve terms of no more than three years on the session or board of deacons, and may be eligible for reelection according to congregational rule. However, no ruling elder or deacon shall be eligible to serve more than six consecutive years, and a ruling elder or deacon who has served six consecutive years shall be ineligible for election to the same board for at least one year. Election shall be to classes as nearly equal in number as possible, with the term of only one class ending each year. The presbytery may, upon written request and by majority vote, grant a congregation a waiver of this limitation on terms.

Once ordained and while they are active members of any congregation of this denomination, ruling elders or deacons not in active service on a session or board of deacons continue to bear the responsibilities of the ministry to which they have been ordained, except as provided in G-2.0406, G-2.0407, or in accordance with the Rules of Discipline.

G-2.0405   *Dissolution of Relationship*

A ruling elder or deacon may resign from the session or board of deacons, with the session's consent. On ceasing to be an active member of a congregation, a ruling elder or deacon ceases to be a member of its session or board. When a ruling elder or deacon, because of change of residence or disability, is unable for a period of one year to perform the duties of the ministry to which he or she was installed, the active relationship shall be dissolved by the session unless there is good reason not to do so, which shall be recorded.

G-2.0406   Release from Ministry as a Ruling Elder or Deacon

If a ruling elder or deacon who is in good standing, against whom no inquiry has been initiated, and against whom no charges have been filed, shall make application to the session to be released from the exercise of the ordered ministry, the session of the congregation in which he or she holds membership, upon granting the release, shall delete that person's name from the appropriate register of ruling elders or deacons of the congregation. No judgment of failure on the part of the ruling elder or deacon is implied in this action. Release from the exercise of the ministry of ruling elder or deacon requires a discontinuation of all functions of that ministry. The status of one so released shall be the same as any church member. Should a person released under this section later desire to be restored to that ordered ministry, that person shall make application to the session that granted the release, and upon approval of the session, that person shall be restored to the exercise of the ministry from which he or she was released without re-ordination.

G-2.0407   Renunciation of Jurisdiction

When a ruling elder or deacon submits to the clerk of session a written statement renouncing the jurisdiction of this church, the renunciation shall be effective upon receipt. When a ruling elder or deacon persists in work disapproved by the session, the session shall consult with him or her and shall give notice of its disapproval. If, after having been provided opportunity for consultation and upon written notice of its disapproval, the ruling elder or deacon persists in the work, the session may then conclude that the ruling elder or deacon has renounced the jurisdiction of this church.

Renunciation of jurisdiction shall remove the ruling elder or deacon from membership and ordered ministry and shall terminate the exercise of the ministry. The renunciation shall be reported by the clerk of session at the next meeting of the session, which shall record the renunciation, delete the name of the ruling elder or deacon from the appropriate register, and take such other administrative actions as may be required by this Constitution.

G-2.05   TEACHING ELDERS: THE MINISTRY OF THE WORD AND SACRAMENT

G-2.0501   Teaching Elder Defined

Teaching elders (also called ministers of the Word and Sacrament) shall in all things be committed to teaching the faith and equipping the saints for the work of ministry (Eph. 4:12). They may serve in a variety of ministries, as authorized by the presbytery. When they serve as preachers and teachers of the Word, they shall preach and teach the faith of the church, so that the people are shaped by the pattern of the gospel and strengthened for witness and service. When they serve at font and table, they shall interpret the mysteries of grace and lift the people's vision toward the hope of God's new creation. When they serve as pastors[i], they shall support the people in the disciplines of the faith amid the struggles of daily life. When they serve as presbyters, they shall participate in the responsibilities of governance, seeking always to discern the mind of Christ and to build up Christ's body through devotion, debate, and decision.

G-2.0502 Presbytery and the Teaching Elder

As the Lord has set aside through calling certain members to be teaching elders, so the church confirms that call through the action of the presbytery. The presbytery shall determine whether a particular work may be helpful to the church in mission and is a call to validated ministry requiring ordination as a teaching elder. In the performance of that ministry, the teaching elder shall be accountable to the presbytery. Teaching elders have membership in the presbytery by action of the presbytery itself, and no pastoral relationship may be established, changed, or dissolved without the approval of the presbytery.

G-2.0503 Categories of Membership

A teaching elder is a member of a presbytery and shall be engaged in a ministry validated by that presbytery, a member-at-large as determined by the presbytery, or honorably retired.

a. *Engaged in a Validated Ministry*

A validated ministry shall:

(1) demonstrate conformity with the mission of God's people in the world as set forth in Holy Scripture, *The Book of Confessions*, and the *Book of Order* of this church;

(2) serve and aid others, and enable the ministry of others;

(3) give evidence of theologically informed fidelity to God's Word;

(4) be carried on in accountability for its character and conduct to the presbytery in addition to any organizations, agencies, and institutions served; and

(5) include responsible participation in the deliberations, worship, and work of the presbytery and in the life of a congregation of this church or a church in correspondence with the PC(USA) (G-5.0201).

When teaching elders are called to validated ministry beyond the jurisdiction of the church, they shall give evidence of a quality of life that helps to share the ministry of the good news. They shall participate in a congregation, in their presbytery, and in ecumenical relationships and shall be eligible for election to the higher councils of the church and to the boards and agencies of those councils.

The presbytery shall review annually the work of all teaching elders engaged in validated ministries outside the congregation.

b. *Member-at-large*

A member-at-large is a teaching elder who has previously been engaged in a validated ministry, and who now, without intentional abandonment of the exercise of ministry, is no longer engaged in a ministry that complies with all the criteria in G-2.0503a. A teaching elder may be designated a member-at-large because he or she is limited in his or her ability to engage in a ministry fulfilling all of the criteria for a validated ministry due to family responsibilities or other individual circumstances recognized by the presbytery. A member-at-large shall comply with as many of the criteria in G-2.0503a as possible and shall actively participate in the life of a congregation. A member-at-large is entitled to take part in the meetings of the presbytery and to speak, vote, and hold office. The status of member-at-large shall be reviewed annually.

c. *Honorably Retired*

Upon request of a member of presbytery, the presbytery may designate the member honorably retired because of age or physical or mental disability.

G-2.0504   *Pastoral Relationships*

When teaching elders are called as pastor, co-pastor, or associate pastor of a congregation, they are to be responsible for a quality of life and relationships that commends the gospel to all persons and that communicates its joy and justice. They are responsible for studying, teaching, and preaching the Word, for celebrating Baptism and the Lord's Supper, and for praying with and for the congregation. With the ruling elders, they are to encourage people in the worship and service of God; to equip and enable them for their tasks within the church and their mission in the world; to exercise pastoral care, devoting special attention to the poor, the sick, the troubled, and the dying; to participate in governing responsibilities, including leadership of the congregation in implementing the principles of participation and inclusiveness in the decision-making life of the congregation, and its task of reaching out in concern and service to the life of the human community as a whole. With the deacons they are to share in the ministries of compassion, witness, and service. In addition to these pastoral duties, they are responsible for sharing in the ministry of the church in councils higher than the session and in ecumenical relationships.

a.   *Installed Pastoral Relationships*

The installed pastoral relationships are pastor, co-pastor, and associate pastor. A teaching elder may be installed in a pastoral relationship for an indefinite period or for a designated term determined by the presbytery in consultation with the congregation and specified in the call. When a congregation determines that its strategy for mission under the Word so requires, the congregation may call additional pastors. Such additional pastors shall be called co-pastors or associate pastors, and the duties of each pastor and the relationship between the pastors of the congregation shall be determined by the session with the approval of the presbytery. When a congregation has two pastors serving as co-pastors, and the relationship of one of them is dissolved, the other remains as pastor. The relationship of an associate pastor to a congregation is not dependent upon that of a pastor. An associate pastor is ordinarily not eligible to be the next installed pastor of that congregation.

b. *Temporary Pastoral Relationships*

Temporary pastoral relationships are approved by the presbytery and do not carry a formal call or installation. When a congregation does not have a pastor, or while the pastor is unable to perform her or his duties, the session, with the approval of presbytery, may obtain the services of a teaching elder, candidate, or ruling elder in a temporary pastoral relationship. No formal call shall be issued and no formal installation shall take place.

Titles and terms of service for temporary relationships shall be determined by the presbytery. A person serving in a temporary pastoral relationship is invited for a specified period not to exceed twelve months in length, which is renewable with the approval of the presbytery. A teaching elder employed in a temporary pastoral relationship is ordinarily not eligible to serve as the next installed pastor, co-pastor, or associate pastor.

c. *Exceptions*

A presbytery may determine that its mission strategy permits a teaching elder currently called as an Associate Pastor to be eligible to serve as the next installed pastor or co-pastor, or a teaching elder employed in a temporary pastoral relationship to be eligible to serve as the next installed pastor, co-pastor, or associate pastor. Presbyteries that permit this eligibility shall establish such relationships only by a three-fourths vote of the members of presbytery present and voting.

G-2.0505 *Transfer of Ministers of Other Denominations*

a. When a minister of another Christian church is called to a work properly under the jurisdiction of a presbytery, the presbytery, after the constitutional conditions have been met, shall recognize the minister's previous ordination to ministry. Such ministers shall furnish credentials and evidence of good standing acceptable to the presbytery, and shall submit satisfactory evidence of possessing the qualifications of character and scholarship required of candidates of this church. (G-2.0607 and G-2.0610). In exceptional circumstances the following provisions will apply:

(1) In the case of ministers for immigrant fellowships and congregations, a presbytery may, if it determines that its strategy for mission with that group requires it, recognize the ordination and receive as a member of presbytery a new immigrant minister who furnishes evidence of good standing in a denomination, even though at the time of enrollment that minister lacks the educational history required of candidates, and provide such educational opportunities as seem necessary and prudent for that minister's successful ministry in the presbytery.

(2) A minister of another Reformed church who has been ordained for five or more years may be granted an exemption for some or all of the examinations required of candidates for ordination by a two-thirds vote of the presbytery.

b.   Upon enrollment, the minister shall furnish the presbytery with evidence of having surrendered membership in any and all other Christian churches with which the minister has previously been associated.

G-2.0506   Temporary Membership in Presbytery for a Period of Service

A presbytery may enroll a minister of another Christian church who is serving temporarily in a validated ministry in this church, or in an installed relationship under the provisions of the Formula of Agreement (*Book of Order*, Appendix B; G-5.0202), when the minister has satisfied the requirements of preparation for such service established by the presbytery's own rule.

G-2.0507   Release from Ministry as a Teaching Elder

When a teaching elder against whom no inquiry has been initiated pursuant to D-10.0101 and D-10.0201, against whom no charges have been filed, and who otherwise is in good standing shall make application to be released from the exercise of the ordered ministry of teaching elder, the presbytery shall delete that person's name from the roll and upon request of a session dismiss that person to a congregation. Release from the exercise of ordered ministry requires discontinuance of all functions of that ministry. The designations that refer to teaching elders shall not be used. The person so released shall engage in the ministry shared by all active members of congregations. Should a person released under this section later desire to be restored to the ordered ministry of teaching elder, that person shall apply through the presbytery which granted the release, and upon approval of that presbytery, the reaffirmation of the ordination questions, and the resumption of a ministry that qualifies that person for membership in the presbytery, shall be restored to the exercise of the ordered ministry as a teaching elder without re-ordination.

G-2.0508   Failure to Engage in Validated Ministry

A teaching elder whom the presbytery determines no longer to be engaged in a validated ministry (G-2.0503a) or to fulfill the criteria for membership-at-large (G-2.0503b), and who is not honorably retired (G-2.0503c), shall not have voice or vote in meetings of the presbytery, except when the matter under consideration pertains to his or her relationship to the presbytery. Names of such persons shall be reported annually to the presbytery by the stated clerk. If after three years the teaching elder does not meet the criteria for validated ministry or membership-at-large, the presbytery may delete that person's name from the roll of membership and, upon request of a session, dismiss that person to a congregation.

G-2.0509   Renunciation of Jurisdiction

When a teaching elder (or authorized representative) submits to the stated clerk of the presbytery of membership a written statement renouncing the jurisdiction of this church, the renunciation shall be effective upon receipt. When a teaching elder persists in work disapproved by the presbytery having jurisdiction, the presbytery shall consult with the teaching elder and shall give notice of its disapproval. If after having been provided opportunity for consultation and upon written notice of its disapproval, the teaching elder persists in the work, the presbytery may then conclude that he or she has renounced the jurisdiction of this church.

When a teaching elder accepts or continues membership of any character in another denomination, except as provided in this Constitution, the presbytery shall record the fact and delete the teaching elder's name from the roll.

Renunciation of jurisdiction shall remove the teaching elder from membership and ordered ministry and shall terminate the exercise of that ministry. The renunciation shall be reported by the stated clerk at the next meeting of the presbytery, which shall record the renunciation, delete her or his name from the appropriate roll, and take such other administrative actions as may be required by this Constitution, including public communication of such a renunciation.

G-2.06 PREPARATION FOR MINISTRY

G-2.0601   Nature and Purpose of Preparation

It is important that those who are to be ordained as teaching elders receive full preparation for their task under the direction of the presbytery. For this purpose, a presbytery shall enter into covenant relationship with those preparing to become teaching elders and with their sessions and congregations. This relationship shall be divided into the two phases of inquiry and candidacy.

G-2.0602   Time Requirements

To be enrolled as an inquirer, the applicant shall be a member of the sponsoring congregation, shall have been active in the work and worship of that congregation for at least six months, and shall have received the endorsement of the session of the sponsoring congregation. The inquiry and candidacy phases shall continue for a period of no less than two years, including at least one year as a candidate.

G-2.0603   Purpose of Inquiry

The purpose of the inquiry phase is to provide an opportunity for the church and those who believe themselves called to ordered ministry as teaching elders to explore that call together so that the presbytery can make an informed decision about the inquirer's suitability for ordered ministry.

G-2.0604   Purpose of Candidacy

The purpose of the candidacy phase is to provide for the full preparation of persons to serve the church as teaching elders. This shall be accomplished through the presbytery's support, guidance, and evaluation of a candidate's fitness and readiness for a call to ministry requiring ordination[j].

G-2.0605   Oversight

During the phases of inquiry and candidacy the individual continues to be an active member of his or her congregation and subject to the concern and discipline of the session. In matters relating to preparation for ministry, the individual is subject to the oversight of the presbytery within the context of their covenant relationship.

G-2.0606   Service in Covenant Relationship

Inquirers and candidates shall, with the permission of the presbytery of care, engage in some form of supervised service to the church. No inquirer or candidate who has not been previously ordained as a ruling elder may serve as moderator of a session, administer the Sacraments, or perform a marriage service. An inquirer or candidate previously ordained as a ruling elder may be authorized by the presbytery to preside at the Lord's Supper when invited by a session.

G-2.0607   Final Assessment and Negotiation for Service

A candidate may not enter into negotiation for his or her service as a teaching elder without approval of the presbytery. The presbytery shall record when it has certified a candidate ready for examination for ordination, pending a call. Evidence of readiness to begin ordered ministry as a teaching elder shall include:

    a.   a candidate's wisdom and maturity of faith, leadership skills, compassionate spirit, honest repute, and sound judgment;

    b.   a transcript showing graduation, with satisfactory grades, at a regionally accredited college or university;

    c.   a transcript from a theological institution accredited by the Association of Theological Schools acceptable to the presbytery, showing a course of study including Hebrew and Greek, exegesis of the Old and New Testaments using Hebrew and Greek, satisfactory grades in all areas of study, and graduation or proximity to graduation; and

    d.   satisfactory grades, together with the examination papers in the areas covered by any standard ordination examination approved by the General Assembly. Such examinations shall be prepared and administered by a body created by the presbyteries.

G-2.0608   Transfer of Relationship

At the request of the inquirer or candidate and with the approval of the sessions and presbyteries involved, a presbytery may transfer the covenant relationship of an inquirer or candidate.

G-2.0609   Removal from Relationship

An inquirer or candidate may, after consultation with the session and the presbytery, withdraw from covenant relationship. A presbytery may also, for sufficient reasons, remove an individual's name from the roll of inquirers and candidates, reporting this action and the reasons to the session, to the individual, and, if appropriate, to the educational institution in which the individual is enrolled. Prior to taking such action, the presbytery or its designated entity shall make a reasonable attempt to give the candidate or inquirer an opportunity to be heard concerning the proposed removal.

G-2.0610   Exceptions

By a three-fourths vote, a presbytery may waive any of the requirements for ordination in G-2.06, except for those of G-2.0607d. If a presbytery judges that there are good and sufficient reasons why a candidate should not be required to satisfy the requirements of G-2.0607d, it shall approve by three-quarters vote some alternate means by which to ascertain the readiness of the candidate for ministry in the areas covered by the standard ordination examinations. A full account of the reasons for exception shall be included in the minutes of the presbytery and communicated to the presbytery to which an inquirer or candidate may be transferred.

G-2.07   ORDINATION

G-2.0701   Ordination

Ordination to the ordered ministry of teaching elder is an act of the whole church carried out by the presbytery, setting apart a person to ordered ministry. Such a person shall have fulfilled the ordination requirements of the presbytery of care and received the call of God to service to a congregation or other work in the mission of the church that is acceptable to the candidate and to the presbytery of call.

G-2.0702   Place of Ordination

The presbytery placing the call to the candidate for ministry shall ordinarily examine, ordain, and install the candidate.

G-2.0703   Service of Ordination

The order for that service of worship in the Directory for Worship (W-4.4000) shall be followed.

G-2.0704   Record of Ordination

The presbytery of call shall record the ordination and installation, along with written affirmation of the new teaching elder to the obligations undertaken in the ordination questions, and enroll the teaching elder as a member of the presbytery. The stated clerk of the presbytery shall report these actions to the General Assembly, the presbytery of care, and to the congregation of which the candidate was formerly a member.

G-2.08   CALL AND INSTALLATION

G-2.0801   Pastoral Vacancy

When a congregation has a vacancy in a pastoral position, or after the presbytery approves the effective date of the dissolution of an existing pastoral relationship, the congregation shall, with the guidance and permission of the presbytery, proceed to fill the vacancy in the following manner.

G-2.0802   *Election of a Pastor Nominating Committee*

The session shall call a congregational meeting to elect a pastor nominating committee that shall be representative of the whole congregation. The committee's duty shall be to nominate a pastor for election by the congregation.

G-2.0803   *Call Process*

According to the process of the presbytery and prior to making its report to the congregation, the pastor nominating committee shall receive and consider the presbytery's counsel on the merits, suitability, and availability of those considered for the call. When the way is clear for the committee to report to the congregation, the committee shall notify the session, which shall call a congregational meeting.

G-2.0804   *Terms of Call*

The terms of call shall always meet or exceed any minimum requirement of the presbytery in effect when the call is made. The session shall review annually the minister's terms of call and shall propose for congregational action (G-1.0501) such changes as the session deems appropriate, provided that they meet the presbytery's minimum requirements. The call shall include participation in the benefits plan of the Presbyterian Church (U.S.A.), including both pension and medical coverage, or any successor plan approved by the General Assembly.

G-2.0805   *Installation Service*

When the congregation, the presbytery, and the teaching elder (or candidate) have all concurred in a call to a permanent or designated pastoral position, the presbytery shall complete the call process by organizing and conducting a service of installation. Installation is an act of the presbytery establishing the pastoral relationship. A service of installation occurs in the context of worship. The order for that service of worship in the Directory for Worship (W-4.4000) shall be followed.

G-2.09   DISSOLUTION OF PASTORAL RELATIONSHIPS

G-2.0901   *Congregational Meeting*

An installed pastoral relationship may be dissolved only by the presbytery. Whether the teaching elder, the congregation, or the presbytery initiates proceedings for dissolution of the relationship, there shall always be a meeting of the congregation to consider the matter and to consent, or decline to consent, to dissolution.

G-2.0902   *Pastor, Co-Pastor or Associate Pastor Requests*

A pastor, co-pastor, or associate pastor may request the presbytery to dissolve the pastoral relationship. The teaching elder must also state her or his intention to the session.

The session shall call a congregational meeting to act upon the request and to make recommendations to the presbytery. If the congregation does not concur, the presbytery shall hear from the congregation, through its elected commissioners, the reasons why the presbytery should not dissolve the pastoral relationship. If the congregation fails to appear, or if its reasons for retaining the relationship are judged insufficient, the request may be granted and the pastoral relationship dissolved.

G-2.0903   *Congregation Requests*

If any congregation desires the pastoral relationship to be dissolved, a procedure similar to G-2.0902, above, shall be followed. When a congregation requests the session to call a congregational meeting to dissolve its relationship with its pastor, the session shall call the meeting and request the presbytery to appoint a moderator for the meeting. If the pastor does not concur with the request to dissolve the relationship, the presbytery shall hear from him or her the reasons why the presbytery should not dissolve the relationship. If the pastor fails to appear, or if the reasons for maintaining the relationship are judged insufficient, the relationship may be dissolved.

G-2.0904   *Presbytery Action*

The presbytery may inquire into reported difficulties in a congregation and may dissolve the pastoral relationship if, after consultation with the teaching elder, the session, and the congregation, it finds the church's mission under the Word imperatively demands it.

G-2.0905   *Officiate by Invitation Only*

After the dissolution of the pastoral relationship, former pastors and associate pastors shall not provide their pastoral services to members of their former congregations without the invitation of the moderator of session.

G-2.10   COMMISSIONING RULING ELDERS TO PARTICULAR PASTORAL SERVICE

G-2.1001   *Functions*

When the presbytery, in consultation with the session or other responsible committee, determines that its strategy for mission requires it, the presbytery may authorize a ruling elder to be commissioned to limited pastoral service as assigned by the presbytery. A ruling elder so designated may be commissioned to serve in a validated ministry of the presbytery. Presbytery, in its commission, may authorize the ruling elder to moderate the session of the congregation to which he or she is commissioned, to administer the Sacraments, and to officiate at marriages where permitted by state law. This commission shall also specify the term of service, which shall not exceed three years but shall be renewable. The presbytery shall review the commission at least annually.

G-2.1002   *Training, Examination and Commissioning*

A ruling elder who seeks to serve under the terms of G-2.1001 shall receive such preparation and instruction as determined by the presbytery to be appropriate to the particular commission. The ruling elder shall be examined by the presbytery as to personal faith, motives for seeking the commission, and the areas of instruction determined by presbytery. A ruling elder who has been commissioned and later ceases to serve in the specified ministry may continue to be listed as available to serve, but is not authorized to perform the functions specified in G-2.1001 until commissioned again to a congregation or ministry by the presbytery.

G-2.1003   *Commissioning Service*

When the presbytery is satisfied with the qualifications of a ruling elder to serve a congregation providing the services described above, it shall commission the ruling elder to pastoral service as designated by the presbytery, employing the questions contained in W-4.4000.

G-2.1004   *Supervision*

The ruling elder commissioned under the terms of G-2.1001 shall work under the supervision of the presbytery. The presbytery may at any time withdraw the commission for reasons it deems good and sufficient. A teaching elder shall be assigned as a mentor and supervisor.

G-2.11   CERTIFIED CHURCH SERVICE

G-2.1101   *Forms of Certified Church Service*

Persons may be certified and called to service within congregations, councils, and church-related entities, serving in staff positions. These individuals endeavor to reflect their faith through their work and to strengthen the church through their dedication. They should be encouraged by their session and presbytery to meet, or be prepared to meet, the certification requirements in a handbook provided by a national certifying body approved by the General Assembly. Names of those who have earned certification through a national certifying body shall be transmitted to the appropriate body of the General Assembly, which will forward them to the stated clerk of the presbyteries in which those persons labor.

G-2.1102   *Presbytery and Certified Church Service*

The presbytery shall encourage sessions to make continuing education funds and time available to those seeking certification, and shall affirm the skill and dedication of these certified persons by providing a service of recognition at the time of certification. The presbytery may grant the privilege of voice at all its meetings to persons in certified church service.

G-2.1103   Christian Educators

a.   *Skills and Training*

Certified Christian educators are persons certified and called to service in the ministry of education in congregations or councils. They shall have skills and training in biblical interpretation, Reformed theology, worship and sacraments, human development, faith development, religious educational theory and practice, and the polity, programs, and mission of the Presbyterian Church (U.S.A.).

b.   *Presbytery Responsibility*

The presbytery shall establish minimum requirements for compensation and benefits for Certified Christian Educators and Certified Associate Christian Educators and shall provide access to the area of presbytery that oversees ministry (G-3.0307). During their term of service in an educational ministry under the jurisdiction of the presbytery, Certified Christian Educators are entitled to the privilege of the floor with voice only at all presbytery meetings, and in the case of Certified Christian Educators who are ruling elders, the privilege of voice and vote at all its meetings.

CHAPTER THREE
COUNCILS OF THE CHURCH

G-3.01 GENERAL PRINCIPLES OF COUNCILS

G-3.0101 *Councils as an Expression of Unity of the Church*

The mutual interconnection of the church through its councils is a sign of the unity of the church. Congregations of the Presbyterian Church (U.S.A.), while possessing all the gifts necessary to be the church, are nonetheless not sufficient in themselves to be the church. Rather, they are called to share with others both within and beyond the congregation the task of bearing witness to the Lordship of Jesus Christ in the world. This call to bear witness is the work of all believers. The particular responsibility of the councils of the church is to nurture, guide, and govern those who witness as part of the Presbyterian Church (U.S.A.), to the end that such witness strengthens the whole church and gives glory to God.

The Presbyterian Church (U.S.A.) is governed by councils composed of presbyters elected by the people (F-3.0202). These councils are called the session, the presbytery, the synod, and the General Assembly. All councils of the church are united by the nature of the church and share with one another responsibilities, rights, and powers as provided in this Constitution. The councils are distinct, but have such mutual relations that the act of one of them is the act of the whole church. The jurisdiction of each council is limited by the express provisions of the Constitution, with the acts of each subject to review by the next higher council. Powers not mentioned in this Constitution are reserved to the presbyteries.

Councils of the church exist to help congregations and the church as a whole to be more faithful participants in the mission of Christ. They do so as they

Provide that the Word of God may be truly preached and heard,
 responding to the promise of God's new creation in Christ, and
 inviting all people to participate in that new creation;

Provide that the Sacraments may be rightly administered and received,
 welcoming those who are being engrafted into Christ,
 bearing witness to Christ's saving death and resurrection,
 anticipating the heavenly banquet that is to come, and
 committing itself in the present to solidarity with the marginalized and the
  hungry; and

Nurture a covenant community of disciples of Christ,
 living in the strength of God's promise, and
 giving itself in service to God's mission.

G-3.0102   Ecclesiastical Jurisdiction

Councils of this church have only ecclesiastical jurisdiction for the purpose of serving Jesus Christ and declaring and obeying his will in relation to truth and service, order and discipline. They may frame statements of faith, bear testimony against error in doctrine and immorality in life, resolve questions of doctrine and discipline, give counsel in matters of conscience, and decide issues properly brought before them under the provisions of this *Book of Order*. They may authorize the administration of the sacraments in accordance with the Directory for Worship. They have power to establish plans and rules for the worship, mission, government, and discipline of the church and to do those things necessary to the peace, purity, unity, and progress of the church under the will of Christ. They have responsibility for the leadership, guidance, and government of that portion of the church that is under their jurisdiction.

G-3.0103   Participation and Representation

The councils of the church shall give full expression to the rich diversity of the church's membership and shall provide for full participation and access to representation in decision-making and employment practices (F-1.0403). In fulfilling this commitment, councils shall give due consideration to both the gifts and requirements for ministry (G-2.0104) and the right of people in congregations and councils to elect their officers (F-3.0106).

Each council shall develop procedures and mechanisms for promoting and reviewing that body's implementation of the church's commitment to inclusiveness and representation. Councils above the session shall establish by their own rule committees on representation to fulfill the following functions: to advise the council regarding the implementation of principles of unity and diversity, to advocate for diversity in leadership, and to consult with the council on the employment of personnel, in accordance with the principles of unity and diversity in F-1.0403. A committee on representation should not be merged with another committee or made a subcommittee of another committee.

G-3.0104   Officers

The pastor of a congregation shall be the moderator of the session of that congregation. In congregations where there are co-pastors, they shall both be considered moderators and have provisions for designating who presides at a particular meeting. If it is impractical for the pastor to moderate, he or she shall invite another teaching elder who is a member of the presbytery or a person authorized by the presbytery to serve as moderator. If there is no installed pastor, or if the installed pastor is unable to invite another moderator, the presbytery shall make provision for a moderator.

The moderator possesses the authority necessary for preserving order and for conducting efficiently the business of the body. He or she shall convene and adjourn the body in accordance with its own action.

Each council higher than the session shall elect a moderator for such terms as the council determines. At the time of their election, moderators must be continuing members of, or commissioners to, the council over which they are elected to preside. They shall preside at meetings of the council during their term of office; councils shall provide by rule who shall preside in the absence of the moderator.

Each council shall elect a clerk who shall record the transactions of the council, keep its rolls of membership and attendance, **maintain any required registers**, preserve its records, and furnish extracts from them when required by another council of the church. Such extracts, verified by the clerk, shall be evidence in any council of the church. The clerk of the session shall be a ruling elder elected by the session for such term as it may determine. The clerk of a presbytery, a synod, and the General Assembly shall be called stated clerk, shall be elected by the council for a definite term as it may determine, and must be a ruling elder or teaching elder. A stated clerk may be removed from office prior to completion of his or her term of service through the use of the process outlined in G-3.0110.

Councils may elect such other officers as the council requires.

G-3.0105   Meetings

Meetings of councils shall be opened and closed with prayer.[a] Meetings shall be conducted in accordance with the most recent edition of *Robert's Rules of Order Newly Revised*, except when it is in contradiction to this Constitution. Councils may also make use of processes of discernment in their deliberations prior to a vote as agreed upon by the body.

When a council makes a decision, a member of the body who voted against the decision is entitled to file a dissent or a protest. Filing a dissent or protest neither initiates nor prevents judicial process.

a.   A dissent is a declaration expressing disagreement with a decision of a council. It shall be made at the particular session during which the decision is made. The names of members dissenting shall be recorded.

b.   A protest is a written declaration, supported by reasons, alleging that a decision of a council is or contains an irregularity or a delinquency. Written notice of the protest shall be given at the particular session of the council during which it arose and shall be filed with the clerk before adjournment. If the protest is expressed in decorous and respectful language, it shall be entered in the minutes of the meeting, and may be accompanied by an answer prepared by the council. No further action is required.

G-3.0106   Administration of Mission

Mission determines the forms and structures needed for the church to do its work. Administration is the process by which a council implements its decisions. Administration enables the church to give effective witness in the world to God's new creation in Jesus Christ and strengthens the church's witness to the mission of the triune God.

Councils higher than the session may provide examples of policies and procedures that may be gathered into advisory handbooks. These examples illumine practices required by the Constitution but left to councils for specific implementation. Such handbooks may also offer information that enhances or secures the ministry of the particular council.

Each council shall develop a manual of administrative operations that will specify the form and guide the work of mission in that council.

All councils shall adopt and implement a sexual misconduct policy.

A council may delegate aspects of its tasks to such entities as it deems appropriate, provided that those entities remain accountable to the council.

The administration of mission demonstrates the unity and interdependence of the church, in that councils share with one another responsibilities, rights, and powers (F-3.0203). Through their members and elected commissioners, lower councils participate in planning and administration of the work of higher councils, and in consultation between bodies concerning mission, budget, staffing and fair employment practices, and matters of equitable compensation.

The funding of mission similarly demonstrates the unity and interdependence of the church. The failure of any part of the church to participate in the stewardship of the mission of the whole church diminishes that unity and interdependence. All mission funding should enable the church to give effective witness in the world to God's new creation in Jesus Christ, and should strengthen the church's witness to the mission of God.

Each council above the session shall prepare a budget for its operating expenses, including administrative personnel, and may fund it with a per capita apportionment among the particular congregations within its bounds. Presbyteries are responsible for raising their own funds and for raising and timely transmission of per capita funds to their respective synods and the General Assembly. Presbyteries may direct per capita apportionments to sessions within their bounds, but in no case shall the authority of the session to direct its benevolences be compromised.

G-3.0107 Records

Each council shall keep a full and accurate record of its proceedings. Minutes and all other official records of councils are the property in perpetuity of said councils or their legal successors. When a council ceases to exist, its records shall become the property of the next higher council within whose bounds the lower council was prior to its cessation. The clerk of each council shall make recommendation to that body for the permanent safekeeping of the body's records with the Presbyterian Historical Society or in a temperature and humidity controlled environment of a seminary of the Presbyterian Church (U.S.A.).

G-3.0108 Administrative Review

Higher councils shall review the work of lower councils in the following ways:

a. *General Administrative Review*

Each council shall review annually or biennially, based on the body's meeting frequency, the proceedings and actions of all entities related to the body, all officers able to act on behalf of the body, and lower councils within its jurisdiction. In reviewing the procedures of the lower council, the higher body shall determine whether the proceedings have been correctly recorded, have been in accordance with this Constitution[b], have been prudent and equitable, and have been faithful to the mission of the whole church. It shall also determine whether lawful injunctions of a higher body have been obeyed.

b. *Special Administrative Review*

If a higher council learns at any time of an alleged irregularity or delinquency of a lower council, it may require the lower body to produce any records and to take appropriate action.

c. *Directed Response*

The higher council may direct the lower council to reconsider and take corrective action if matters are determined to be out of compliance. In addition to administrative review, review and correction may be sought by initiating judicial process as described in the Rules of Discipline.

G-3.0109   Committees and Commissions

Councils may designate by their own rule such committees and commissions as they deem necessary and helpful for the accomplishment of the mission of the church, and may create such structures jointly with other councils, in consultation with the next higher council. In appointing such committees and commissions councils shall be mindful of the principles of unity in diversity consistent with the provisions of this Constitution (F-1.0403, G-3.0103).

A committee shall study and recommend action or carry out decisions already made by a council. It shall make a full report to the council that created it, and its recommendations shall require action by that body. Committees of councils higher than the session shall consist of both teaching elders and members of congregations, with at least one half being members of congregations.

A commission is empowered to consider and conclude matters referred to it by a council. The designating council shall state specifically the scope of the commission's powers and any restrictions on those powers.

A council may designate two types of commissions:

a. *Judicial Commissions*

Judicial commissions shall consider and decide cases of process for the council **or councils** according to the Rules of Discipline. Sessions shall perform the function of a judicial commission for the congregation; each council higher than the session shall elect a permanent judicial commission (see D-5.0000). **Cooperating synods may elect a joint permanent judicial commission pursuant to G-3.0404 and D-5.0101.**

b. *Administrative Commissions*

Administrative commissions are designated to consider and conclude matters not involving ecclesiastical judicial process, except that in the discharge of their assigned responsibilities they may discover and report to the designating council matters that may require judicial action by the council.

Functions that may be entrusted to administrative commissions include, but are not limited to:

(1) (by sessions) ordaining and installing ruling elders and deacons, receiving and dismissing members, and visiting organizations within the congregation to settle differences therein;

(2) (by presbyteries) ordaining and installing teaching elders;

(3) (by presbyteries) examining and receiving into membership teaching elders seeking admission to presbytery, including approval of terms of call and commissions for ordination and installation; and receiving candidates under care;

(4) (by presbyteries) developing immigrant fellowships, organizing new congregations, merging congregations, or forming union or federated congregations (G-5.05);

(5) (by presbyteries, synods, and the General Assembly) visiting particular councils, congregations, or agencies over which they have immediate jurisdiction reported to be affected with disorder[c], and inquiring into and settling the difficulties therein, except that no commission of a presbytery shall be empowered to dissolve a pastoral relationship without the specific authorization by the designating body (G-2.0901);

(6) (by all councils) making pastoral inquiry into persons accused of sexual abuse of another person (D-10.0401c) when jurisdiction in a judicial proceeding against such persons has ended due to death or renunciation of the accused; such inquiries shall not be understood as judicial proceedings but shall seek to reach a determination of truth related to the accusation and to make appropriate recommendations to the designating council.

A commission of presbytery, synod, or General Assembly shall be composed of ruling elders and teaching elders in numbers as nearly equal as possible and sufficient to accomplish their work. A quorum of any commission shall be established by the designating council **or councils** but in no case shall be less than a majority of its members (except as limited by D-5.0204).

A commission of a session shall be composed of at least two ruling elders, and a teaching elder in an installed or temporary relationship with the congregation governed by that session or a ruling elder commissioned to pastoral service.

A commission shall keep a full record of its proceedings and shall submit that record to the council **or councils** for incorporation into its records. Actions of a commission shall be regarded as actions of the council **or councils** that created it. A commission may be assigned additional duties as a committee, which duties shall be reported and handled as the report of a committee.

The decisions of an administrative commission shall be reported to the clerk of the designating council, who shall report it to the council at its next stated meeting. A council may rescind or amend an action of its administrative commission in the same way actions of the council are modified.

When an administrative commission has been designated to settle differences within a particular organization or council, it shall, before making its decision final, afford to all persons affected by its decision fair notice and an opportunity to be heard on matters at issue.

G-3.0110   *Administrative Staff*

Councils higher than the session may employ such staff as is required by the mission of the body in accordance with the principles of unity in diversity (F-1.0403). Councils may, in consultation with the next higher council, share staff as required by the mission of the body. A council shall make provision in its manual of administrative operations (G-3.0106) for the process of electing executive staff and the hiring of other staff, the description of the responsibilities of the positions, the method of performance review, and the manner of termination of employment. (G-3.0104)

G-3.0111   *Nominating Process*

All councils higher than the session shall have a process for nominating persons to serve in positions requiring election by the council. The process shall ensure that nominations are made by an entity broadly representative of the constituency of the council, and in conformity with the church's commitment to unity in diversity (F-1.0403).

G-3.0112   *Insurance*

Each council shall obtain property and liability insurance coverage to protect its facilities, programs, staff, and elected and appointed officers.

G-3.0113   *Finances*

Each council shall prepare and adopt a budget to support the church's mission within its area.

A full financial review of all financial books and records shall be conducted every year by a public accountant or committee of members versed in accounting procedures. Reviewers should not be related to the treasurer(s). Terminology in this section is meant to provide general guidance and is not intended to require or not require specific audit procedures or practices as understood within the professional accounting community.

G-3.02 THE SESSION

G-3.0201   Composition and Responsibilities

The session is the council for the congregation. It shall be composed of those persons elected by the congregation to active service[d] as ruling elders, together with all installed pastors and associate pastors. All members of the session are entitled to vote. The pastor shall be the moderator of the session, and the session shall not meet without the pastor or designated moderator. If there is no installed pastor, or if the installed pastor is unable to invite another moderator, the presbytery shall make provisions for a moderator. Presbyteries shall provide by rule for moderators when the session is without a moderator for reasons of vacancy or inconvenience.

The session shall have responsibility for governing the congregation[e] and guiding its witness to the sovereign activity of God in the world, so that the congregation is and becomes a community of faith, hope, love, and witness. As it leads and guides the witness of the congregation, the session shall keep before it the marks of the Church (F-1.0302), the notes by which Presbyterian and Reformed congregations have identified themselves throughout history (F-1.0303) and the six Great Ends of the Church (F-1.0304).

In light of this charge, the session has responsibility and power to:

a.   *provide that the Word of God may be truly preached and heard.* This responsibility shall include providing a place where the congregation may regularly gather for worship, education, and spiritual nurture; providing for regular preaching of the Word by a teaching elder or other person prepared and approved for the work; planning and leading regular efforts to reach into the community and the world with the message of salvation and the invitation to enter into committed discipleship; planning and leading ministries of social healing and reconciliation in the community in accordance with the prophetic witness of Jesus Christ; and initiating and responding to ecumenical efforts that bear witness to the love and grace of God.

b.   *provide that the Sacraments may be rightly administered and received.* This responsibility shall include authorizing the celebration of the Lord's Supper at least quarterly and the administration of Baptism as appropriate, in accordance with the principles of the Directory for Worship; and exercising pastoral care among the congregation in order that the Sacraments may be received as a means of grace, and the congregation may live in the unity represented in the Sacraments.

c.   *nurture the covenant community of disciples of Christ.* This responsibility shall include receiving and dismissing members; reviewing the roll of active members at least annually and counseling with those who have neglected the responsibilities of membership; providing programs of nurture, education, and fellowship; training, examining, ordaining, and installing those elected by the congregation as ruling elders and deacons; encouraging the graces of generosity and faithful stewardship of personal and financial resources; managing the physical property of the congregation for the furtherance of its mission; directing the ministry of deacons, trustees, and all organizations of the congregation; employing the administrative staff of the congregation; leading the congregation in participating in the mission of the whole church; warning and bearing witness against error in doctrine and immorality in practice within the congregation and community; and serving in judicial matters in accordance with the Rules of Discipline[f].

G-3.0202   Relations with Other Councils

Sessions have a particular responsibility to participate in the life of the whole church through participation in other councils. It is of particular importance that sessions:

    a.   elect, as commissioners to presbytery, ruling elders from the congregation, preferably for at least a year, and receive their reports;

    b.   nominate to presbytery ruling elders from the congregation who may be considered for election as commissioners to synod and General Assembly, and to serve on committees or commissions of the same, bearing in mind principles of inclusiveness and fair representation in the decision making of the church (F-1.0403);

    c.   see that the guidance and communication of presbytery, synod, and General Assembly are considered, and that any binding actions are observed and carried out;

    d.   welcome representatives of the presbytery on the occasions of their visits;

    e.   propose to the presbytery, or through it to the synod and General Assembly, such measures as may be of common concern to the mission of the church; and

    f.   send to presbytery[g] and General Assembly requested statistics and other information according to the requirements of those bodies, as well as voluntary financial contributions.

G-3.0203   Meetings

The session shall hold stated meetings at least quarterly. The moderator[h] shall call a special meeting when he or she deems necessary or when requested in writing by any two members of the session. The business to be transacted at special meetings shall be limited to items specifically listed in the call for the meeting. There shall be reasonable notice given of all special meetings. The session shall also meet when directed by presbytery. Sessions shall provide by rule for a quorum for meetings; such quorum shall include the moderator and either a specific number of ruling elders or a specific percentage of those ruling elders in current service on the session.

G-3.0204   Minutes and Records

Minutes of the session shall be subject to the provisions of G-3.0107. They shall contain the minutes of all meetings of the congregation and all joint meetings with deacons and trustees.

Each session shall maintain the following roll and registers:

a. *Membership Roll*

There shall be rolls of baptized, active, and affiliate members in accordance with G-1.0401, G-1.0402 and G-1.0403. The session shall delete names from the roll of the congregation upon the member's death, admission to membership in another congregation or presbytery, or renunciation of jurisdiction. The session may delete names from the roll of the congregation when a member so requests, or has moved or otherwise ceased to participate actively in the work and worship of the congregation for a period of two years. The session shall seek to restore members to active participation and shall provide written notice before deleting names due to member inactivity.

b. *Registers*

There shall be registers of baptisms authorized by the session, of ruling elders and deacons, of installed pastors with dates of service, and such other registers as the session may deem necessary.

G-3.0205   Finances

In addition to those responsibilities described in G-3.0113, the session shall prepare and adopt a budget and determine the distribution of the congregation's benevolences. It shall authorize offerings for Christian purposes and shall account for the proceeds of such offerings and their disbursement. It shall provide full information to the congregation concerning its decisions in such matters.

The session shall elect a treasurer for such term as the session shall decide and shall supervise his or her work or delegate that supervision to a board of deacons or trustees. Those in charge of various congregational funds shall report at least annually to the session and more often as requested. Sessions may provide by rule for standard financial practices of the congregation, but shall in no case fail to observe the following procedures:

a.   All offerings shall be counted and recorded by at least two duly appointed persons, or by one fidelity bonded person;

b.   Financial books and records adequate to reflect all financial transactions shall be kept and shall be open to inspection by authorized church officers at reasonable times;

c.   Periodic, and in no case less than annual, reports of all financial activities shall be made to the session or entity vested with financial oversight.

G-3.03 THE PRESBYTERY

G-3.0301   Composition and Responsibilities

The presbytery is the council serving as a corporate expression of the church within a certain district and is composed of all the congregations[i] and teaching elders within that district. The presbytery shall adopt and communicate to the sessions a plan for determining how many ruling elders each session should elect as commissioners to presbytery, with a goal of numerical parity of teaching elders and ruling elders. This plan shall require each session to elect at least one commissioner[j] and shall take into consideration the size of congregations as well as a method to fulfill the principles of participation and representation found in F-1.0403 and G-3.0103. Ruling elders elected as officers of the presbytery shall be enrolled as members during the period of their service. A presbytery may **enroll, or may** provide by its own rule for the enrollment of, ruling elders **during terms of elected service to the presbytery or its congregations.**

The minimum composition of a presbytery is ten duly constituted sessions and ten teaching elders.

The presbytery is responsible for the government of the church throughout its district, and for assisting and supporting the witness of congregations[k] to the sovereign activity of God in the world, so that all congregations become communities of faith, hope, love, and witness. As it leads and guides the witness of its congregations, the presbytery shall keep before it the marks of the Church (F-1.0302), the notes by which Presbyterian and Reformed communities have identified themselves through history (F-1.0303) and the six Great Ends of the Church (F-1.0304).

In light of this charge, the presbytery has responsibility and power to:

a. *provide that the Word of God may be truly preached and heard.* This responsibility shall include organizing, receiving, merging, dismissing, and dissolving congregations in consultation with their members; overseeing congregations without pastors; establishing pastoral relationships and dissolving them; guiding the preparation of those preparing to become teaching elders; establishing and maintaining those ecumenical relationships that will enlarge the life and mission of the church in its district; providing encouragement, guidance, and resources to congregations in the areas of mission, prophetic witness, leadership development, worship, evangelism, and responsible administration to the end that the church's witness to the love and grace of God may be heard in the world.

b. *provide that the Sacraments may be rightly administered and received.* This responsibility shall include authorizing the celebration of the Lord's Supper at its meetings at least annually and for fellowship groups, new church developments, and other non-congregational entities meeting within its bounds; authorizing and training specific ruling elders to administer or preside at the Lord's Supper when it deems it necessary to meet the needs for the administration of the Sacrament; and exercising pastoral care for the congregations and members of presbytery in order that the Sacraments may be received as a means of grace, and the presbytery may live in the unity represented in the Sacraments.

c. *nurture the covenant community of disciples of Christ.* This responsibility shall include ordaining, receiving, dismissing, installing, removing, and disciplining its members who are teaching elders[l]; commissioning ruling elders to limited pastoral service; promoting the peace and harmony of congregations and inquiring into the sources of congregational discord; supporting congregations in developing the graces of generosity, stewardship, and service; assisting congregations in developing mission and participating in the mission of the whole church; taking jurisdiction over the members of dissolved congregations and granting transfers of their membership to other congregations; warning and bearing witness against error in doctrine and immorality in practice within its bounds; and serving in judicial matters in accordance with the Rules of Discipline.

G-3.0302   *Relations with Synod and General Assembly*

The presbytery has a responsibility to maintain regular and continuing relationship to synod and General Assembly by:

a.   electing commissioners to synod and General Assembly and receiving their reports;

b.   electing ruling and teaching elders to be readers of standard ordination examinations;

c.   seeing that the guidance and communication of synod and General Assembly are considered and that any binding actions are observed and carried out;

d.   proposing to synod such measures as may be of common concern to the mission of the church, and/**or proposing to General Assembly overtures that have received a concurrence from at least one other presbytery, and**

e.   sending annually to synod and General Assembly statistical and other information according to the requirements of those bodies.

G-3.0303   *Relations with Sessions*

Presbytery, being composed of the teaching elders and commissioners elected by the session of congregations within its district, has a particular responsibility to coordinate, guide, encourage, support, and resource the work of its congregations for the most effective witness to the broader community. In order to accomplish this responsibility, the presbytery has authority to:

a.   develop strategy for the mission of the church in its district;

b.   control the location of new congregations and of congregations desiring to move as well as to divide, dismiss, or dissolve congregations in consultation with their members;

c.   establish minimum compensation standards for pastoral calls and Certified Christian Educators and Certified Associate Christian Educators within the presbytery;

d.   counsel with a session concerning reported difficulties within a congregation, including:

(1) advising the session as to appropriate actions to be taken to resolve the reported difficulties,

(2) offering to help as a mediator, and

(3) acting to correct the difficulties if requested to do so by the session or if the session is unable or unwilling to do so, following the procedural safeguards of the Rules of Discipline;

e. assume original jurisdiction in any situation in which it determines that a session cannot exercise its authority. After a thorough investigation, and after full opportunity to be heard has been accorded to the session, the presbytery may conclude that the session of a congregation is unable or unwilling to manage wisely its affairs, and may appoint an administrative commission with the full power of session. This commission shall assume original jurisdiction of the existing session, if any, which shall cease to act until such time as the presbytery shall otherwise direct.

f. consider and act upon requests from congregations for permission to take the actions regarding real property as described in G-4.0206.

G-3.0304   Meetings and Quorum

The presbytery shall hold stated meetings at least twice each year, shall meet at the direction of synod, and may call special meetings in accordance with its own rules.

A presbytery may set its own quorum[m], but it shall be not fewer than three teaching elders who are members of the presbytery and three ruling elder commissioners from three different congregations.

G-3.0305   Minutes and Records

Minutes and other official records of the presbytery are the property of the presbytery, and are subject to the review specified in G-3.0108. The stated clerk is responsible for the preservation of the presbytery's minutes and records. **These records shall include the rolls of the presbytery's membership and registers of all Certified Christian Educators, Certified Associate Christian Educators, and ruling elders commissioned to particular pastoral service.**

G-3.0306   Membership of Presbytery

Each presbytery determines the teaching elders who are its members and validates the ministries in which they are to be engaged. It shall be guided in this determination by written criteria developed by the presbytery for validating ministries within its bounds (G-2.0503a).

The presbytery shall examine each teaching elder or candidate who seeks membership in it on his or her Christian faith and views in theology, the Sacraments, and the government of this church.

The presbytery may designate teaching elders to work as teachers, evangelists, administrators, chaplains, and in other forms of ministry recognized as appropriate by the presbytery. Those so designated may administer the Sacraments at times and places authorized by the presbytery.

Every teaching elder shall ordinarily be a member of the presbytery where his or her work is situated or of the presbytery where she or he resides.

A teaching elder who is serving in a church outside the United States may, with the approval of the presbytery, accept membership in that church for the period of such service without affecting his or her membership in a presbytery of this church.

G-3.0307   *Pastor, Counselor, and Advisor to Teaching Elders and Congregations*

Presbyteries shall be open at all times to communication regarding the life and ministry of their congregations.

Each presbytery shall develop and maintain mechanisms and processes to serve as pastor and counselor to teaching elders, ruling elders commissioned to pastoral service, and certified Christian educators of the presbytery; to facilitate the relations between the presbytery and its congregations, teaching elders, ruling elders commissioned to pastoral service, and certified Christian educators; and to settle difficulties on behalf of the presbytery where possible and expedient.

Each presbytery shall develop and maintain mechanisms and processes to guide, nurture and oversee the process of preparing to become a teaching elder.

To facilitate the presbytery's oversight of inquirers and candidates, reception and oversight of teaching elder members, approval of calls for pastoral services and invitations for temporary pastoral services, oversight of congregations without pastors, dissolution of relationships, dismissal of members, and its close relationship with both member congregations and teaching elders, it may delegate its authority to designated entities within the presbytery. Such entities shall be composed of ruling elders and teaching elders in approximately equal numbers, bearing in mind the principles of unity in diversity in F-1.0403. All actions carried out as a result of delegated authority must be reported to the presbytery at its next regular meeting.

G-3.04   THE SYNOD[n]

G-3.0401   *Composition and Responsibilities*

The synod is the intermediate council serving as a corporate expression of the church throughout its region. It shall consist of not fewer than three presbyteries within a specific geographic region.

When a synod meets, it shall be composed of commissioners elected by the presbyteries. Each presbytery shall elect at least one ruling elder and one teaching elder to serve as commissioners to synod. A synod shall determine a plan for the election of commissioners to the synod, as well as the method to fulfill the principles of participation and representation found in F-1.0403 and G-3.0103; both plans shall be subject to approval by a majority of the presbyteries in the synod. The commissioners from each presbytery shall be divided equally between ruling elders and teaching elders. Each person elected moderator or other officer shall be enrolled as a member of the synod until a successor is elected and installed.

Synod is responsible for the life and mission of the church throughout its region and for supporting the ministry and mission of its presbyteries as they seek to support the witness of congregations, to the end that the church throughout its region becomes a community of faith, hope, love, and witness. As it leads and guides the witness of the church throughout its region, it shall keep before it the marks of the Church (F-1.0302), the notes by which Presbyterian and Reformed communities have identified themselves through history (F-1.0303) and the six Great Ends of the Church (F-1.0304).

In light of this charge, the synod has responsibility and power to:

a.   *provide that the Word of God may be truly preached and heard.* This responsibility may include developing, in conjunction with its presbyteries, a broad strategy for the mission of the church within its bounds and in accord with the larger strategy of the General Assembly; assisting its member presbyteries when requested in matters related to the calling, ordaining, and placement of teaching elders; establishing and maintaining, in conjunction with its presbyteries, those ecumenical relationships that will enlarge the life and mission of the church in its region; facilitating joint action in mission with other denominations and agencies in its region; facilitating communication among its presbyteries and between its presbyteries and the General Assembly; providing services for presbyteries within its area that can be performed more effectively from a broad regional base.

b.   *provide that the Sacraments may be rightly administered and received.* This responsibility may include authorizing the celebration of the Lord's Supper at its meetings and at other events and gatherings under its jurisdiction; and exercising pastoral care among its presbyteries in order that the Sacraments may be received as a means of grace, and the synod may live in the unity represented in the Sacraments.

c.   *nurture the covenant community of disciples of Christ.* This responsibility shall include providing such services of education and nurture as its presbyteries may require; providing encouragement, guidance, and resources to presbyteries in the areas of mission, prophetic witness, leadership development, worship, evangelism, and responsible administration; reviewing the work of its presbyteries; warning or bearing witness against error in doctrine or immorality in practice within its bounds; and serving in judicial matters in accordance with the Rules of Discipline.

G-3.0402   Relations with General Assembly

The synod has responsibility to maintain regular and continuing relationship with the General Assembly by seeing that the guidance and communication of the General Assembly are considered and that any binding actions are observed and carried out, and by proposing to the General Assembly such measures as may be of common concern to the mission of the whole church.°

G-3.0403   Relations with Presbyteries

Each presbytery shall participate in the synod's responsibility and service through its elected commissioners to the synod. The synod has responsibility for supporting the work of the presbyteries within its bounds and as such is charged with:

a.   developing, in conjunction with its presbyteries, joint plans and objectives for the fulfillment of mission, providing encouragement and guidance to its presbyteries and overseeing their work;

b.   developing and providing, when requested, resources as needed to facilitate the mission of its presbyteries;

c.   organizing new presbyteries, dividing, uniting, or otherwise combining presbyteries or portions of presbyteries previously existing, and, with the concurrence of existing presbyteries, creating non-geographic presbyteries, subject to the approval of the General Assembly, or taking other such actions as may be deemed necessary in order to meet the mission needs of racial ethnic or immigrant congregations. Such presbyteries shall be formed in compliance with the requirements of G-3.0301 and be accountable to the synod within which they were created.

G-3.0404   Reduced Function

A synod may decide, with the approval of a two-thirds majority of its presbyteries, to reduce its function. In no case shall synod function be less than the provision of judicial process and administrative review of the work of the presbyteries (G-3.0401c). Such a synod shall meet at least every two years for the purposes of setting budget, electing members to its permanent judicial commission, and admitting to record the actions of its permanent judicial and administrative commissions. Presbyteries of such a synod shall assume for themselves, by mutual agreement, such other synod functions as may be deemed necessary by the presbyteries and the synod.

Two or more synods sharing common boundaries, with the approval of a two-thirds majority of the presbyteries in each of the synods, may share administrative services **and form a shared permanent judicial commission, with the membership of the commission being proportional, insofar as possible, to the number of presbyteries within each participating synod. Each synod shall pay the costs for processing a judicial case arising within its bounds.**.

G-3.0405   Meetings and Quorum

The synod shall hold stated meetings at least biennially, shall meet at the direction of the General Assembly, and may call special meetings in accordance with its own rules.

A synod may set its own quorum, but it shall include an equal number of ruling elders and teaching elders representing at least three presbyteries or one-third of its presbyteries, whichever is larger.

G-3.0406   Minutes and Records

The synod shall keep a full and accurate record of its proceedings that shall be submitted to the next succeeding meeting of the General Assembly for its general review and control. It shall report to the General Assembly the number of its presbyteries and, in general, all important changes that have occurred within its bounds.

G-3.05 THE GENERAL ASSEMBLY

G-3.0501   Composition and Responsibilities

The General Assembly[p] is the council of the whole church and it is representative of the unity of the synods, presbyteries, sessions, and congregations of the Presbyterian Church (U.S.A.). It shall consist of equal numbers of ruling elders and teaching elders elected by the presbyteries and reflective of the diversity within their bounds (F-1.0403 and G-3.0103), to serve as commissioners according to the following proportions:

8,000 members or less: 1 ruling elder and 1 teaching elder

8,001–16,000: 2 ruling elders and 2 teaching elders

16,001–24,000: 3 ruling elders and 3 teaching elders

24,001–32,000: 4 ruling elders and 4 teaching elders

32,001–40,000: 5 ruling elders and 5 teaching elders

40,001–48,000: 6 ruling elders and 6 teaching elders

48,001 or more: 7 ruling elders and 7 teaching elders

Each person elected Moderator shall be enrolled as a member of the General Assembly until a successor is elected and installed.

The General Assembly constitutes the bond of union, community, and mission among all its congregations and councils, to the end that the whole church becomes a community of faith, hope, love, and witness. As it leads and guides the witness of the whole church, it shall keep before it the marks of the Church (F-1.0302), the notes by which Presbyterian and Reformed communities have identified themselves through history (F-1.0303) and the six Great Ends of the Church (F-1.0304).

In light of this charge, the General Assembly has responsibility and power to:

a.   *provide that the Word of God may be truly preached and heard.* This responsibility shall include establishing a comprehensive mission strategy and priorities for the church; establishing and maintaining ecumenical relationships and correspondence with other ecclesiastical bodies; uniting with or receiving under its jurisdiction other ecclesiastical bodies consistent with the faith and order of this church, subject to the provisions of G-5.02 and G-5.03; and commissioning, sending, and support of such mission personnel as will spread the good news of the grace of Jesus Christ to the world and foster the growth and development of God's people.

b.   *provide that the Sacraments may be rightly administered and received.* This responsibility shall include authorizing the celebration of the Lord's Supper at meetings of the General Assembly and other events and gatherings under its jurisdiction; authorizing the participation in the celebration of the Lord's Supper in ecumenical gatherings attended by authorized representatives of the General Assembly; and exercising pastoral care throughout the whole church in order that the Sacraments may be received as a means of grace, and the church may live in the unity represented in the Sacraments.

c.   *nurture the covenant community of disciples.* This responsibility shall include providing those services, resources, and programs performed most effectively at a national level; communicating with the whole church on matters of common concern; warning and bearing witness against errors in doctrine or immorality in the church and in the world; providing such services of education and nurture as its presbyteries may require; providing encouragement, guidance, and resources to presbyteries in the areas of mission, prophetic witness, leadership development, worship, evangelism, and responsible administration; discerning and presenting with the guidance of the Holy Spirit, matters of truth and vision that may inspire, challenge, and educate both church and world; serving in judicial matters in accordance with the Rules of Discipline; deciding controversies brought before it and advising and instructing in cases submitted to it, in conformity with this Constitution; authoritatively interpreting the most recent edition of the *Book of Order* in a manner binding on the whole church, in accordance with the provisions of G-6.02 or through a decision of the General Assembly Permanent Judicial Commission in a remedial or disciplinary case, with the most recent interpretation of the *Book of Order* being binding; and establishing and maintaining an office of the Stated Clerk.

G-3.0502   Relations with Other Councils

The General Assembly has responsibility to maintain relationships with presbyteries and synods by:

a.   consulting with and providing resources for presbyteries and synods as they execute their constitutional responsibilities;

b.   overseeing the work of synods;

c.   reviewing the records of synods, taking care to ensure that they conform to this Constitution;

d.   organizing new synods, or dividing, uniting, or otherwise combining previously existing synods or portions of synods; and

e.   approving the acts of synods to organize, divide, unite, or combine presbyteries or portions of presbyteries.

G-3.0503   Meetings and Quorum

The General Assembly shall hold a stated meeting at least biennially. The Moderator, or in the event of the incapacity of the Moderator, the Stated Clerk of the General Assembly, shall call a special meeting at the request or with the concurrence of at least one fourth of the ruling elder commissioners and one fourth of the teaching elder commissioners to the last preceding stated meeting of the General Assembly representing at least fifteen presbyteries, under the jurisdiction of at least five synods. Commissioners to the special meeting shall be the commissioners elected to the last preceding stated meeting of the General Assembly or their alternates. Notice of special meetings shall be sent no fewer than sixty days prior to convening and shall set out the purpose of the meeting. No other business than that listed in the notice shall be transacted.

A quorum of the General Assembly shall be one hundred commissioners, fifty of whom shall be ruling elders and fifty teaching elders, representing presbyteries of at least one fourth of its synods.

CHAPTER FOUR

THE CHURCH AND CIVIL AUTHORITY

G-4.01 INCORPORATION AND TRUSTEES

G-4.0101 Incorporation and Power

Where permitted by civil law, each congregation shall cause a corporation to be formed and maintained. If incorporation is not permitted, individual trustees shall be elected by the congregation. Any such individual trustees shall be elected from the congregation's members in the same manner as those elected to the ordered ministries of deacon and ruling elder. Terms of service shall be governed by the provisions of G-2.0404.

The corporation so formed, or the individual trustees, shall have the following powers: to receive, hold, encumber, manage, and transfer property, real or personal, for the congregation, provided that in buying, selling, and mortgaging real property, the trustees shall act only after the approval of the congregation, granted in a duly constituted meeting; to accept and execute deeds of title to such property; to hold and defend title to such property; to manage any permanent special funds for the furtherance of the purposes of the congregation, all subject to the authority of the session and under the provisions of the Constitution of the Presbyterian Church (U.S.A.). The powers and duties of the trustees shall not infringe upon the powers and duties of the session or the board of deacons.

Where permitted by civil law, each presbytery, synod, and the General Assembly shall cause a corporation to be formed and maintained and shall determine a method to constitute the board of trustees by its own rule. The corporation so formed, or individual trustees, shall have the following powers: to receive, hold, encumber, manage, and transfer property, real or personal, for and at the direction of the council.

G-4.0102 Members of the Corporation

Only persons eligible for membership in the congregation or council shall be eligible to be members of the corporation and to be elected as trustees. The ruling elders on the session of a congregation, who are eligible under the civil law, shall be the trustees of the corporation, unless the corporation shall determine another method for electing its trustees. Presbyteries, synods, and the General Assembly shall provide by rule for the election of trustees from among persons eligible for membership in the council.

G-4.02 CHURCH PROPERTY

G-4.0201 Property as a Tool for Mission

The property of the Presbyterian Church (U.S.A.), of its councils and entities, and of its congregations, is a tool for the accomplishment of the mission of Jesus Christ in the world.

G-4.0202   Decisions Concerning Property

The provisions of this Constitution prescribing the manner in which decisions are made, reviewed, and corrected within this church are applicable to all matters pertaining to property.

G-4.0203   Church Property Held in Trust

All property held by or for a congregation, a presbytery, a synod, the General Assembly, or the Presbyterian Church (U.S.A.), whether legal title is lodged in a corporation, a trustee or trustees, or an unincorporated association, and whether the property is used in programs of a congregation or of a higher council or retained for the production of income, is held in trust nevertheless for the use and benefit of the Presbyterian Church (U.S.A.).

G-4.0204   Property Used Contrary to the Constitution

Whenever property of, or held for, a congregation of the Presbyterian Church (U.S.A.) ceases to be used by that congregation as a congregation of the Presbyterian Church (U.S.A.) in accordance with this Constitution, such property shall be held, used, applied, transferred, or sold as provided by the presbytery.

G-4.0205   Property of a Dissolved or Extinct Congregation

Whenever a congregation is formally dissolved by the presbytery, or has become extinct by reason of the dispersal of its members, the abandonment of its work, or other cause, such property as it may have shall be held, used, and applied for such uses, purposes, and trusts as the presbytery may direct, limit, and appoint, or such property may be sold or disposed of as the presbytery may direct, in conformity with the Constitution of the Presbyterian Church (U.S.A.).

G-4.0206   Selling, Encumbering, or Leasing Church Property

a.   Selling or Encumbering Congregational Property

A congregation shall not sell, mortgage, or otherwise encumber any of its real property and it shall not acquire real property subject to an encumbrance or condition without the written permission of the presbytery transmitted through the session of the congregation.

b.   Leasing Congregational Property

A congregation shall not lease its real property used for purposes of worship, or lease for more than five years any of its other real property, without the written permission of the presbytery transmitted through the session of the congregation.

G-4.0207   Property of Congregation in Schism

The relationship to the Presbyterian Church (U.S.A.) of a congregation can be severed only by constitutional action on the part of the presbytery (G-3.0303b). If there is a schism within the membership of a congregation and the presbytery is unable to effect a reconciliation or a division into separate congregations within the Presbyterian Church (U.S.A.), the presbytery shall determine if one of the factions is entitled to the property because it is identified by the presbytery as the true church within the Presbyterian Church (U.S.A.). This determination does not depend upon which faction received the majority vote within the congregation at the time of the schism.

G-4.0208   Exceptions

The provisions of this chapter shall apply to all congregations of the Presbyterian Church (U.S.A.) except that any congregation which was not subject to a similar provision of the constitution of the church of which it was a part, prior to the reunion of the Presbyterian Church in the United States and The United Presbyterian Church in the United States of America to form the Presbyterian Church (U.S.A.), has been excused from that provision of this chapter if the congregation, within a period of eight years following the establishment of the Presbyterian Church (U.S.A.), voted to be exempt from such provision in a regularly called meeting and thereafter notified the presbytery of which it was a constituent congregation of such vote. The congregation voting to be so exempt shall hold title to its property and exercise its privileges of incorporation and property ownership under the provisions of the Constitution to which it was subject immediately prior to the establishment of the Presbyterian Church (U.S.A.). This paragraph may not be amended (G-6.05).

G-4.03   CONFIDENCE AND PRIVILEGE

G-4.0301   Trust and Confidentiality

In the exercise of pastoral care, teaching elders (also called ministers of the Word and Sacrament) and ruling elders who have been commissioned by a presbytery to limited pastoral service (G-2.10), shall maintain a relationship of trust and confidentiality, and shall hold in confidence all information revealed to them in the course of providing care and all information relating to the exercise of such care.

When the person whose confidences are at issue gives express consent to reveal confidential information, then a teaching elder or a ruling elder commissioned to pastoral service may, but cannot be compelled to, reveal confidential information.

A teaching elder or a ruling elder commissioned to pastoral service may reveal confidential information when she or he reasonably believes that there is risk of imminent bodily harm to any person.

G-4.0302   Mandatory Reporting

Any member of this church engaged in ordered ministry and any certified Christian educator employed by this church or its congregations, shall report to ecclesiastical and civil legal authorities knowledge of harm, or the risk of harm, related to the physical abuse, neglect, and/or sexual molestation or abuse of a minor or an adult who lacks mental capacity when (1) such information is gained outside of a confidential communication as defined in G-4.0301, (2) she or he is not bound by an obligation of privileged communication under law, or (3) she or he reasonably believes that there is risk of future physical harm or abuse.

CHAPTER FIVE
ECUMENICITY AND UNION

G-5.01 ECUMENICAL COMMITMENT

G-5.0101 *Ecumenicity*

The Presbyterian Church (U.S.A.) at all levels seeks to manifest more visibly the unity of the body of Christ and will be open to opportunities for conversation, cooperation, and action with other ecclesiastical groups. It will seek to initiate, maintain, and strengthen relations with other Reformed and Christian entities.

G-5.0102 *Interfaith Relations*

The Presbyterian Church (U.S.A.) at all levels seeks new opportunities for conversation and understanding with non-Christian religious entities.

G-5.0103 *Secular Organizations*

The Presbyterian Church (U.S.A.) at all level seeks to initiate and respond to approaches for conversation and common action with secular organizations and agencies where such approaches show promise of serving the mission of the Church in the world.

G-5.02 RELATIONS WITH OTHER DENOMINATIONS

G-5.0201 *Correspondence*

In seeking the unity of the Church of Jesus Christ (G-5.0101), the General Assembly may authorize and direct that covenants, agreements, and statements of purpose and intent be developed with other Christian bodies. Such actions, when authorized and approved by the General Assembly, may address, but are not limited to, the mutual recognition of baptism and the orderly exchange of ministers. All councils of this church are encouraged to engage in opportunities to minister together in mutual affirmation and admonition with other Christian bodies.

The General Assembly, through the Office of the General Assembly, shall maintain a relationship of correspondence with the highest council or governing body:

    a.   of those churches with which it has had historical relations outside the United States, as recognized by the General Assembly;

    b.   of those churches that are members of the ecumenical bodies in which the Presbyterian Church (U.S.A.) holds membership;

    c.   of those churches with which the Presbyterian Church (U.S.A.) has formal ecumenical dialogue approved by the General Assembly.

G-5.0202   Full Communion

The General Assembly of the Presbyterian Church (U.S.A.) is in full communion with those churches so recognized by the General Assembly. Full communion shall include the mutual recognition of baptism and the orderly exchange of ministers, as defined by ecumenical agreement. Councils of this church are encouraged to engage in opportunities to minister together in mutual affirmation and admonition with churches with which the Presbyterian Church (U.S.A.) is in full communion.

G-5.0203   Ecumenical Statements

In seeking the unity of the Church in Jesus Christ (F-1.0302a and G-5.0101), and in addition to the above relations, the Office of the General Assembly shall develop formal agreements and ecumenical statements of understanding with other Christian bodies. Such statements and agreements shall be approved by the General Assembly as guides for shared action, and shall be submitted to the presbyteries for their affirmative or negative votes.

G-5.03 FULL ORGANIC UNION

Full organic union of the Presbyterian Church (U.S.A.) with any other ecclesiastical body shall be effected subject to the following approvals:

    a.   the approval of the proposed plan of union by the General Assembly and its recommendation to the presbyteries;

    b.   the approval in writing of two-thirds of the presbyteries; and

    c.   the approval and consummation by the next General Assembly, or other General Assembly specified in the proposed plan of union.

G-5.04 UNION PRESBYTERIES

A presbytery of the Presbyterian Church (U.S.A.) may unite to form a union presbytery with one or more comparable councils or governing bodies[a], each of which is a member of another Reformed body, with the approval of the synod or comparable council or governing body of which each is a part.

G-5.0401   Constitutional Authority

The union presbytery shall be subject to the constitution of each denomination represented in the union. Wherever the constitutions of the denominations differ, any mandatory provisions of one shall apply in all cases where the others are permissive. Where there are conflicting mandatory provisions, the union presbytery shall overture the highest council or governing body of the denominations involved to resolve the conflict either by authoritative interpretation or by constitutional amendment.

G-5.0402   Plan of Union

A union presbytery shall be created by the adoption of a plan of union by two-thirds vote of each presbytery or governing body that is party to the union. The synod and/or governing body having jurisdiction over each of the uniting bodies shall approve the plan of union.

G-5.05 JOINT CONGREGATIONAL WITNESS

When its strategy for mission requires it, a presbytery may approve the creation of a joint witness between congregations of this denomination and congregations of other Christian churches that recognize Jesus Christ as Lord and Savior, accept the authority of Scripture, and observe the Sacraments of Baptism and the Lord's Supper[b].

a.   Such joint witnesses shall be subject to the constitution of each denomination involved. Wherever the constitutions of the denominations differ, the mandatory provisions of one shall apply in all cases when the others are permissive. Wherever there are conflicting mandatory provisions, the congregational council shall petition the next higher councils or governing bodies to resolve the conflict.

b.   Such joint witnesses shall be formed according to a plan approved by a two-thirds majority of the members of each of the congregations at duly called meetings of the congregation, and by the presbytery or comparable council or governing body of each church. No provision of a plan for joint witness shall be construed as modifying or amending the Constitution of the Presbyterian Church (U.S.A).

c.   After consultation with the congregation involved in joint witness and the next higher council or governing body of the other denomination involved, a presbytery may receive a congregation from or transfer a congregation to a denomination with which the Presbyterian Church (U.S.A.) is in full communion or correspondence when it determines that the strategy for mission of that congregation is better served by such a transfer (G-3.0303b).

CHAPTER SIX
INTERPRETING AND AMENDING THE CONSTITUTION

G-6.01 REFORM

The Presbyterian Church (U.S.A.) seeks to be "the church reformed, always to be reformed, according to the Word of God" in the power of the Spirit (F-2.02.) In light of this commitment, the following interpretation and amendment procedures are understood as a means to faithfulness.

G-6.02 INTERPRETING THE CONSTITUTION

The General Assembly may provide authoritative interpretation of the *Book of Order*, which shall be binding on the councils of the church when rendered in the manner described in this section or through a decision of the General Assembly Permanent Judicial Commission in a remedial or disciplinary case.

The General Assembly shall elect an Advisory Committee on the Constitution composed of nine persons, teaching elders and ruling elders in numbers as nearly equal as possible. The Stated Clerk of the General Assembly shall be a member *ex officio* without vote. No person who has served on the Advisory Committee on the Constitution for a full term of six years shall be eligible for reelection until four years have elapsed after the expired six-year term. The General Assembly shall provide by its own rule for the qualifications of members of the Advisory Committee on the Constitution.

All questions requiring an interpretation by the General Assembly of the *Book of Order* arising from councils of the church shall be communicated in writing to the Stated Clerk of the General Assembly no later than 120 days prior to the convening of the next session of the General Assembly. The Stated Clerk shall refer all such questions of interpretation to the Advisory Committee on the Constitution, except those pertaining to matters pending before a judicial commission. The Advisory Committee on the Constitution shall communicate its report and recommendations to the next session of the General Assembly, no less than sixty days prior to the General Assembly.

G-6.03 AMENDING *THE BOOK OF CONFESSIONS*

Amendments to the confessional documents[a] of this church may be made only if all the following steps are completed:

a. The proposal to amend *The Book of Confessions* is approved by the General Assembly for study in the church.

b. The General Assembly appoints a committee of ruling elders and teaching elders, numbering not fewer than fifteen, of whom not more than two shall be from any one synod, to consider the proposal. This committee shall consult with the committee or council from which the proposal originated. It shall report its findings to the next General Assembly.

c.   The next ensuing General Assembly considers the report of the study committee and approves the proposed amendment and recommends it to the presbyteries for vote.

d.   The proposed amendment receives the approval in writing of two thirds of the presbyteries.

e.   The proposed amendment is approved and enacted by the next ensuing General Assembly following the amendment's receipt of the necessary two-thirds approval of the presbyteries.

G-6.04   AMENDING THE *BOOK OF ORDER*

Amendments to the *Book of Order* shall be made only if all the following steps are completed:

a.   All proposals requesting amendment of the *Book of Order* are communicated in writing to the Stated Clerk of the General Assembly no later than 120 days prior to the convening of the next session of the General Assembly.

b.   The Stated Clerk shall refer all such proposals to amend the *Book of Order* to the Advisory Committee on the Constitution (G-6.02), which shall examine the proposed amendment for clarity and consistency of language and for compatibility with other provisions of the Constitution of the Presbyterian Church (U.S.A.). At least sixty days prior to the meeting of the General Assembly, the advisory committee shall report its findings to the General Assembly along with its recommendations, which may include an amended version of any proposed constitutional changes as well as advice to accept or decline the proposals referred to the committee. The General Assembly shall not consider any amendment until it has considered the report and any recommendations from the Advisory Committee on the Constitution.

c.   The same General Assembly approves the proposal to amend and transmits the proposed amendment to the presbyteries for their vote.

d.   Presbyteries shall transmit their votes to the Stated Clerk no later than one year following the adjournment of the assembly transmitting the proposed amendments.

e.   The Stated Clerk receives written advice that a proposed amendment to the *Book of Order* has received the affirmative votes of a majority of all the presbyteries. The proposed amendment so approved shall become effective one year following the adjournment of the assembly transmitting the proposed amendment.

G-6.05   EXCEPTIONS

The provisions of G-4.0208 of this Constitution shall not be amended.

G-6.06 AMENDMENTS TO SPECIAL PROVISIONS

The processes for amending the confessional documents and for effecting full organic union (G-5.03) can be amended only by the same method that they prescribe.

DIRECTORY
FOR WORSHIP
[TEXT]

Note 1 & 2:
1. In light of the addition of the Foundations of Presbyterian Polity and the revision of the Form of Government (2011), the following terms in use in the Directory for Worship have been replaced with terms employed in the new and revised documents:

    - "Minister" or "minister of the Word and Sacrament" = "teaching elder"
    - "Elder" = "ruling elder"
    - "Governing body" = "council"
    - "Commissioned Lay Pastor" = "ruling elder commissioned to particular pastoral service" or "ruling elder commissioned to pastoral service"
    - "Office" or "Ordained Office" = "ordered ministry"
    - "Officer/s," "Church Officer/s," or "Ordained Officer/s" = "[person/those in] ordered ministry"

2. "†" - In the Form of Government, the functions described in the following provisions may be performed by ruling elders in certain circumstances as well as by teaching elders: W-1.4005; W-2.3011a(4); W-2.3011b; W-2.4012 b; W-3.3401 b,d; W-3.3604; W-3.3606; W-3.5403; W-4.4001b; W-4.9002; W-4.9003; W-4.9004; W-4.9006.

DIRECTORY FOR WORSHIP[1][2]

PREFACE

a.   This Directory for Worship reflects the conviction that the life of the Church is one, and that its worship, witness, and service are inseparable. The theology is based on the Bible, is instructed by the *Book of Confessions* of the Presbyterian Church (U.S.A.), and seeks to be sensitive to ecumenical discussion. A rich heritage of traditions and a diversity of cultures in the Presbyterian church are reflected and encouraged by this directory. A Directory for Worship is not a service book with fixed orders of worship, a collection of prayers and rituals, or a program guide. Rather it describes the theology that underlies Reformed worship and outlines appropriate forms for that worship. This directory suggests possibilities for worship, invites development in worship, and encourages continuing reform of worship. It sets standards and presents norms for the conduct of worship in the life of congregations and the councils of the Presbyterian Church (U.S.A.). As the constitutional document ordering the worship of the Presbyterian Church (U.S.A.), this Directory for Worship shall be authoritative for this church.

b.   In addition to the terms defined in the Preface to the *Book of Order*, this directory also uses language about worship which is simply descriptive.

c.   This Directory for Worship has been written in an intentional effort to listen to the Spirit speaking in Scripture and to be guided by the *Book of Confessions*. When the words have come directly from the Bible or from one of the confessions, that is so noted in the text. References to other sections of this Directory for Worship (W-) or to the Foundations of Presbyterian Polity (F-), the Form of Government (G-), and the Rules of Discipline (D-) are included in parentheses in the text to guide those who use the directory. Notes at the bottom of the pages are to identify biblical and confessional sources which have shaped the development of this directory. These notes are also included to guide the reader to Scripture and the confessions in order to enhance the use of this directory as a teaching text and resource at various levels in the life of the church.

---

[1] The following abbreviations are used throughout:
F- Foundations of Presbyterian Polity
G- Form of Government
W- Directory for Worship
D- Rules of Discipline.

[2] In light of the addition of the Foundations of Presbyterian Polity and the revision of the Form of Government (2011), the following terms in use in the Directory for Worship have been replaced with terms employed in the new and revised documents:

- "minister" or "minister of the Word and Sacrament" = "teaching elder"
- "elder" = "ruling elder"
- "governing body" = "council"
- "commissioned lay pastor" = "ruling elder commissioned to particular pastoral service" or "ruling elder commissioned to pastoral service"
- "office" or "ordained office" = "ordered ministry"
- "officer/s," "church officer/s," or "ordained officer/s" = "[person/those in] ordered ministry"

CHAPTER I

W-1.0000   THE DYNAMICS OF CHRISTIAN WORSHIP

W-1.1000   1.   **Christian Worship: An Introduction**

W-1.1001   Christian worship joyfully ascribes all praise and honor, glo-
Christian Worship   ry and power to the triune God. In worship the people of God
acknowledge God present in the world and in their lives. As they
respond to God's claim and redemptive action in Jesus Christ,
believers are transformed and renewed. In worship the faithful
offer themselves to God and are equipped for God's service in the
world.

W-1.1002   a.   The Spirit of God quickens people to an awareness of
God's Initiative   God's grace and claim upon their lives. The Spirit moves them to
respond by naming and calling upon God, by remembering and
proclaiming God's acts of self-revelation in word and deed, and
by committing their lives to God's reign in the world.

God's Encounter   b.   The earliest recollections of the people of God speak of
with Humans   God's encounter with human beings. God takes the initiative in
creation and in covenant, in calling to repentance and in offering
forgiveness. God plants and plucks up; God judges and blesses.
(Jeremiah 1:10)

God's Entrance   c.   In Jesus Christ, God entered fully into the human condi-
Into the Human   tion in an act of self-revelation, redemption, and forgiveness. En-
Condition   tering the brokenness of the world, God in Jesus Christ atoned for
sin and restored human life. By so entering the created world God
brought time and space, matter and human life to fulfillment as
instruments for knowing and praising their Creator.

W-1.1003   a.   In the person and work of Jesus, God and a human life
Jesus Christ   are united but not confused, distinguished but not separated.

Perfect Human   b.   Jesus of Nazareth offered the perfect human response to
Response   God. The Life that redeems reveals the form and purpose of re-

---

W-1.1001:   Isa. 6; Rev. 4:11; Scots Conf. 3.01; 2 Helv.Conf. 5.023, 5.135; West.Conf.
            6.112, 6.113; L.Cat. 7.214, 7.215; S.Cat. 7.046, 7.047, 7.050, 7.051;
            Conf.1967 9.35–9.37
W-1.1002:   Rom. 10:13; 1 Cor. 11:26, 12:3; Scots Conf. 3.02, 3.04–3.06, 3.12;
            Conf.1967 9.07–9.09, 9.18, 9.20
W-1.1003:   Jer. 33:1–9; John 1:1–14; Phil. 2:9–11; Heb. 1, 2; Rev. 19:11–16; Scots
            Conf. 3.06, 3.09–3.11; 2 Helv. Conf. 5.062, 5.064, 5.146; West.Conf.
            6.043–6.047; Conf.1967 9.07–9.11, 9.19

deemed life. Jesus' life discloses the character of authentic Christian worship.

The Living God in Common Life

c. Jesus Christ is the living God present in common life. The One who is proclaimed in the witness of faith is

(1) the Word of God spoken at creation,

(2) the Word of God promising and commanding throughout covenant history,

(3) the Word of God

(a) who became flesh and dwelt among us,

(b) who was crucified and raised in power,

(c) who shall return in triumph to judge and reign.

W-1.1004
Jesus Christ in Word and Sacrament

Scripture—the Word written, preaching—the Word proclaimed, and the Sacraments—the Word enacted and sealed, bear testimony to Jesus Christ, the living Word. Through Scripture, proclamation, and Sacraments, God in Christ is present by the Holy Spirit acting to transform, empower, and sustain human lives. In Christian worship the people of God

(1) hear the Word proclaimed,

(2) receive the Word enacted in Sacrament,

(3) discover the Word in the world, and

(4) are sent to follow the Word into the world.

W-1.1005
Christian Response to God in Community

a. From the beginning God created women and men for community and called a people into covenant. Jesus called, commissioned, and promised to be present to a people gathered in his name. The Holy Spirit calls, gathers, orders, and empowers the new community of the covenant. To each member, that Spirit gives gifts for building up the body of Christ and for equipping it for the work of ministry. A Christian's personal response to God is in community.

Response in Worship and Service

b. The people of God respond with words and deeds of praise and thanksgiving in acts of prayer, proclamation, remembrance, and offering. In the name of Christ, by the power of the Holy Spirit, the Christian community worships and serves God

---

W-1.1004: John 1:14–18; Rom. 10:8; 2 Cor. 4:4b–6; Phil. 2:5–11; Col. 1:15; Barm.Dec. 8.11, 8.14, 8.17; Conf.1967 9.07, 9.20, 9.27, 9.30, 9.35–9.37

W-1.1005: Matt. 28:20; John 14:18 ff.; Rom. 12:6, 8; 1 Cor. 12; Eph. 4:12 ff.; 1 Pet. 4:10; Heid.Cat. 4.055; Conf.1967 9.17–9.19, 9.20, 9.22, 9.31–9.33

(1) in shared experiences of life,

(2) in personal discipleship,

(3) in mutual ministry, and

(4) in common ministry in the world.

W-1.2000

2. The Language of Worship

W-1.2001
The Language of
Response to God

God brings all things into being by the Word. God offers the Word of grace, and people respond to that divine initiative through the language of worship. They call God by name, invoke God's presence, beseech God in prayer, and stand before God in silence and contemplation. They bow before God, lift hands and voices in praise, sing, make music, and dance. Heart, soul, strength, and mind, with one accord, they join in the language, drama, and pageantry of worship.

W-1.2002
Symbolic
Language

When people respond to God and communicate to each other their experiences of God, they must use symbolic means, for God transcends creation and cannot be reduced to anything within it. No merely human symbols can be adequate to comprehend the fullness of God, and none is identical to the reality of God. Yet the symbols human beings use can be adequate for understanding, sharing, and responding to God's gracious activity in the world since God has chosen to accommodate to humanity in self-revelation

a.   through the created order,

b.   in the events of covenant history, and

c.   most fully in the incarnate Word, Jesus Christ.

Symbols spoken or acted are authentic and appropriate for Christian worship to the extent that they are faithful to the life, death, and resurrection of Jesus Christ.

W-1.2003

Old Testament
Symbols

As the people of God worshiped the Holy One, they used symbols out of human experience, speaking of God as creator, covenant-maker, liberator, judge, redeemer, shepherd, comforter, sovereign, begetter, bearer. From the world of nature they as-

---

W-1.2000:   2 Helv.Conf. 5.217; Conf.1967 9.50
W-1.2002:   Isa. 40:18–25, 55:8, 9; John 1:1–18; Rom. 11:33–36; Col. 1:15–20; Heb. 1:1–3
W-1.2003:   Psalms, Isaiah, and other poetic and prophetic books

cribed to God the character of rock, well-spring, fire, eagle, hen, lion, or light. Their worship was also filled with the language of symbolic action:

> fasting and feasting,
> > rejoicing and wailing,
> > > marching and resting,
> > > > dancing and clapping hands,

> purification and dedication,
> > circumcisions and anointings,
> > > burnt offerings and sin offerings,
> > > > doing justice and mercy,

> making music and singing to the Lord.

W-1.2004
New Testament
Symbols

a.   Jesus used Old Testament symbols and images to speak to and about God. He participated in the symbolic actions of Israel's worship. In many cases, he personalized and gave new depth to the familiar symbols for God, especially as in his intimate use of Abba, Father. He spoke of himself in terms of many Old Testament symbols—the good shepherd, Israel's bridegroom, the Son of Man—and intensified their meanings. He brought new meaning to current religious practices like almsgiving, baptism, and breaking bread. In daily life, Jesus took ordinary acts of human compassion—healing the sick, feeding the hungry, washing feet—and translated them into ways of serving God.

Christ the Focus of
New Symbols

b.   As the Risen Lord, Jesus Christ became the focus of new symbols. The New Testament writers often used Old Testament symbolic language for the new reality as they sought to communicate the good news, describing Christ as the second Adam and as the Lamb of God. They used new symbolic language as well: the eternal Word, the firstborn of all creation, our peace who has broken down the dividing wall of hostility. In hymns and other forms of praise, Jesus Christ was glorified as the true symbol who reveals all that God is to the world. (W-1.1003-.1005)

W-1.2004:   John 1:1, 36; 1 Cor. 15:45; Eph. 2:14; Col. 1:15

W-1.2005
Authentic and
Appropriate
Language

The Church in every culture through the ages has used and adapted biblical symbols, images, stories, and words in worship. The Church's use of this language has not always been authentic and appropriate. For the Reformed tradition in its various expressions the historical and cultural use of language proves to be authentic when it reflects the biblical witness to God in Jesus Christ. Language proves to be appropriate when a worshiping community can claim it as its own when offering praise and thanksgiving to God. Appropriate language by its nature

a. is more expressive than rationalistic,

b. builds up and persuades as well as informs and describes,

c. creates ardor as well as order,

d. is the utterance of the whole community of faith as well as the devotion of individuals.

Appropriate language seeks to recognize the variety of traditions which reflect biblical truth authentically in their own forms of speech and actions. In doing so the church honors and properly uses the language of the tradition. The church is, nonetheless, free to be innovative in seeking appropriate language for worship. While respecting time-honored forms and set orders, the church may reshape them to respond freely to the leading of God's Spirit in every age.

W-1.2006
Inclusive
Language

a. Since the Presbyterian Church (U.S.A.) is a family of peoples united in Jesus Christ, appropriate language for its worship should display the rich variety of these peoples. To the extent that forms, actions, languages, or settings of worship exclude the expression of diverse cultures represented in the church or deny emerging needs and identities of believers, that worship is not faithful to the life, death, and resurrection of Jesus Christ.

Diverse
Language

b. The church shall strive in its worship to use language about God which is intentionally as diverse and varied as the Bible and our theological traditions. The church is committed to using language in such a way that all members of the community of faith may recognize themselves to be included, addressed, and equally cherished before God. Seeking to bear witness to the whole world, the church struggles to use language which is faithful to biblical truth and which neither purposely nor inadvertently excludes people because of gender, color, or other circumstance in life.

W-1.2006:   1 Cor. 9:19–23; 10:23, 24, 31–33; Gal. 3:28; James. 2:1–9

W-1.3000   **3. Time, Space, and Matter**

W-1.3010   **a. Time**

W-1.3011   (1) Christians may worship at any time, for all time has
Sabbath,   been hallowed by God. The covenant community worshiped dai-
Lord's Day   ly. But God set aside one day in seven to be kept holy to the
                 Lord. In the Old Testament the Sabbath was understood as a day
                 totally set aside and offered to the Lord. In the New Testament,
                 believers observed the first day of the week, the day of resurrec-
                 tion, as the time when the new people of the covenant gathered to
                 worship God in Jesus Christ. They came to speak of this as the
                 Lord's Day.

Word and   (2) From earliest times, the church has gathered on the
Sacraments   Lord's Day for the proclamation and exposition of the Word and
                 the celebration of the Sacraments. The Reformed tradition has
                 emphasized the importance of the Lord's Day as the time for
                 hearing the Word and celebrating the Sacraments in the expecta-
                 tion of encountering the risen Lord, and for responding in prayer
                 and service. (W-3.2001; W-5.5001)

W-1.3012   (1) In Israel's worship, daily hours were set aside for
Daily Worship   sacrifices of praise and thanksgiving. Even after the loss of the
                 Temple, morning, noon, and evening were established times for
                 prayer. Jesus set aside regular times for prayer, and the believing
                 community gathered daily for prayer in the Temple, in an upper
                 room, and in their homes. New Testament writers exhorted the
                 Church to pray without ceasing. Through the ages, the Church
                 has maintained special hours for daily prayer, historically known
                 as the daily office.

Prayer and   (2) The Reformed tradition adapted the pattern of the
Scripture   daily office, to provide an occasion not only for prayer but also
                 for the public reading and expounding of Scripture. Daily public
                 worship is to be commended as a dimension of the life and wit-
                 ness of the church as it ministers in and to the community.
                 Changing patterns of life have also led to the expression of daily
                 prayer in family and personal devotion, which are encouraged as
                 a part of the regular discipline of the Christian life. (W-3.4000;
                 W-5.2000; W-5.7000)

W-1.3011:   Gen. 1:3,14 ff.; 2:3; Ex. 20:8–11; Deut. 5:12–15; Acts 20:7; Rev.1:10; Heid.Cat.
             4.103; 2 Helv.Conf. 5.223–5.226; West.Conf. 6.118–6.119; S.Cat. 7.060;
             L.Cat.7.226–7.227
W-1.3012:   Acts 1:14; 2:42; 3:1; 10:9; West.Conf. 6.117

W-1.3013
Church Year

As God created and appointed days, God created a rhythm of time and appointed seasons for worship. In the Old Testament, people observed seasons of fasting and feasting as occasions for festival worship of God. Jesus kept these festivals. For the Church in the New Testament, the festivals were transformed in meaning and purpose by Jesus' life and teaching, his death and resurrection, and by the gift of the Holy Spirit. Jesus' birth, life, death, resurrection, ascension, and promised return give meaning to the seasons which order the annual rhythm of worship and guide the selection of lessons to be read and proclaimed in the life of the Church. (W-3.2002; W-3.2003)

W-1.3020   **b. Space**

W-1.3021
Old Testament

Christians may worship in any place, for the God who created time also created and ordered space. The Old Testament tells us God met with people in many different places. Yet particular locations became recognized as places where people had special encounter with God, so they arranged space in such a way as to remember and enhance that meeting. Whether the stone altars of the patriarchs, the Tent of Meeting for the wandering people of God, the Temple of the Kingdom in Jerusalem, or the house-synagogue worship of the Dispersion, each place was ordered to invite and express God's presence.

W-1.3022
Jesus

Jesus' life reflects the covenant community's understanding of places for worship. He regularly worshiped in the synagogue and in the Temple, in the wilderness and on the hillsides of Galilee. Jesus especially disclaimed the notion that God could be confined to any one place.

W-1.3023
Early Church

Because the identifying reality of Christian worship was neither the place nor the space but the presence of God, the early Christians could worship in the Temple, in synagogues, in homes, in catacombs, and in prisons. Wherever Christ was present among them in the interpretation of the Word and the breaking of bread, that space was hallowed. Yet the Church began to set aside special places for gathering in the presence of the risen Christ and responding in praise and service. To this day, when the Church gathers, it is not the particular place, but the presence of the risen

---

W-1.3013:   Rom. 14:5, 6; Col. 2:16, 17
W-1.3020:   West.Conf. 6.117
W-1.3022:   John 4:21–24
W-1.3024:   2 Helv.Conf. 5.214–5.216

Lord in the midst of the community which marks the reality of worship.

W-1.3024
Arrangement
of Space

When a place is set aside for worship it should facilitate accessibility and ease of gathering, should generate a sense of community, and should open people to reverence before God. It should include a place for the reading of Scripture and the preaching or exposition of the Word. It should provide for the celebration and proper administration of the Sacraments, with a font or pool for Baptism and a table suitable for the people's celebration of the Lord's Supper. The arrangement of space should visibly express the integral relation between Word and Sacrament and their centrality in Christian worship. (W-1.4004)

W-1.3030

c. Matter

W-1.3031
Old Testament

God created the material universe and pronounced it good. The covenant community understood that the material world reflects the glory of God. They also came to see that material realities can be a means for expressing suitable praise and thanksgiving to God. Ark, showbread, woven and embroidered linen, basins, oil, lights, musical instruments, grain, fruit, and animals all became expressions of the community's worship of God. The prophets warned, however, against offering the material as a substitute for offering the self to God.

W-1.3032
Jesus

In Jesus Christ the Word became flesh, and God hallowed material reality. Jesus presented his body as a living sacrifice. In his ministry, he used common things like nets, fish, baskets, jars, ointment, clay, towel and basin, water, bread, and wine. Working in and through these material things, he blessed and healed people, reconciled and bound them into community, and exhibited the grace, power, and presence of the Kingdom of God.

W-1.3033
Church:
Sacraments

(1) The early Church, following Jesus, took three primary material elements of life—water, bread, and wine—to become basic symbols of offering life to God as Jesus had offered his life. Being washed with the water of Baptism, Christians received new life in Christ and presented their bodies to be living sacrifices to God. Eating bread and drinking wine they received the sustaining presence of Christ, remembered God's covenant promise, and pledged their obedience anew.

W-1.3031:   Amos 5:21–24, Isa. 1:11–17, Mic. 6:6–8; cf. Ps. 50; Conf.1967 9.16
W-1.3033:   Scots Conf. 3.21; Heid.Cat. 4.066–4.068; 2 Helv.Conf. 5.169–5.180; West.Conf.
            6.149–6.153; S.Cat. 7.092–7.093; L.Cat. 7.272–7.274

Reformed Tradition: Sacraments	(2) The Reformed tradition understands Baptism and the Lord's Supper to be Sacraments, instituted by God and commended by Christ. Sacraments are signs of the real presence and power of Christ in the Church, symbols of God's action. Through the Sacraments, God seals believers in redemption, renews their identity as the people of God, and marks them for service. (W-3.3601)
W-1.3034 Use of Material in Worship	(1) The Church has acknowledged that the lives of Christians and all they have belong to the Creator and are to be offered to God in worship. As sign and symbol of this self-offering, the people of God have presented their creations and material possessions to God. The richness of color, texture, form, sound, and motion has been brought into the act of worship.
Artistic Expressions	(2) The Reformed heritage has called upon people to bring to worship material offerings which in their simplicity of form and function direct attention to what God has done and to the claim that God makes upon human life. The people of God have responded through creative expressions in architecture, furnishings, appointments, vestments, music, drama, language, and movement. When these artistic creations awaken us to God's presence, they are appropriate for worship. When they call attention to themselves, or are present for their beauty as an end in itself, they are idolatrous. Artistic expressions should evoke, edify, enhance, and expand worshipers' consciousness of the reality and grace of God.
W-1.3040 Mission	All time, all space, all matter are created by God and have been hallowed by Jesus Christ. Christian worship, at particular times, in special places, with the use of God's material gifts, should lead the church into the life of the world to participate in God's purpose to redeem time, to sanctify space, and to transform material reality for the glory of God.

W-1.3034:　2 Helv.Conf. 5.020–5.022; Conf.1967 9.50
W-1.3040:　Mic. 6:8; Rom. 12:1; Eph. 6:16; James. 1:22–27; West.Conf. 6.174

W-1.4000   **4. Responsibility and Accountability for Worship**

W-1.4001   In worship, the church is to remember both its liberty in
· Responsibility   Christ and the biblical command to do all things in an orderly
                      way. While Christian worship need not follow prescribed forms,
                      careless or disorderly worship is both an offense to God and a
                      stumbling block to the people. Those responsible for worship are
                      to be guided by the Holy Spirit speaking in Scripture, the historic
                      experience of the Church universal, the Reformed tradition, *The
                      Book of Confessions*, the needs and particular circumstances of
                      the worshiping community, as well as the provisions of the Form
                      of Government and this directory. (W-3.1001; W-3.1002)

W-1.4002   To ensure that these guiding principles are being followed,
Review and   those responsible on behalf of presbytery for the oversight and
Oversight   review of the ministry of particular worshiping congregations
                      should discuss with those sessions the quality of worship, the
                      standards governing it, and the fruit it is bearing in the life of
                      God's people as they proclaim the gospel and communicate its
                      joy and justice. (G-3.0301)

W-1.4003   In Jesus Christ, the Church is a royal priesthood in which
Who May   worship is the work of everyone. The people of God are called to
Participate and   participate in the common ministry of worship. No one shall be
Lead in Worship   excluded from participation or leadership in public worship in the
                      Lord's house on the grounds of race, color, class, age, sex, or
                      handicapping condition. Some by gifts and training may be called
                      to particular acts of leadership in worship. It is appropriate to
                      encourage members and those in ordered ministry with such
                      abilities to assist in leading worship.

W-1.4004   In a particular church, the session is to provide for worship
Session   and shall encourage the people to participate fully and regularly
                      in it. The session shall make provision for the regular

                      a.   preaching of the Word,

                      b.   celebration of the Sacraments,

                      c.   corporate prayer, and

                      d.   offering of praise to God in song. (W-2.0000; W-3.0000)

W-1.4001:   Gal. 5:1; 1 Cor. 14
W-1.4003:   1 Pet. 2:9 ff.; Conf.1967 9.39
W-1.4004:   Conf.1967 9.50

The session has authority

    e.   to oversee and approve all public worship in the life of the particular church with the exception of those responsibilities delegated to the pastor alone (W-1.4005)

    f.   to determine occasions, days, times, and places for worship.

It is responsible

    g.   for the space where worship is conducted, including its arrangement and furnishings,

    h.   for the use of special appointments such as flowers, candles, banners, paraments, and other objects of art,

    i.   for the overall program of music and other arts in the church,

    j.   for those who lead worship through music, drama, dance, and other arts.

W-1.4005
Pastor

    a.   The teaching elder† as pastor has certain responsibilities which are not subject to the authority of the session. In a particular service of worship the pastor is responsible for

    (1) the selection of Scripture lessons to be read,

    (2) the preparation and preaching of the sermon or exposition of the Word,

    (3) the prayers offered on behalf of the people and those prepared for the use of the people in worship,

    (4) the music to be sung,

    (5) the use of drama, dance, and other art forms

The pastor may confer with a worship committee in planning particular services of worship. (G-2.0504)

Pastor and Choir
Director

    b.   Where there is a choir director or other musical leader, the pastor and that person will confer to ensure that anthems and other musical offerings are appropriate for the particular service. The session should see that these conferences take place appropriately and on a regular basis.

W-1.4005:   2 Helv.Conf. 5.163

W-1.4006
Session and
Pastor

The sequence and proportion of the elements of worship are the responsibility of the pastor with the concurrence of session. The selection of hymnals, song books, service books, Bibles, and other materials for use of the congregation in public worship is the responsibility of the session with the concurrence of the pastor and in consultation with musicians and educators available to the session.

W-1.4007
Session
Responsibility
for Education

In the exercise of its responsibility to encourage the participation of its people in worship, the session should provide for education in Christian worship by means appropriate to the age, interests, and circumstances of the members of the congregation. (W-3.5202; W-6.2000; G-3.0201a, b) It shall also provide for the regular study of this directory in the education of ruling elders and deacons (G-3.0201c)

W-1.4008
Accountability
to Presbytery

In fulfilling their responsibilities for worship, pastors and sessions are accountable to presbytery in its exercise of constitutional supervision of its members. (G-3.0307)

W-1.4009
Presbytery
Responsibility
for Education

In the exercise of their responsibility to provide encouragement, guidance, and resources in worship to member churches, presbyteries should arrange appropriate educational events. They shall also provide education in worship through regular use of this directory as they examine candidates for ordination and teaching elders for continuing membership. (G-2.0503 and G-3.0306)

CHAPTER II

W-2.0000   **THE ELEMENTS OF CHRISTIAN WORSHIP**

W-2.1000   **1. Prayer**

W-2.1001   Prayer is at the heart of worship. In prayer, through the Holy
Christian Prayer   Spirit, people seek after and are found by the one true God who has
                      been revealed in Jesus Christ. They listen and wait upon God, call
                      God by name, remember God's gracious acts, and offer themselves
                      to God. Prayer may be spoken, sung, offered in silence, or enacted.
                      Prayer grows out of the center of a person's life in response to the
                      Spirit. Prayer is shaped by the Word of God in Scripture and by the
                      life of the community of faith. Prayer issues in commitment to join
                      God's work in the world.

W-2.1002   In prayer we respond to God in many ways. In adoration we
Content of Prayer   praise God for who God is. In thanksgiving we express gratitude for
                      what God has done. In confession we acknowledge repentance for
                      what we as individuals and as a people have done or left undone. In
                      supplication we plead for ourselves and the gathered community. In
                      intercession we plead for others, on behalf of others, and for the
                      whole world. In self-dedication we offer ourselves to the purpose
                      and glory of God.

W-2.1003   Song is a response which engages the whole self in prayer.
Music as Prayer: Song unites the faithful in common prayer wherever they gather for
Congregational   worship whether in church, home, or other special place. The cove-
Song   nant people have always used the gift of song to offer prayer.
                      Psalms were created to be sung by the faithful as their response to
                      God. Though they may be read responsively or in unison, their full
                      power comes to expression when they are sung. In addition to
                      psalms the Church in the New Testament sang hymns and spiritual
                      songs. Through the ages and from varied cultures, the church has
                      developed additional musical forms for congregational prayer.
                      Congregations are encouraged to use these diverse musical forms
                      for prayer as well as those which arise out of the musical life of
                      their own cultures.

W-2.1004   To lead the congregation in the singing of prayer is a primary
Music as Prayer: role of the choir and other musicians. They also may pray on behalf
Choir and   of the congregation with introits, responses, and other musical
Instrumental   forms. Instrumental music may be a form of prayer since words are
Music   not essential to prayer. In worship, music is not to be for entertain-

---

W-2.1000:   Heid.Cat. 4.116–4.118; 2 Helv.Conf. 5.218–5.221; West.Conf. 6.114–6.115; S.Cat.
            7.098–7.099; L.Cat. 7.264, 7.288–7.296; Conf.1967 9.50
W-2.1003:   Eph. 5:19; Col. 3:16

ment or artistic display. Care should be taken that it not be used merely as a cover for silence. Music as prayer is to be a worthy offering to God on behalf of the people. (See also W-2.2008; W-3.3101)

W-2.1005
Enacted Prayer

In the Old and New Testaments and through the ages, the people of God expressed prayer through actions as well as speech and song. So in worship today it is appropriate

    a.   to kneel, to bow, to stand, to lift hands in prayer,

    b.   to dance, to clap, to embrace in joy and praise,

    c.   to anoint and to lay hands in intercession and supplication, commissioning and ordination.

W-2.2000

2. Scripture Read and Proclaimed

W-2.2001
Centrality of
Scripture

The church confesses the Scriptures to be the Word of God written, witnessing to God's self-revelation. Where that Word is read and proclaimed, Jesus Christ the Living Word is present by the inward witness of the Holy Spirit. For this reason the reading, hearing, preaching, and confessing of the Word are central to Christian worship. The session shall ensure that in public worship the Scripture is read and proclaimed regularly in the common language(s) of the particular church.

W-2.2002
Selection of
Scripture

The teaching elder is responsible for the selection of Scripture to be read in all services of public worship and should exercise care so that over a period of time the people will hear the full message of Scripture. It is appropriate that in the Service of the Lord's Day there be readings from the Old Testament and the Epistles and Gospels of the New Testament. The full range of the psalms should be also used in worship.

W-2.2003
Lectionaries

Selections for reading in public worship should be guided by the seasons of the church year, pastoral concerns for a local congregation, events and conditions in the world, and specific program emphases of the church. Lectionaries offered by the church ensure a broad range of readings as well as consistency and connection with the universal Church.

W-2.2004
Discipline in
Reading

The people of God should exercise this same principle of selection in their choice of Scripture reading in family and personal worship. (W-5.3000) Those responsible for teaching and preaching the

---

W-2.2000:   Scots Conf. 3.18–3.19; 2 Helv.Conf. 5.001–5.007; West.Conf. 6.001–6.010, 6.116; S.Cat. 7.088–7.090; L.Cat. 7.113–7.115, 7.264–7.270; Bar.Dec. 8.11–8.12, 8.26; Conf.1967 9.27–9.30, 9.49

Word have a special responsibility to ensure that in their personal worship they observe a discipline of reading from the fullness of Scripture.

**W-2.2005
Versions**

The teaching elder has responsibility for the selection of the version of text from which the Scripture lessons are read in public worship. If paraphrases are used, adaptations are made, or new translations are prepared, the congregation should be informed.

**W-2.2006
Public Reading
and Hearing
of Scripture**

The public reading of Scripture should be clear, audible, and attentive to the meanings of the text, and should be entrusted to those prepared for such reading. Listening to the reading of Scripture requires expectation and concentration and may be aided by the availability of a printed text for the worshipers. The congregation may read Scripture responsively, antiphonally, or in unison as a part of the service. (W-3.3401)

**W-2.2007
Preaching the
Word**

The preached Word or sermon is to be based upon the written Word. It is a proclamation of Scripture in the conviction that through the Holy Spirit Jesus Christ is present to the gathered people, offering grace and calling for obedience. Preaching requires diligence and discernment in the study of Scripture, the discipline of daily prayer, cultivated sensitivity to events and issues affecting the lives of the people, and a consistent and personal obedience to Jesus Christ. The sermon should present the gospel with simplicity and clarity, in language which can be understood by the people. For reasons of order the preaching of the Word shall ordinarily be done by a teaching elder. A teaching elder or other person authorized by presbytery may be invited by the pastor with the concurrence of the session or, when there is no pastor, by the session. A person may be sent to preach by the presbytery. (G-2.0301; G-3.0301; G-3.0307; G-2.0606; G-2.0504b; G-2.1001)

**W-2.2008
Other Forms of
Proclamation**

The Word is also proclaimed through song in anthems and solos based on scriptural texts, in cantatas and oratorios which tell the biblical story, in psalms and canticles, and in hymns, spirituals, and spiritual songs which present the truth of the biblical faith. Song in worship may also express the response of the people to the Word read, sung, enacted, or proclaimed. Drama and dance, poetry and pageant, indeed, most other human art forms are also expressions through which the people of God have proclaimed and responded to the Word. Those entrusted with the proclamation of the Word through art forms should exercise care that the gospel is faithfully presented in ways through which the people of God may receive and respond.

W-2.2009
Creeds and
Confessions

The people also express the Word in response to the reading and proclamation of the Word through creeds and confessions. (F-2.01) The church confesses its faith in relation to

a.   the Church universal,

b.   its particular historic heritage, and

c.   its local situation.

When the church confesses its faith during the celebration of Baptism and the Lord's Supper the creeds of the universal Church should be used. (W-3.3603) The Word confessed is always judged by the living Word, Jesus Christ, as attested in Scripture.

W-2.2010
Hearing the
Word

The people's participation in the proclamation of the Word is above all to hear:

a.   to discern Jesus Christ,

b.   to receive his offered grace,

c.   to respond to his call with obedience.

Such participation depends upon the illumination of the Holy Spirit, which is to be sought earnestly in prayer. The words "hearing" and "heard" are not intended exclusively to mean acts of sensory perception.

W-2.3000

3.   Baptism

W-2.3001
Jesus and
Baptism

Baptism is the sign and seal of incorporation into Christ. Jesus through his own baptism identified himself with sinners in order to fulfill all righteousness. Jesus in his own baptism was attested Son by the Father and was anointed with the Holy Spirit to undertake the way of the servant manifested in his sufferings, death, and resurrection. Jesus the risen Lord assured his followers of his continuing presence and power and commissioned them "Go therefore and make disciples of all nations, baptizing them in the name of the Father and of the Son and of the Holy Spirit, and teaching them to obey everything that I have commanded you. And remember, I am with you always to the end of the age" (Matt. 28:19, NRSV). The disciples were empowered by the outpouring of the Spirit to undertake a life of service and to be an inclusive worshiping community, sharing life in which love, justice, and mercy abounded. (W-1.3033)

W-2.3000:   Scots Conf. 3.21–3.23; Heid.Cat. 4.069–4.074; 2 Helv.Conf. 5.185–5.192; West.Conf. 6.154–6.160; S.Cat. 7.094–7.095; L.Cat. 7.275–7.277, 7.286–7.287; Conf.1967 9.51

W-2.3001:   Matt. 3:15; 28:19–20; Mark 10:38–40; Acts 2:38–47.

W-2.3002
Dying and Rising
in Baptism

In Baptism, we participate in Jesus' death and resurrection. In Baptism, we die to what separates us from God and are raised to newness of life in Christ. Baptism points us back to the grace of God expressed in Jesus Christ, who died for us and who was raised for us. Baptism points us forward to that same Christ who will fulfill God's purpose in God's promised future.

W-2.3003
Covenant and the
Water of Baptism

In Baptism, the Holy Spirit binds the Church in covenant to its Creator and Lord. The water of Baptism symbolizes the waters of Creation, of the Flood, and of the Exodus from Egypt. Thus, the water of Baptism links us to the goodness of God's creation and to the grace of God's covenants with Noah and Israel. Prophets of Israel, amidst the failure of their own generation to honor God's covenant, called for justice to roll down like waters and righteousness like an everflowing stream. (Amos 5:24) They envisioned a fresh expression of God's grace and of creation's goodness—a new covenant accompanied by the sprinkling of cleansing water. In his ministry, Jesus offered the gift of living water. So, Baptism is the sign and seal of God's grace and covenant in Christ.

W-2.3004
Inclusion in the
Covenant of Grace

As circumcision was the sign and symbol of inclusion in God's grace and covenant with Israel, so Baptism is the sign and symbol of inclusion in God's grace and covenant with the Church. As an identifying mark, Baptism signifies

    a.   the faithfulness of God,

    b.   the washing away of sin,

    c.   rebirth,

    d.   putting on the fresh garment of Christ,

    e.   being sealed by God's Spirit,

    f.   adoption into the covenant family of the Church,

    g.   resurrection and illumination in Christ.

W-2.3005
Union with Christ
and One Another

The body of Christ is one, and Baptism is the bond of unity in Christ. As they are united with Christ through faith, Baptism unites the people of God with each other and with the church of every time and place. Barriers of race, gender, status, and age are to be transcended. Barriers of nationality, history, and practice are to be overcome.

W-2.3002:   Rom. 6:3–11; Col. 2:12.
W-2.3003:   Gen. 1:2; Jer. 31:31–34; Ezek. 36:25–27; John 4:7–15; 7:37, 38; 1 Cor.10:1, 2; 1 Pet. 3:20–21
W-2.3004:   Gen. 17:7–14; John 3:5; Acts 2:39; 22:16; 1 Cor. 6:11, 12:12–13; 2 Cor. 1:22; Gal. 3:27; Eph. 1:13–14; 5:14; Col. 2:11–12; Tit. 3:5
W-2.3005:   1 Cor. 12:12–13; Gal. 3:27–28; Eph. 2:11–22; 4:4–6

W-2.3006
Baptism: Grace,
Repentance,
Commissioning

Baptism enacts and seals what the Word proclaims: God's redeeming grace offered to all people. Baptism is God's gift of grace and also God's summons to respond to that grace. Baptism calls to repentance, to faithfulness, and to discipleship. Baptism gives the church its identity and commissions the church for ministry to the world.

W-2.3007
Sign and Seal
of God's
Faithfulness

God's faithfulness signified in Baptism is constant and sure, even when human faithfulness to God is not. Baptism is received only once. The efficacy of Baptism is not tied to the moment when it is administered, for Baptism signifies the beginning of life in Christ, not its completion. God's grace works steadily, calling to repentance and newness of life. God's faithfulness needs no renewal. Human faithfulness to God needs repeated renewal. Baptism calls for decision at every subsequent stage of life's way, both for those whose Baptism attends their profession of faith and for those who are nurtured from childhood within the family of faith.

W-2.3008
"One Baptism":
Its Meanings

a.   Both believers and their children are included in God's covenant love. Children of believers are to be baptized without undue delay, but without undue haste. Baptism, whether administered to those who profess their faith or to those presented for Baptism as children, is one and the same Sacrament.

Children

b.   The Baptism of children witnesses to the truth that God's love claims people before they are able to respond in faith.

Adults

c.   The Baptism of those who enter the covenant upon their own profession of faith witnesses to the truth that God's gift of grace calls for fulfillment in a response of faithfulness.

W-2.3009
Remembering
One's Baptism

Baptism is received only once. There are many times in worship, however, when believers acknowledge the grace of God continually at work. As they participate in the celebration of another's Baptism, as they experience the sustaining nurture of the Lord's Supper, and as they reaffirm the commitments made at Baptism, they confess their ongoing need of God's grace and pledge anew their obedience to God's covenant in Christ.

W-2.3010
One Body,
One Baptism

As there is one body, there is one Baptism. (Eph. 4:4–6) The Presbyterian Church (U.S.A.) recognizes all Baptisms with water in the name of the Father, of the Son, and of the Holy Spirit administered by other Christian churches.

W-2.3006:   Matt. 28:18–20; Luke 3:3,8–14; Acts 2:38,41–47; cf. Isa. 44:3; John 4:7–15;
7:37–38; Rev. 7:17, 22:17

W-2.3011
Responsibility
for Baptism

a.   For reasons of order, Baptism shall be authorized by the session, administered by a teaching elder or ruling elder commissioned to pastoral service when invited by the session and authorized by the presbytery, and accompanied by the reading and proclaiming of the Word. (G-3.0301; W-3.3602–.3608) Baptism is celebrated in a service of public worship. Extraordinary circumstances may call for the administration of Baptism apart from the worship of the whole congregation. In such cases care should be taken that

(1) the congregation be represented by one or more members of the session;

(2) a proper understanding of the meaning of the Sacrament be offered by the teaching elder;

(3) the session be consulted when possible;

(4) the Baptism be reported by the officiating teaching elder† and recorded by the session.

By Chaplains
and Others

b.   A council may also authorize the celebration of the Sacrament of Baptism by chaplains or others engaged in ordered ministries serving in hospitals, prisons, schools, or other institutions where the council has an authorized ministry or an institutional witness, by chaplains ministering to members of the armed forces and their families, and by teaching elders† engaged in new church development under the jurisdiction of the council. In all such cases of Baptism, the teaching elder† shall take responsibility that the newly baptized person is enrolled as a member of a particular church. Such enrollment may be arranged in advance in consultation with the session of the church, or the council may provide that any such newly baptized member shall be enrolled in absentia as a member of a particular church designated by the council and under its jurisdiction or upon the roll held by the council until a new church is organized.

W-2.3012
Session
Responsibility

The session's responsibilities for Baptism are

a.   encouraging parents to present their children for Baptism, reminding them that children of believers are to be baptized without undue haste, but without undue delay, and authorizing the Baptism of those presented; (W-2.3014)

b.   admitting to Baptism children of believers, after appropriate instruction and discussion with the parent(s) or one(s) rightly exercising parental responsibility, acquainting them with the significance of what God is doing in this act, and with the special responsibilities on parents and congregations for nurturing the baptized person in the Christian life;

c.   admitting to Baptism, after appropriate instruction and examination, those not yet baptized who come making public their personal profession of faith;

d.   placing all baptized persons on the appropriate roll as members of the congregation;

e.   making certain that those baptized are nurtured in understanding the meaning of Baptism, of the Lord's Supper, and of their interrelation, and that they are surrounded by Christian encouragement and support. (G-3.0201; G-3.0204; W-2.3011)

W-2.3013
Church
Responsibility

The congregation as a whole, on behalf of the Church universal, assumes responsibility for nurturing the baptized person in the Christian life. In exercising this ministry, the session may designate certain members of the congregation as representatives of the church charged with special responsibility for nurture. For any person who is being baptized, sponsor(s) may be appointed by the session in consultation with those desiring Baptism for themselves or for their children and given the specific role of nurturing the baptized person. (W-6.2001; W-6.2005)

W-2.3014
Parental
Responsibility

When a child is being presented for Baptism, ordinarily the parent(s) or one(s) rightly exercising parental responsibility shall be an active member of the congregation. Those presenting children for Baptism shall promise to provide nurture and guidance within the community of faith until the child is ready to make a personal profession of faith and assume the responsibility of active church membership. (W-4.2002; W-4.2003) The session may also consider a request for the baptism of a child from a Christian parent who is an active member of another congregation. If the session approves such a request, it shall consult with the council of the other congregation and shall notify them when the Sacrament has been administered.

W-2.4000

4.   The Lord's Supper

W-2.4001
Jesus and
the Supper

a.   The Lord's Supper is the sign and seal of eating and drinking in communion with the crucified and risen Lord. During his earthly ministry Jesus shared meals with his followers as a sign of community and acceptance and as an occasion for his own ministry. He celebrated Israel's feasts of covenant commemoration.

W-2.4000:   Scots Conf. 3.21–3.23; Heid.Cat. 4.075–4.082; 2 Helv.Conf. 5.193–5.210; West.Conf. 6.161–6.168; S.Cat. 7.096–7.097; L.Cat. 7.278–7.287; Conf.1967 9.52

W-2.4001:   Matt. 14:13–21; 15:32–39; Luke 5:27–32; 7:36–50; 10:38–42; and parallels. John 2:13; 5:1; 7:2–37; 10:22–33; 12:1–3; 13:1–4 ff. and synoptic parallels. Matt. 26:17–29; Mark 14:12–25; Luke 22:7–20, 24:41–43; John 21:13; Acts 1:4

Last Supper

b. In his last meal before his death, Jesus took and shared with his disciples the bread and wine, speaking of them as his body and blood, signs of the new covenant. He commended breaking bread and sharing a cup to remember and proclaim his death.

Resurrection

c. On the day of his resurrection, the risen Jesus made himself known to his followers in the breaking of bread. He continued to show himself to believers, by blessing and breaking bread, by preparing, serving, and sharing common meals. (W-1.3033)

W-2.4002
Church in the
New Testament

The Church in the New Testament devoted itself to the apostles' teaching, to fellowship, to prayers, and to the common meal. The apostle Paul delivered to the Church the tradition he had received from the risen Lord, who commanded that his followers share the bread and cup as a remembrance and a showing forth of his death until he comes. The New Testament describes the meal as a participation in Christ and with one another in the expectation of the Kingdom and as a foretaste of the messianic banquet.

W-2.4003
Thanksgiving

In the Lord's Supper the Church, gathered for worship,

a. blesses God for all that God has done through creation, redemption, and sanctification;

b. gives thanks that God is working in the world and in the Church in spite of human sin;

c. gratefully anticipates the fulfillment of the Kingdom Christ proclaimed, and offers itself in obedient service to God's reign.

W-2.4004
Remembering

At the Lord's Table, the Church is

a. renewed and empowered by the memory of Christ's life, death, resurrection, and promise to return;

b. sustained by Christ's pledge of undying love and continuing presence with God's people;

c. sealed in God's covenant of grace through partaking of Christ's self-offering.

In remembering, believers receive and trust the love of Christ present to them and to the world; they manifest the reality of the covenant of grace in reconciling and being reconciled; and they proclaim the power of Christ's reign for the renewal of the world in justice and in peace.

W-2.4002: Acts 2:42, 46; 1 Corinthians 11:23–26; Matt. 8:11; 22:1; 1 Cor. 10:16–17; Rev. 19:9; cf. Ps. 107:1–3; Isa. 25:6–8; 43:5–7

W-2.4005
Invocation

As the people of God bless and thank God the Father and remember Jesus Christ the Son, they call upon the Holy Spirit

a.   to lift them into Christ's presence;

b.   to accept their offering of bread and wine;

c.   to make breaking bread and sharing the cup a participation in the body and blood of Christ;

d.   to bind them with Christ and with one another;

e.   to unite them in communion with all the faithful in heaven and on earth;

f.   to nourish them with Christ's body and blood that they may mature into the fullness of Christ;

g.   to keep them faithful as Christ's body, representing Christ and doing God's work in the world.

W-2.4006
Communion of
the Faithful

Around the Table of the Lord, God's people are in communion with Christ and with all who belong to Christ. Reconciliation with Christ compels reconciliation with one another. All the baptized faithful are to be welcomed to the Table, and none shall be excluded because of race, sex, age, economic status, social class, handicapping condition, difference of culture or language, or any barrier created by human injustice. Coming to the Lord's Table the faithful are actively to seek reconciliation in every instance of conflict or division between them and their neighbors. Each time they gather at the Table the believing community

a.   are united with the Church in every place, and the whole Church is present;

b.   join with all the faithful in heaven and on earth in offering thanksgiving to the triune God;

c.   renew the vows taken at Baptism;

and they commit themselves afresh to love and serve God, one another, and their neighbors in the world.

W-2.4005:   1 Cor. 10:16.
W-2.4006:   Matt. 5:23–24; 18:15–18; 1 Cor. 11:18–22, 27–29; Gal. 3:28; Jas. 2:1–7

W-2.4007
Foretaste of the
Kingdom Meal

In this meal the Church celebrates the joyful feast of the people of God, and anticipates the great banquet and marriage supper of the Lamb. Brought by the Holy Spirit into Christ's presence, the Church eagerly expects and prays for the day when Christ shall come in glory and God be all in all. Nourished by this hope, the Church rises from the Table and is sent by the power of the Holy Spirit to participate in God's mission to the world, to proclaim the gospel, to exercise compassion, to work for justice and peace until Christ's Kingdom shall come at last.

W-2.4008
Word and
Sacrament
Together

In the life of the worshiping congregation, Word and Sacrament have an integral relationship. Whenever the Lord's Supper is observed, it shall be preceded by the reading and the proclamation of the Word. (W-1.1005)

W-2.4009
Time, Place, and
Frequency

The Lord's Supper is to be observed on the Lord's Day, in the regular place of worship, and in a manner suitable to the particular occasion and local congregation. It is appropriate to celebrate the Lord's Supper as often as each Lord's Day. It is to be celebrated regularly and frequently enough to be recognized as integral to the Service for the Lord's Day.

W-2.4010
Special Occasions

It is also appropriate to observe the Lord's Supper on other occasions of special significance in the life of the Christian community, as long as the celebration of the Sacrament is open to the whole believing community. The Lord's Supper may be observed in connection with the visitation of the sick and those isolated from public worship as a means of extending the church's ministry to them. On all such occasions of the celebration of the Sacrament, the Word shall be read and proclaimed. Even though such a celebration may involve only a few members of the congregation, nevertheless it is not to be understood as a private ceremony or devotional exercise, but as an act of the whole church, which shall be represented not only by the teaching elder or the one authorized by presbytery to administer the Sacrament, but also by one or more members of the congregation authorized by the session to represent the church. (W-2.4012; W-3.3609–.3618; W-3.6204)

W-2.4007:   Matt. 22:1–10; Luke 14:15–24; 1 Cor. 15:20–28; Eph. 1:23; Phil. 2:10, 11; Col.
3:1–4; 1 Thess. 4:16, 17; Rev. 19:9; Ps. 72:2–4, 12–14; Isa. 2:1–4; Mic. 4:1–4, 6:8;
Matt. 5:21–26; 28:18–20; Luke 3:10–14; 4:18–21; Acts 1:3–8; Jas. 2:14–17; 1 Jn.
3:16–18

W-2.4011 Who May Receive	a. The invitation to the Lord's Supper is extended to all who have been baptized, remembering that access to the Table is not a right conferred upon the worthy, but a privilege given to the undeserving who come in faith, repentance, and love. In preparing to receive Christ in this Sacrament, the believer is to confess sin and brokenness, to seek reconciliation with God and neighbor, and to trust in Jesus Christ for cleansing and renewal. Even one who doubts or whose trust is wavering may come to the Table in order to be assured of God's love and grace in Christ Jesus.
Baptized Children	b. Baptized children who are being nurtured and instructed in the significance of the invitation to the Table and the meaning of their response are invited to receive the Lord's Supper, recognizing that their understanding of participation will vary according to their maturity. (W-4.2002)
W-2.4012 Responsibility	a. The session is responsible for authorizing all observances of the Lord's Supper in the life of a particular church and shall ensure regular and frequent celebration of the Sacrament, in no case less than quarterly. Any other council of the church, also, may appoint times for the celebration of the Lord's Supper during their meetings. A council may also authorize the celebration of the Sacrament in connection with the public worship of some gathering of believers which is under its jurisdiction or in institutions where it has a missional witness or authorized ministry. A council may delegate the authority to approve the celebration of the Lord's Supper to an appropriate overseeing body in the institutions for which it has responsibility. (cf. W-3.6205)
Chaplains or Others	b. Chaplains or other teaching elders† serving in hospitals, prisons, schools, or other institutions, and chaplains ministering to members of the armed forces and their families, may administer the Sacrament of the Lord's Supper when authorized to do so by the council which has jurisdiction over the ministry exercised by the particular teaching elder†. The terms of the authority to administer the Sacrament of the Lord's Supper shall be stated in the teaching elder's† terms of call or endorsement.
Administered by Teaching Elder or Ruling Elder Commissioned to Pastoral Service	c. For reasons of order the Sacrament of the Lord's Supper shall be administered by a teaching elder or ruling elder commissioned to pastoral service when invited by the session and authorized by the presbytery. Missional concerns may lead to exceptions as determined and authorized by presbytery. (G-3.0301; G-2.1001)

W-2.4011:   L.Cat. 7.281–7.282

W-2.5000	**5. Self-Offering**
W-2.5001 Response to Christ	The Christian life is an offering of one's self to God. In worship the people are presented with the costly self-offering of Jesus Christ, are claimed and set free by him, and are led to respond by offering to him their lives, their particular gifts and abilities, and their material goods.
W-2.5002 Offering Spiritual Gifts	Worship should always offer opportunities to respond to Christ's call to become disciples by professing faith, by uniting with the church, and by taking up the mission of the people of God, as well as opportunities for disciples to renew the commitment of their lives to Jesus Christ and his mission in the world. As the Holy Spirit has graced each member with particular gifts for strengthening the body of Christ for mission, so worship should provide opportunities to recognize these gifts and to offer them to serve Christ in the church and in the world.
W-2.5003 Offering Material Gifts and Goods	a. The offering of material goods in worship is a corporate act of self-dedication in response to God. It expresses thanksgiving to God, the giver of life and all goods, the redeemer from sin and evil. It is an affirmation by Christ's disciples of

      (1)   their commitment to be stewards in all creation;

      (2)   their responsibility to share the Word with and to care for all people;

      (3)   their desire to share God's gifts with those to whom believers are bound in the Church universal;

      (4)   their common bond in the body of Christ.

Disciplined and Generous Support	b. In the Old Testament the people of Israel were commanded to bring a tenth of their income to support the work of the house of God and those who served God in it. In the New Testament the apostles recognized that the work of the Church required disciplined support. Both in Israel and in the early Church the people were encouraged to give generously to meet the needs of the poor. God calls believers today to be disciplined and generous in giving support to the ministries of the church. (W-5.5004)
Received in Worship	c. During public worship, at an appropriate time, and as an act of thanksgiving, the tithes and offerings of the people are gathered and received.

W-2.5001:   2 Helv.Conf. 5.110–5.123; West.Conf. 6.088
W-2.5002:   Rom. 12:4–8; 1 Cor. 12; Eph. 4:7–16
W-2.5003:   Gen. 1:28 ff., 2:15; Lev. 23:22; Num. 18:21–29; Deut. 28:7–12; 2 Chron. 24:8–14;
           Mal. 3:8–10; Matt. 28:19; Acts 1:8; 2:44–45; 4:34–37; 1 Cor. 16:1, 2; 2 Cor.
           8:1–15; 9:5–15; 1 Tim. 5:17, 18; Jas. 2:4; 3 Jn. 5–8; 2 Helv.Conf. 5.211

W-2.6000   **6. Relating to Each Other and the World**

W-2.6001   Worship is an activity of the common life of the people of God
Community   in which the care of the members for each other and for the quality
Concerns   of their life and ministry together expresses the reality of God's
                  power to create and sustain community in the midst of a sinful
                  world. As God is concerned for the events in daily life, so members
                  of the community in worship appropriately express concern for one
                  another and for their ministry in the world.

Greetings   a. as they
                          (1) greet one another and are greeted by those who are
                  leading them in worship;
                          (2) welcome visitors, note their presence, and extend
                  Christian hospitality;

Reconciliation   b. as they
                          (1) take opportunity to seek and to offer forgiveness for
                  hurts, misunderstandings, and broken relationships among them-
                  selves;
                          (2) respond to God's act of reconciliation by exchanging
                  signs and words of reconciliation and of Christ's peace;

Preparation   c. as they
for Prayer   (1) prepare for intercessions by expressing concerns and
                  requesting prayer on behalf of those with needs in the congregation,
                  the church, and the world;
                          (2) offer thanksgiving for life and life's transitions, rejoic-
                  ing with those who rejoice and mourning with those who mourn;

Interpretation   d. as they
                          (1) apply God's Word to daily life;
                          (2) interpret the mission and work of the church;
                          (3) give witness to faith and service;

Mission   e. as they
                          (1) make and renew covenants;
                          (2) commit themselves to and are commissioned for spe-
                  cific corporate and personal ministries of compassion, justice,
                  peacemaking, reconciliation, and witness.

W-2.6000:   2 Helv.Conf. 5.135; West.Conf. 6:146–6.147; Conf.1967 9.35–9.38

CHAPTER III

W-3.0000

THE ORDERING OF CHRISTIAN WORSHIP

W-3.1000

1. Principles and Sources of Ordering

W-3.1001
Scripture and
History

Those responsible for ordering Christian worship shall be faithful to the authority of the Holy Spirit speaking in and through Scripture. Beyond Scripture no single warrant for ordering worship exists, but the worship of the Church is informed and shaped by history, culture, and contemporary need. Thus the worship of the Presbyterian Church (U.S.A.) should be guided by the historic experience of the Church at worship through the ages, especially in the Reformed tradition. (W-1.4001)

W-3.1002
Form and
Freedom

a. The Church has always experienced a tension between form and freedom in worship. In the history of the Church, some have offered established forms for ordering worship in accordance with God's Word. Others, in the effort to be faithful to the Word, have resisted imposing any fixed forms upon the worshiping community. The Presbyterian Church (U.S.A.) acknowledges that all forms of worship are provisional and subject to reformation. In ordering worship the church is to seek openness to the creativity of the Holy Spirit, who guides the church toward worship which is orderly yet spontaneous, consistent with God's Word and open to the newness of God's future. (W-1.4001)

Guidance of
Session

b. Manifestations of the Spirit in worship edify the whole church. When actions in worship are present only for personal expression, call attention to themselves, or are insensitive to the congregation at worship, they are not in order and call for the counsel and guidance of the session.

W-3.1003
Participation and
Leadership

The ordering of worship should also reflect the richness of the cultural diversity in which the church ministers, as well as the local circumstances and needs of its congregations. While the authority for ordering worship belongs to those so designated (G-2.0504; G-3.0201; W-1.4000) and leadership in worship is assigned to those with gifts, training, and authorization (W-1.4003), the order for worship should provide for and encourage the participation of all.

W-3.1004
Children in
Worship

Children bring special gifts to worship and grow in the faith through their regular inclusion and participation in the worship of the congregation. Those responsible for planning and leading the

---

W-3.1000: Scots Conf. 3.20; West.Conf. 6.006
W-3.1002: 1 Cor. 12–14

participation of children in worship should consider the children's level of understanding and ability to respond, and should avoid both excessive formality and condescension. The session should ensure that regular programs of the church do not prevent children's full participation with the whole congregation in worship, in Word and Sacrament, on the Lord's Day. (W-3.3201; W-3.5202; W-6.2001; W-6.2006)

W-3.2000

W-3.2001
Days

2. Days and Seasons

God has appointed one day in seven to be kept holy, set aside as the occasion for the people of God to worship corporately. God has also commended daily worship by the people, whether gathered in assembly or at home. (W-1.3011–.3012; W-5.5001)

W-3.2002
Church Year

God has provided a rhythm of seasons which orders life and influences the church's worship. (Cf. W-1.3013) God's work of redemption in Jesus Christ offers the Church a central pattern for ordering worship in relationship to significant occasions in the life of Jesus and of the people of God. The Church thus has come to observe the following days and seasons:

    a.   Advent, a season to recollect the hope of the coming of Christ, and to look forward to the Lord's coming again;

    b.   Christmas, a celebration of the birth of Christ;

    c.   Epiphany, a day for commemorating God's self-manifestation to all people;

    d.   Lent, a season of spiritual discipline and preparation, beginning with Ash Wednesday, anticipating the celebration of the death and resurrection of Christ;

    e.   Holy Week, a time of remembrance and proclamation of the atoning suffering and death of Jesus Christ;

    f.   Easter, the day of the Lord's resurrection and the season of rejoicing which commemorates his ministry until his Ascension, and continues through

    g.   the Day of Pentecost, the celebration of the gift of the Holy Spirit to the Church.

The church also observes other days such as Baptism of the Lord, Transfiguration of the Lord, Trinity Sunday, All Saints Day, and Christ the King.

W-3.2002:   2 Helv.Conf. 5.226

W-3.2003
Other Seasons

Human life in community reflects a variety of rhythms which also affect Christian worship. Among these are the annual cycles of civic, agricultural, school, and business life; special times of family remembrance and celebration; and the patterns of a variety of cultural expressions, commemorations, and events. The church in carrying out its mission also creates a cycle of activities, programs, and observances. While such events may be appropriately recognized in Christian worship, care shall be taken to ensure that they do not obscure the proclamation of the gospel on the Lord's Day.

W-3.3000   **3.   Service for the Lord's Day**

W-3.3100   **a.   Appropriate Actions**

W-3.3101
What Is Included:

In the Service for the Lord's Day:

Scripture

(1) The Scriptures shall be read and proclaimed (W-2.2001). Lessons should be read from both Testaments. (W-2.2002) Scripture shall be interpreted in a sermon or other form of exposition. (W-2.2007–.2008)

Prayer

(2) Prayer shall be offered. (W-2.1001) Prayers may be offered on behalf of the congregation, whose participation may be affirmed by their corporate response, "Amen." Prayer forms may encourage the participation of the worshipers through unison and responsive, bidding and spontaneous prayers. Times of silence may be provided for prayer and meditation. (W-2.1000)

Music

(3) Music may serve as presentation and interpretation of Scripture, as response to the gospel, and as prayer, through psalms and canticles, hymns and anthems, spirituals and spiritual songs. (W-2.1003–.1004; W-2.2008)

Baptism

(4) The Sacrament of Baptism shall be administered as people present children or themselves for incorporation into the church. (W-2.3000)

Lord's Supper

(5) The Sacrament of the Lord's Supper shall be celebrated regularly and frequently as determined by the session. (W-2.4000)

Tithes and
Offerings

(6) The tithes and offerings of the people shall be gathered and received. (W-2.5000)

Special Times

(7) Times for gathering, greeting, and calling to worship; for sharing common concerns; and for blessing and sending forth should be provided at points in the service suitable to the life of the particular church. (W-2.6000)

Special Services   (8) Services of receiving new members; of ordaining, installing, and commissioning; of making and renewing covenants; and of recognizing and sharing life's transitions should be provided as called for in the life of the congregation. (W-2.5000–.6000; W-4.0000)

W-3.3200   **b. Ordering the Actions**

W-3.3201   In setting an order for worship on the Lord's Day, the pastor
Setting an Order   with the concurrence of the session shall provide opportunity for
for Worship   the people from youngest to oldest to participate in a worthy offering of praise to God and for them to hear and to respond to God's Word. (W-1.4004–.4007; W-3.1004)

W-3.3202   The order offered here is a logical progression, is rooted in
A Suggested   the Old and New Testaments, and reflects the tradition of the uni-
Order   versal Church and our Reformed heritage. Other orders of worship may also serve the needs of a particular church and be orderly, faithful to Scripture, and true to historic principles. The order that follows is presented in terms of five major actions centered in the Word of God:

  (1) gathering around the Word;

  (2) proclaiming the Word;

  (3) responding to the Word;

  (4) the sealing of the Word;

  (5) bearing and following the Word into the world.

W-3.3300   **(1) Gathering Around the Word**

W-3.3301   (a) Worship begins as the people gather. One or
Gathering   more of the following actions are appropriate: People may greet one another; people may prepare in silent prayer or meditation; announcements of concern to the congregation may be made; or music may be offered.

  (b) The people are called to worship God. Words of Scripture are spoken or sung to proclaim who God is and what God has done.

  (c) A prayer or hymn of adoration and praise is offered.

  (d) A prayer of confession of the reality of sin in personal and common life follows. In a declaration of pardon, the gospel is proclaimed and forgiveness is declared in the name of Jesus Christ. God's redemption and God's claim upon human life are remembered.

(e) The people give glory to God, and they may at this point share signs of reconciliation and the peace of Christ.

W-3.3400

W-3.3401
Proclaiming

(2) Proclaiming the Word

(a) In preparation for the reading, proclaiming, and hearing of God's Word, a prayer seeking the illumination of the Holy Spirit is appropriately offered.

(b) Scripture lessons suitable for the day are read by a teaching elder†, by a member of the congregation, or by the people responsively, antiphonally, or in unison. (W-2.2006)

(c) Psalms or anthems, and other musical forms or artistic expression which proclaim or interpret the Scripture lessons or their themes, may be included with the reading lessons.

(d) The Word shall be interpreted in a sermon preached by the teaching elder† or in other forms authorized by the session and by the pastor. (W-1.4004–.4006; W-2.2007–.2008) This proclamation concludes with a prayer, acclamation, or ascription of praise. It is appropriate also to call the people to discipleship. (W-2.2007; W-2.2009)

W-3.3500

W-3.3501
Responding:
Affirmation

(3) Responding to the Word

The response to the proclamation of the Word is expressed in an affirmation of faith and commitment. A common affirmation may be offered by the congregation through singing a hymn or other appropriate musical response, or through saying or singing a creed of the church. The choir may lead the congregation with an anthem or other musical form of affirmation. An opportunity for personal response may also be provided during this time.

W-3.3502
Affirming and
Reaffirming
Commitments

Response to the Word also involves acts of commitment and recognition. The Sacrament of Baptism may be observed. (W-3.3601–.3607) Baptized believers may be received as members of the particular church as they make public their profession of faith for the first time, or as they reaffirm that faith or transfer their church membership. (For the services of reception and commissioning see W-4.2000; W-4.3000; cf. G-1.03; G-3.0201c.) It is also appropriate to offer opportunities for individuals or the gathered congregation to engage in reaffirming the commitments made at Baptism. (W-4.2005)

W-3.3503
Other Acts of
Commitment

Other acts of commitment which may appropriately be included as response to the Word are

(a) Christian marriage (W-4.9000),

(b) ordination and installation to ordered ministry (W-4.4000),

(c) commissioning for service in and to the church in such roles as Christian educator, church school teacher, organizational officer, or group adviser (W-4.3000; cf. W-3.3701).

W-3.3504
Acts of
Recognition

It is appropriate as a response to the Word to recognize and give thanks for life and life's transitions,

(a) commemorating significant events in the lives of individuals and in the life of the community,

(b) celebrating reunions and bidding farewell,

(c) noting and remembering the lives of those who have died. (Cf. W-4.5000; W-4.7000; W-4.8000)

W-3.3505
Mission Concerns

Witness to faith and service and interpretation of the mission and programs of the church may be included in the service as a response to the Word. They should be presented in such a way as to reflect this response and may prepare for the people's prayers of intercession and supplication, as well as for their self-offering and gifts in support of the ministry of Christ and the church.

W-3.3506
Prayers

As the people respond to the Word, prayers of intercession are offered for

(a) the Church universal, its ministry and those who minister, that the world might believe;

(b) the world, those in distress or special need, and all in authority, that peace and justice might prevail;

(c) the nation, the state, local communities, and those who govern in them, that they may know and have strength to do what is right.

Prayers of supplication are offered for

(d) the local church, that it have the mind of Christ in facing special issues and needs;

(e) those who struggle with their faith, that they be given assurance;

(f) those in the midst of transitions in life, that they be guided and supported;

(g) those who face critical decisions, that they receive wisdom;

(h) those who are sick, grieving, lonely, and anxious, that they be comforted and healed;

(i) all members, that grace conform them to God's purpose. (W-2.1000)

Prayers of confession may be included at this time. (W-3.3301) When the service does not include the Lord's Supper, prayers of thanksgiving are offered and the prayers are concluded with the Lord's Prayer. (W-3.3613)

W-3.3507
Offerings

The tithes and offerings of God's people are gathered and received with prayer, spoken or sung. (W-2.5003) Signs of reconciliation and peace may be exchanged, if this was not done as a response to the Word of assurance of God's pardon. (W-3.3301) When the Lord's Supper is to be celebrated, gifts of bread and wine may be brought to the Table in thanksgiving for God's Word. (W-2.4003; W-3.3609)

W-3.3600

(4) The Sealing of the Word: Sacraments

W-3.3601
Sacraments
as Seals

The Sacraments of Baptism and the Lord's Supper are God's acts of sealing the promises of faith within the community of faith as the congregation worships, and include the responses of the faithful to the Word proclaimed and enacted in the Sacraments.

W-3.3602
Baptism

The Sacrament of Baptism (W-2.3000), the sign and seal of God's grace and our response, is the foundational recognition of Christian commitment. It is appropriately celebrated following the reading and the proclaiming of the Word, and shall include statements concerning the biblical meaning of Baptism, the responsibility to be assumed by those desiring Baptism for themselves or their children, and the nurture to be undertaken by the church.

W-3.3603
Commitments
and Vows

Those desiring the Sacrament of Baptism for their children or for themselves shall make vows that

(a) profess their faith in Jesus Christ as Lord and Savior,

(b) renounce evil and affirm their reliance on God's grace,

(c) declare their intention to participate actively and responsibly in the worship and mission of the church,

(d) declare their intention to provide for the Christian nurture of their child.

The congregation shall

(e) profess its faith, using the Apostles' Creed,

(f) voice its support of those baptized,

(g) express its willingness to take responsibility for the nurture of those baptized.

A ruling elder may lead the congregation in these professions and affirmations. (W-2.2009; W-2.3011–.3014)

W-3.3604
The Prayer

The teaching elder† offers a baptismal prayer. This prayer

    (a) expresses thanksgiving for God's covenant faithfulness,

    (b) gives praise for God's reconciling acts,

    (c) asks that the Holy Spirit attend and empower the Baptism, make the water a water of redemption and rebirth, equip the church for faithfulness.

W-3.3605
The Water

The water used for Baptism should be common to the location, and shall be applied to the person by pouring, sprinkling, or immersion. By whatever mode, the water should be applied visibly and generously.

W-3.3606
The Words
of Baptism

The teaching elder† shall use the name given the person to be baptized and shall baptize in the name of the triune God. The baptismal formula is: "_____, I baptize you in the name of the Father, and of the Son, and of the Holy Spirit."

W-3.3607
Other Actions

Care shall be taken that the central act of baptizing with water is not overshadowed. Other actions that are rooted deeply in the history of Baptism such as the laying on of hands in blessing, the praying for the anointing of the Holy Spirit, anointing with oil, and the presentation of the newly baptized to the congregation may also be included. When such actions are introduced, they should be explained carefully in order to avoid misinterpretation and misunderstanding.

W-3.3608
Welcoming

Declaration shall be made of the newly baptized person's membership in the Church of Jesus Christ. The welcome of the congregation is extended. Whenever the service is so ordered, the Lord's Supper may follow Baptism at the appropriate time in the service.

W-3.3609
Lord's Supper:
Preparing

The congregation should prepare themselves to celebrate the Sacrament of the Lord's Supper. (W-2.4006; W-2.4011; W-5.2001) If the Lord's Supper is celebrated less frequently than on each Lord's Day, public notice is to be given at least one week in advance. When the Lord's Supper is celebrated, the Table should be prepared and the elements provided to be placed on the Table before worship begins or during the gathering of the tithes and offerings.

W-3.3610 Bread	Bread common to the culture of the community should be provided to be broken by the one who presides. The use of the one bread expresses the unity of the body of Christ. Bread for the congregation may be broken from the same loaf or prepared in some manner suitable for distribution.
W-3.3611 Cup	A cup and pitcher may be provided for the one who presides to use in presenting the cup. The use of a common cup expresses the communal nature of the Sacrament and reflects the consistent New Testament reference to a single cup. Pouring into the cup signifies the shed blood of Christ poured out for the world. The manner of distribution used by the particular community of faith may involve the provision of one cup or a number of cups suitably prepared for the people. The session is to determine what form of the fruit of the vine is to be used. In making this decision the session should be informed by the biblical precedent, the history of the church, ecumenical usage, local custom, and concerns for health and the conscience of members of the congregation. Whenever wine is used in the Lord's Supper, unfermented grape juice should always be clearly identified and served also as an alternative for those who prefer it.
W-3.3612 Invitation	The teaching elder or one presiding shall invite the people to the Lord's Table using suitable words from Scripture. (W-2.4011) If the words of institution (1 Cor. 11:23–26, or Gospel parallels) will not be spoken at the breaking of bread or included in the prayer of thanksgiving, they are to be said as part of the invitation.
W-3.3613 The Prayer	The one presiding is to lead the people in the prayer,

(a) thanking God for creation and providence, for covenant history, and for seasonal blessings, with an

acclamation of praise;

(b) remembering God's acts of salvation in Jesus Christ: his birth, life, death, resurrection, and promise of coming, and institution of the Supper (if not otherwise spoken), together with an

acclamation of faith;

(c) calling upon the Holy Spirit to draw the people into the presence of the risen Christ so that they

---

W-3.3610:   1 Cor. 10:16–17
W-3.3611:   Mark 14:23 ff. and parallels; 1 Cor. 10:16, 21; 11:25–28; Rom. 14:1–23; 1 Cor. 8:1–13; 10:14–33; 11:17–32

(1') may be fed,

(2') may be joined in the communion of saints to all God's people and to the risen Christ, and

(3') may be sent to serve as faithful disciples; followed by an

ascription of praise to the triune God, and

(d) the Lord's Prayer.

W-3.3614
Breaking Bread

The one presiding is to take the bread and break it in the view of the people. If the words of institution have not previously been spoken as part of the invitation or in the communion prayer, 1 Cor. 11:23, 24 shall be used at this time.

W-3.3615
Presenting
the Cup

Having filled the cup, the one presiding is to present it in the view of the people. If the words of institution have not previously been spoken as part of the invitation or in the communion prayer, 1 Cor. 11:25, 26 shall be used at this time.

W-3.3616
Distributing
Bread and Cup

The elements are distributed in the manner most suitable to the particular occasion.

The Gathering

a. The people may gather about the Table to receive the bread and the cup; they may come to those serving to receive the elements; or those serving may distribute the elements to them where they are.

The Bread

b. The bread may be broken from that on the Table and placed in the people's hands; people may break off a portion from the broken loaf or other bread offered for distribution; or they may receive pieces of bread prepared for distribution.

The Cup

c. A common cup may be offered to all who wish to partake of it; several cups may be offered and shared; or individual cups may be prepared for distribution. Rather than drink from a common cup, communicants may dip the broken bread into the cup.

The Serving

d. The bread and the cup may be served by those in the ordered ministry of the church, or by other church members on invitation of the session or authorizing council.

e. The serving of the elements may be extended by two or more persons in the ordered ministry of the church, to those isolated from the community's worship, provided

(1) the elements are to be served following worship on the same calendar day, or as soon thereafter as practically feasible, as a direct extension of the serving of the gathered congregation, to church members who have accepted the church's invitation to receive the Sacraments;

(2) care is taken in the serving to ensure that the unity of Word and Sacrament is maintained, by the reading of Scripture and the offering of prayers; and

(3) those serving have been instructed by the session or authorized council in the theological and pastoral foundations of this ministry and in the liturgical resources for it (W-6.3011).

W-3.3617
Receiving the
Supper

While the bread and the cup are being shared,

(a) the people may sing psalms, hymns, spirituals, or other appropriate songs;

(b) the choir may sing anthems or other appropriate musical offerings;

(c) instrumental music suitable to the occasion may be played;

(d) appropriate passages of Scripture may be read; or

(e) people may pray in silence.

W-3.3618
Blessing After
Supper

When all have communed and the remaining elements have been placed on the Table, the one presiding leads the people in prayer, thanking God for the gift of Christ in the Sacrament, asking for God's grace to fulfill the pledges made by the people in the Supper, and making supplication for the coming of the promised Kingdom. The congregation sings a psalm, canticle, hymn, spiritual, or spiritual song.

W-3.3619
Disposition of
the Elements

When the service is ended, the communion elements shall be removed from the Table and used or disposed of in a manner which is approved by the session, and which is consistent with the Reformed understanding of the Sacrament and the principles of good stewardship.

W-3.3700

(5) Bearing and Following the Word Into the World

W-3.3701
Acts of
Commitment and
Recognition

(a) Acts of commitment to discipleship, declaration of intent to seek Baptism, and reaffirmation of the vows taken at Baptism are appropriate responses to the Word received in Sacrament. (W-2.4005; W-2.4007) As the service comes to a close, other acts of commitment and recognition may be observed. People may make commitments to and be commissioned for specific corporate and personal acts of evangelism, compassion, justice, reconciliation, and peacemaking in the world. (W-4.3000)

When One Leaves   (b) Those leaving the fellowship of a particular church

(1') to undertake these commissions; or

(2') to move to another place for purposes of education, national service, career change, family circumstance, or health

may be recognized with a farewell. This also may be an appropriate time to remember those of the congregation who have died.

W-3.3702
Going in the
Name of the
Triune God

The service concludes with a formal dismissal. This may include a charge to the people to go into the world in the name of Christ. It shall include words of blessing, using a trinitarian benediction or other words from Scripture, such as the apostolic benediction in 2 Cor. 13:13. Signs of reconciliation and peace may be exchanged as the people depart.

W-3.4000   **4. Service of Daily Prayer**

W-3.4001
Daily Prayer

a.   The Service of Daily Prayer is a service of public worship observed regularly throughout the week. (W-1.3012; W-3.2001) This service may be offered in the morning, at midday, at the end of the day, in the evening, or at night, in keeping with the needs of the church and the community in which it ministers.

Word and Prayer

b.   The service shall include the reading and hearing of the Word and prayer.

W-3.4002
Scripture

Scripture lessons are read, and time observed for reflection and meditation. An exposition of Scripture may be given. The Word may be expressed in music, drama, or dance. Psalms and canticles are especially appropriate to daily prayer because in using them worshipers both express and respond to the Word. (W-2.2000)

W-3.4003
Prayer

Prayers may be spoken, sung, enacted, and offered in silence. Daily prayer affords a unique opportunity for silence and meditation in community. Prayer in all its dimensions should be offered with special attention to the public and personal concerns of the community. (W-2.1000)

W-3.4004
Order

The Service of Daily Prayer should be ordered to move through

(1) praise,

(2) the reading and hearing of the Word,

(3) responding to the Word in meditation, prayer, and song,

(4) going forth in the name of Christ.

W-3.4005
Leadership

The service, authorized by the session, should be planned in consultation with the pastor, and may be led by appropriately prepared teaching elders, ruling elders, deacons, or other members of the church.

W-3.5000
5. Other Regularly Scheduled Services of Worship

W-3.5100
a. Sunday Services

W-3.5101
Other Sunday
Services

The primary service of worship on Sunday is the Service for the Lord's Day, scheduled at the time(s) when most members can participate. Other services may be regularly scheduled on Sunday, at times in the morning, afternoon, or evening. The time and nature of these services is to be determined by the session as it considers the needs of the congregation and the community. In planning these services, care should be taken to preserve the integrity of the Service for the Lord's Day.

W-3.5102
Elements

These services include the reading and hearing of the Word, prayer, and opportunities for self-offering and for relating to each other and the world. (W-2.1000–.2000; W-2.5000–.6000) They may place special emphasis upon prayer, congregational singing, the teaching of Scripture, and interpretation of the Word through the arts. Such services may include the preaching of the Word, or other forms of proclamation authorized by the pastor and the session. (W-1.4000; W-2.2000; W-3.3400) On those occasions the Sacraments may also be celebrated.

W-3.5103
Order

The order of each service should reflect the principles of worship in this directory as they relate to the particular occasion.

W-3.5200
b. Church School

W-3.5201
Church School

When several classes of the church school assemble together for worship, there should be opportunity for prayer, singing, and reading and hearing the Word. There may be occasions when an offering of gifts is an appropriate expression of self-offering and of relating to the world.

W-3.5202
Elements
and Order

There should be regular opportunities for worship in each church school class. Such worship may be less formal and more spontaneous than in larger groups. Yet it should include prayer and song that grow out of the consideration of the Word. It may include acts and tokens of self-offering and commitment, which may lead

(1) to requesting Baptism,

(2) to participating in the Lord's Supper,

(3) to affirming the vows taken at Baptism.

Worship in the church school is not to be a substitute for participation in the worship of the whole congregation on the Lord's Day. (W-3.1004; W-3.3201; W-6.2001)

W-3.5300

W-3.5301
Prayer Meetings

c. Gatherings for Prayer

In the life of a congregation people may gather for prayer in a number of settings. The session is responsible for the authorization of such gatherings. Regularly scheduled prayer meetings which are open to all may take several forms, including the midweek evening service, a morning, midday, or afternoon gathering, and prayer breakfasts and luncheons. Smaller groups may meet regularly as prayer circles, intercessory fellowships, or covenant groups. Special days and occasions in the life of the local community, the nation, and the ecumenical Church may draw people together for services of prayer.

W-3.5302
Elements

In these services the Word is read and heard, and may be proclaimed, taught, and discussed, or expressed in music and the other arts. Prayer is offered, and may be spoken, sung, enacted, or shared in silence. Opportunities may be given for the recognition and offering of gifts and for the commitment of life to Jesus Christ. Concern for one another may be shown in words and acts of welcome, reconciliation, and mutual ministry. Concern for the world may be enacted in prayer and ministries of compassion, justice, peacemaking, and witness.

W-3.5400

W-3.5401
Healing Services

d. Services for Wholeness

Healing was an integral part of the ministry of Jesus which the church has been called to continue as one dimension of its concern for the wholeness of people. Through services for wholeness, the church enacts in worship its ministry as a healing community.

W-3.5402
Authorization

Services for wholeness are to be authorized by the session, and shall be under the direction of the pastor. Such services may be observed as regularly scheduled services of worship, as occasional services, or as part of the Service for the Lord's Day. (W-3.3506) These services should be open to all and not restricted to those desiring healing for themselves or for others of special concern to them. The services should be held in a place readily accessible to those who may be seeking healing.

W-3.5403 Forms of Prayer	The vital element of worship in the service for wholeness is prayer since this is essentially a time of waiting in faith upon God. Thanksgiving for God's promise of wholeness, intercessions, and supplications should be offered. Adequate time for silent prayer should be provided, as well as occasions for prayers spoken and sung. Enacted prayer in the form of the laying on of hands and anointing with oil is appropriate (James 5:14). The enactment of prayers involves the presiding teaching elder† together with representatives of the believing community.
W-3.5404 Word and Sacrament	These prayers are a response to the Word read and proclaimed. Particular focus should be on announcing the gospel's promise of wholeness through Christ. The sealing of this promise in the Lord's Supper may be celebrated, and should follow the prayers and the laying on of hands. Occasion for offering one's life and gifts for ministry may be provided, as well as opportunities for reconciliation and renewed commitment to the service of Jesus Christ in the world.
W-3.5405 Source of Healing	When a service for wholeness includes anointing and the laying on of hands, these enacted prayers should be introduced carefully in order to avoid misinterpretation and misunderstanding. Healing is to be understood not as the result of the holiness, earnestness, or skill of those enacting the prayers, or of the faith of the ones seeking healing, but as the gift of God through the power of the Holy Spirit.
W-3.5500	**e. Services for Evangelism**
W-3.5501 Invitations to Discipleship	The invitation to respond to Jesus Christ should be offered frequently and regularly in the Service for the Lord's Day. (W-2.5002) It is appropriate for the session to authorize services for the particular purpose of evangelism, and to set such services at regular seasons. (W-3.2003; W-7.2000)
W-3.5502 Order	The central element of worship in services for evangelism is the proclamation of the Word, with a special emphasis on the redeeming grace of God in Christ, the claim Jesus Christ makes on human life, and his invitation to a life of discipleship empowered by the Holy Spirit. This proclamation involves

> (1) the reading and hearing of Scripture,
>
> (2) preaching and witness,
>
> (3) the Word sung, enacted, and confessed.

W-3.5500:   West.Conf. 6.055–6.058, 6.187–6.190

Surrounding this central act should be prayer,

(4) in preparation for the services;

(5) in the service itself

as praise, thanksgiving, confession, intercession, and supplication;

(6) following the service

that the new disciples be supported in their commitment and vitally included in the life of the church.

W-3.5503
Commitment

The service shall move to a clear invitation to commitment or renewed commitment to Jesus Christ as Lord and Savior and to life in the covenant community which is Christ's body, the Church. Such commitment is a sign of grace and an act of self-offering which should issue in

(1) new relationship to one another,

(2) new awareness of one's gifts for ministry,

(3) new involvement in the redemptive activity of Christ in the world.

W-3.5504
Responses
to New
Commitment

Those who respond to the invitation shall be offered nurture and instruction to support them in their commitment and to equip them for the life of discipleship. (G-1.0304) Those who are making their first commitment shall make public the profession of their faith during a Service for the Lord's Day, with those who have not been baptized receiving Baptism in that service. Those who are renewing a commitment shall be given opportunity for public acknowledgment of their reaffirmation during a Service for the Lord's Day. (W-3.3502; W-4.2000)

W-3.5600

f.   Program and Mission Interpretation

W-3.5601
Services for
Mission
Emphasis

Interpretation of the program and mission of the church may occur in services of worship held for this purpose and regularly scheduled at appropriate seasons of the year. (W-3.2003) In these services, a primary focus is on the interpretation of the program or mission which has led the session to authorize the special service(s). Therefore a central emphasis of such worship is relating to the world and to each other. (W-2.6000)

W-3.5602
Elements

The Word should be read and heard. Prayers of thanksgiving, supplication, and intercession should be offered on behalf of the ministries interpreted in the service. Opportunities for offering of material gifts and for commitment of life may be appropriately included.

W-3.5700

g.   Special Groups in the Local Congregation

W-3.5701
Special Groups

In every local congregation there are special groups, con-stituted by age, gender, or interest, which meet regularly. Worship should ordinarily occur in meetings of these groups and should reflect the principles of this directory. All of the elements of worship in Chapter Two are appropriate in these settings except celebration of the Sacraments, which are acts of worship authorized by the session, ordinarily for the partic-ipation of the entire congregation.

W-3.6000

6.   Special Gatherings

W-3.6100

a.   Councils

W-3.6101
Worship in
Councils

Councils shall worship regularly and shall order that worship in accordance with the principles of this directory. Each council should establish a group charged with responsibility for and over-sight of its worship. It may also adopt guidelines for the planning and conduct of worship at its meetings.

W-3.6102
Word and
Sacrament

In councils above the session, provision is to be made for the regular reading, proclaiming, and hearing of the Word, and for the regular and frequent celebration of the Lord's Supper. (G-3.0105)

W-3.6103
Prayer

Every meeting of a council shall open and close with prayer (G-3.0105) and should provide for adequate occasions of prayer during the course of its deliberations. The prayers should express praise and thanksgiving, confession, intercession, and supplica-tion in relation to proceedings of the council.

W-3.6200

b.   Retreats, Camps, Conferences, and Special Gatherings

W-3.6201
Worship in
Conferences
and Retreats

Councils have the responsibility for authorizing worship in special gatherings under their jurisdiction. Worship is an integral part of the life of retreats, camps, and conferences. That worship shall be guided by the principles of this directory and the guide-lines established by the appropriate council.

W-3.6202
Order

The nature and focus of worship will vary with the type of gathering, its purpose, its participants, its location, the season, and the rhythm and order of its life. Worship may use the order of Daily Prayer (W-3.4000), be guided by the Service for the Lord's Day (W-3.3000), or adapt the form of other services described in this directory. (W-3.5000)

W-3.6203
Elements

The elements of worship appropriate for every gathering are prayer, the reading and hearing of Scripture, self-offering, and relating to each other and the world. (W-2.1000; W-2.2000; W-2.5000; W-2.6000) Different elements of worship may be emphasized in different settings, such as

    (1) retreats for silent prayer or marriage enrichment,

    (2) nature camps or mission caravans,

    (3) youth leadership or music conferences.

Yet in every case, the Word shall be presented with integrity, and appropriate prayers should be offered. (W-2.1000–.2000)

W-3.6204
Lord's Supper
at Special
Gatherings

The Sacrament of the Lord's Supper is appropriate for any special gathering

    (1) when it is authorized by the council responsible for the gathering or by the presbytery within whose bounds the event will take place,

    (2) when a teaching elder presides and other ruling elders or deacons of the church are present,

    (3) when it is observed in a service of worship following the preaching of the Word or other form of proclamation authorized by the council,

    (4) when it is understood as participation in the life of the whole believing community rather than as a devotional exercise for a few. (W-2.4010–.4012)

The church bears strong witness to the unity of the body of Christ when Christians gather from a number of different churches or diverse ethnic or cultural groups, or in ecumenical assemblies for the celebration of the Lord's Supper. (W-2.4006)

W-3.6205
Ecumenical
Eucharist

Teaching elders invited to celebrate or participate in the celebration of the Lord's Supper in ecumenical settings have the authority to do so to the extent that the participation does not contradict the Reformed understanding of the Lord's Supper.

CHAPTER IV

W-4.0000

ORDERING WORSHIP FOR SPECIAL PURPOSES

W-4.1000

1. Special Occasions and Recognitions

W-4.1001
Services for
Special Occasions
and Purposes

There are special occasions and transitions in the life of the congregation and the lives of its members which are appropriately recognized in worship. Many of these are ordinarily celebrated at particular points in the Service for the Lord's Day. Others may be celebrated in the Service for the Lord's Day or in other regularly scheduled services or in a service especially appointed for the occasion. No special recognitions should be included in the Service for the Lord's Day when they would diminish the importance of hearing the Word and celebrating the Sacraments in joyful expectation of encountering the risen Lord. (W-1.3011)

W-4.2000

2. Services of Welcome and Reception

W-4.2001
Baptism and
Membership

In Baptism a person is sealed by the Holy Spirit, given identity as a member of the church, welcomed to the Lord's Table, and set apart for a life of Christian service. (W-3.3602–.3608; W-3.5504) These aspects of Baptism are given further expression in worship through welcoming the baptized to the Lord's Table, confirming and commissioning, and receiving new members. (W-6.2001) These occasions are ordinarily observed in the Service for the Lord's Day in responding to the Word. (W-3.3502)

W-4.2002
Welcoming to the
Lord's Table

It is the responsibility of the whole congregation, particularly exercised through the session, to nurture those who are baptized to respond to the invitation to the Lord's Supper. When a person is baptized as a child, the session shall equip and support the parent(s) or those exercising parental responsibility for their task of nurturing the child for receiving the Lord's Supper. (W-2.3012) When the child begins to express a desire to receive this Sacrament, the session should take note of this and provide an occasion for recognition and welcome.

W-4.2003
Confirming and
Commissioning

The church nurtures those baptized as children and calls them to make public their personal profession of faith and their acceptance of responsibility in the life of the church. When these persons are ready, they shall be examined by the session. (G-3.0201c) After the session has received them as active members they shall be presented to the congregation during a service of public worship. In that service the church shall confirm them in their baptismal identity. They shall reaffirm the vows taken at Baptism by

a.   professing their faith in Jesus Christ as Lord and Savior,

b.   renouncing evil and affirming their reliance on God's grace,

c.   declaring their intention to participate actively and responsibly in the worship and mission of the church. (W-3.3603)

They are commissioned for full participation in the mission and governance of the church, and are welcomed by the congregation. (W-3.3502; W-3.3602–.3608; W-3.3701)

W-4.2004
Reception of
Other Members

The service for the reception of members into a congregation by transfer of certificate or by reaffirmation of faith is an occasion to recall one's earlier Baptism, profession of faith, and commitment to discipleship. After examination and reception by the session, these new members shall be recognized at a regularly scheduled service of public worship. (W-3.3502) It is appropriate for them to reaffirm the commitments made at Baptism, to make public again their profession of faith in Jesus Christ as Lord and Savior, and to express their intention to participate actively in the worship and mission of the church. (W-3.3602) They are welcomed into the life of the congregation and are commissioned for service as members.

W-4.2005
Reaffirmation
by All

On each occasion when people entering membership in a particular church make public their profession of faith, it is appropriate for all baptized worshipers formally to reaffirm the commitments made at Baptism.

W-4.2006
Renewal
and Fresh
Commitment

In the life of a believer there are times of special awakening, renewal, and fresh commitment which call for public expression, recognition, and celebration. People should be encouraged to share with the teaching elder(s) and with the session these decisive moments and stirrings of the Holy Spirit. It may often be appropriate for people to make public this sense of deepened commitment in a service of worship, and for the church to acknowledge it with prayer and thanksgiving. (W-3.3502; W-3.3701)

W-4.2007
Enacting
Welcome and
Recognition

In all these services the welcoming, recognizing, commissioning, and acknowledging should be expressed in actions as well as in words. Appropriate actions may include

a.   sharing the peace of Christ,
b.   offering hands in welcome,
c.   anointing,
d.   embracing,

and other acts of recognition and celebration common to the culture(s) of the participants.

W-4.3000

W-4.3001
Recognizing
Discipleship

3. Commissioning for Specific Acts of Discipleship

In the life of the Christian community God calls people to particular acts of discipleship to use their personal gifts for service in the Church and in the world. These specific acts may be strengthened and confirmed by formal recognition in worship.

W-4.3002
Forms of
Discipleship

Discipleship may be expressed

a. in the local church through service such as teacher in the church school, trustee, member of the choir, officer in a church organization, or adviser or helper with various church groups;

b. on behalf of the local church through its ministry in and to the community;

c. in the larger church as people serve in the ministries of presbytery, synod, and the General Assembly, and of ecumenical agencies and councils;

d. beyond the church cooperating with all who work for compassion and reconciliation. (W-7.3000–.4000)

W-4.3003
Recognition and
Commissioning

Recognition and commissioning of people called to such acts of discipleship may occur in the Service for the Lord's Day as a response to the proclamation of the Word (W-3.3500) or as a bearing and following of the Word into the world. (W-3.3700) Recognizing and commissioning for specific acts of discipleship may also occur in services of worship provided for this purpose or in other appropriate services. (W-3.5100; W-3.5300; W-3.5600)

W-4.4000

W-4.4001
Ordination and
Installation

4. Ordination, Installation, and Commissioning

a. In ordination the church sets apart with prayer and the laying on of hands those who have been called through election by the church to serve as deacons, ruling elders, and teaching elders. (W-2.1005) In installation the church sets apart with prayer those previously ordained as deacons, ruling elders, and teaching elders, and called anew to service in that ministry.

Service of
Ordination,
Installation, and
Commissioning

b. The service of ordination and installation for ruling elders, deacons, or teaching elders, and for the commissioning of ruling elders to pastoral service, certified Christian educators, and other certified persons, shall focus upon Christ and the joy and responsibility of serving him through the mission and ministry of the church, and shall include a sermon appropriate to the occasion. The teaching elder† presiding shall state briefly the nature of the ministry.

W-4.4002
Setting of
the Service

The service of ordination and installation, or commissioning, may take place during the Service for the Lord's Day as a response to the proclamation of the Word. (W-3.3503). Ordination and installation, or commissioning, may also take place in a special service that focuses upon Jesus Christ and the mission and ministry of the church and which includes the proclamation of the Word. The service of **ordination or** installation of a **teaching elder** shall be conducted at a convenient time to enable the substantial participation of the presbytery.

W-4.4003
Constitutional
Questions for
Ordination,
Installation, and
Commissioning

The moderator of the council of those to be ordained, installed, or commissioned shall ask them to stand before the body of membership and to answer the following questions:

a. Do you trust in Jesus Christ your Savior, acknowledge him Lord of all and Head of the Church, and through him believe in one God, Father, Son, and Holy Spirit?

b. Do you accept the Scriptures of the Old and New Testaments to be, by the Holy Spirit, the unique and authoritative witness to Jesus Christ in the Church universal, and God's Word to you?[a]

c. Do you sincerely receive and adopt the essential tenets of the Reformed faith as expressed in the confessions of our church as authentic and reliable expositions of what Scripture leads us to believe and do, and will you be instructed and led by those confessions as you lead the people of God?[b]

d. Will you fulfill your ministry in obedience to Jesus Christ, under the authority of Scripture, and be continually guided by our confessions?

e. Will you be governed by our church's polity, and will you abide by its discipline? Will you be a friend among your colleagues in ministry, working with them, subject to the ordering of God's Word and Spirit?[c]

f. Will you in your own life seek to follow the Lord Jesus Christ, love your neighbors, and work for the reconciliation of the world?

g. Do you promise to further the peace, unity, and purity of the church?

h.   Will you pray for and seek to serve the people with energy, intelligence, imagination, and love?

i.   (1) (For ruling elder) Will you be a faithful ruling elder, watching over the people, providing for their worship, nurture, and service? Will you share in government and discipline, serving in councils of the church, and in your ministry will you try to show the love and justice of Jesus Christ?

(2) (For deacon) Will you be a faithful deacon, teaching charity, urging concern, and directing the people's help to the friendless and those in need, and in your ministry will you try to show the love and justice of Jesus Christ?

(3) (For teaching elder) Will you be a faithful teaching elder, proclaiming the good news in Word and Sacrament, teaching faith and caring for people? Will you be active in government and discipline, serving in the councils of the church; and in your ministry will you try to show the love and justice of Jesus Christ?

(4) (For ruling elder commissioned to particular pastoral service) Will you be a faithful ruling elder in this commission, serving the people by proclaiming the good news, teaching faith and caring for the people, and in your ministry will you try to show the love and justice of Jesus Christ?

(5) (For certified Christian educator) Will you be a faithful certified Christian educator, teaching faith and caring for people, and will you in your ministry try to show the love and justice of Jesus Christ?

W-4.4004
Ordination or
Installation of
Ruling Elders or
Deacons

At the service of ordination or installation of ruling elders and deacons:

Questions to
Congregation

a.   The ruling elders- and deacons-elect having answered in the affirmative, a ruling elder shall stand with them before the congregation and shall ask the congregation to answer the following questions:

(1) Do we, the members of the church, accept (names) _____ as ruling elders or deacons, chosen by God through the voice of this congregation to lead us in the way of Jesus Christ?[d]

(2) Do we agree to pray for them, to encourage them, to respect their decisions, and to follow as they guide us, serving Jesus Christ, who alone is Head of the Church?

Prayer and Laying on of Hands	b. The members of the church having answered these questions in the affirmative, those to be ordained shall kneel, if able, for prayer and the laying on of hands by the session. Those previously ordained ordinarily shall stand, along with the congregation, if able, for the prayer of installation. The session may invite other ruling elders and teaching elders to participate in the laying on of hands.
Statement	c. The moderator shall say to those who have thus been ordained and installed:

You are now ruling elders and deacons in the Church of Jesus Christ and for this congregation. Whatever you do, in word or deed, do everything in the name of the Lord Jesus, giving thanks to God the Father through him. Amen.

Session Welcomes	d. Then the members of the session, and others as may be appropriate, shall welcome the newly ordained and installed, or newly installed, ruling elders and deacons into their fellowship in ministry.
Congregation Greets	e. After the service, it is appropriate for the members of the congregation to greet their new ruling elders and deacons, showing affection and support.
W-4.4005 Ordination of Teaching Elder	At the service of ordination to the ministry of the Word and Sacrament
Ordination Questions	a. The presbytery shall utilize the ordination questions laid out at W-4.4003, using these words for Question i.(3): Will you be a faithful teaching elder, proclaiming the good news in Word and Sacrament, teaching faith and caring for people? Will you be active in government and discipline, serving in the councils of the church; and in your ministry will you try to show the love and justice of Jesus Christ?
Prayer and Laying on of Hands	b. The candidate, having answered the questions in the affirmative, shall kneel, if able, and the presbytery, or presbytery commission, shall, with prayer and the laying on of hands, ordain the candidate to the ministry of the Word and Sacrament. The member presiding shall then say:

(Name)_____, you are now ordained a teaching elder in the church of Jesus Christ. Whatever you do, in word or deed, do everything in the name of the Lord Jesus, giving thanks to God the Father through him. Amen.

Presbytery
Welcomes

c. Then the members of the presbytery, and others as may be appropriate, shall welcome the new teaching elder into the ministry of the Word and Sacrament. At the conclusion of the ordination service, the new teaching elder may make a brief statement and shall pronounce the benediction.

W-4.4006
Installation of
Teaching Elder

Every Christian is called by God to serve the church; however, God calls some persons to serve the church in particular and specific ways in congregations. When the congregation, the presbytery, and the teaching elder (or candidate) have all concurred in a call to a permanent or designated pastoral position, the presbytery shall complete the call process by organizing and conducting the service of installation. Installation is an act of the presbytery establishing the pastoral relationship. A commission may be appointed to act for the presbytery.

Installation
Service

a. On the day designated for the installation, the presbytery or commission appointed for this purpose shall convene and shall call the congregation gathered to worship. The service shall have the same focus and form as the service of ordination and the person being installed shall be asked to answer the questions asked at the time of ordination.

Questions for
Congregation

b. Following the affirmative answers to the questions asked of the person being installed, a ruling elder shall face the congregation along with the pastor-elect (associate pastor-elect) and shall ask them to answer the following questions:

(1) Do we, the members of the church, accept (Name) _____ as our pastor (associate pastor), chosen by God through the voice of this congregation to guide us in the way of Jesus Christ?

(2) Do we agree to pray for him (her), to encourage him (her), to respect his (her) decisions, and to follow as he (she) guides us, serving Jesus Christ, who alone is Head of the Church?[e]

(3) Do we promise to pay him (her) fairly and provide for his (her) welfare as he (she) works among us; to stand by him (her) in trouble and share his (her) joys? Will we listen to the word he (she) preaches, welcome his (her) pastoral care, and honor his (her) authority as he (she) seeks to honor and obey Jesus Christ our Lord?[f][g]

Installation of
Teaching Elder

c. The members of the congregation having answered these questions in the affirmative,[h][i]

(1) a candidate being ordained and installed shall kneel, if able, and the presbytery shall, with prayer and the

laying on of hands, ordain the candidate to the ministry of the Word and Sacrament and install him or her in the particular pastoral responsibility.

(2) a teaching elder, previously ordained, who is being installed ordinarily shall stand, if able, for the laying on of hands and the prayer of installation.

Statement to
Teaching Elder

d.   The member presiding shall then say:[j]

(1) (For one being ordained and installed)

(Name) _____, you are now a teaching elder in the Church of Jesus Christ and for this congregation. Whatever you do, in word or deed, do everything in the name of the Lord Jesus, giving thanks to God the Father through him. Amen.

(2) (For a teaching elder previously ordained)

(Name) _____, you are now a teaching elder in and for this congregation. Whatever you do, in word or deed, do everything in the name of the Lord Jesus, giving thanks to God the Father through him. Amen.

Welcome

e.   Then the members of the presbytery, and others as may be appropriate, shall welcome the newly ordained and installed or newly installed teaching elder into their fellowship in the ministry of the Word and Sacrament.[k]

Charge

f.   Persons invited by the presbytery may then give brief charges to the pastor (associate pastor) and to the congregation to be faithful in their relationship and in their reciprocal responsibilities.[l]

Benediction

g.   At the conclusion of the service, the newly installed teaching elder may make a brief statement and shall pronounce the benediction.

W-4.5000

5.   Transitions in Ministry

W-4.5001
Recognition of
Transition

When those especially commissioned for specific acts of discipleship; those ordained as deacons, ruling elders, or teaching elders; or others serving in the church conclude a period of ministry, it is appropriate for the congregation and others associated with the ministry to recognize those persons' gifts and service.

W-4.5002
Form of
Recognition

This recognition may be given in the Service for the Lord's Day as a part of responding to the Word (W-3.3503) or of bearing and following the Word into the world (W-3.3701), or in another appointed service of worship. The service may include expressions of commendation and gratitude for the persons' ministry, and should include prayers of thanksgiving and intercession on their behalf as they make this transition in their ministry.

W-4.6000

W-4.6001
Censure and
Restoration

6. Censure and Restoration

Forms for censure and for restoration are set forth in the Rules of Discipline in this *Book of Order*. (D-12.0102; D-12.0103; D-12.0104; D-12.0105; D-12.0202; D-12.0203) In using these forms, care should be taken that they be spoken and enacted in the spirit of pastoral concern and in the context of worship within the appropriate community.

W-4.7000

W-4.7001
Recognition
of Service

7. Recognition of Service to the Community

Service given to the community beyond the particular mission of the church may be appropriately recognized as an expression of Christian discipleship with prayer and thanksgiving at a suitable time in an occasion of worship. Significant accomplishments in the lives of Christians or honors and other forms of recognition received by them may also be occasions for such celebration with the community of faith.

W-4.8000

W-4.8001
Brokenness
and Wholeness

8. Services of Acceptance and Reconciliation

Christians are forgiven sinners living in a sinful world, involved in brokenness which they suffer, involved in brokenness which they cause. Given this reality, a significant move toward wholeness is the recognition and acknowledgment of one's own responsibility in the brokenness and failure of a relationship

a. in friendship and in marriage,

b. in family and in church,

c. in workplace and in school,

d. in neighborhood, in community, and in the world.

W-4.8002
Services of
Acceptance and
Reconciliation

Beyond this the Christian community must recognize and acknowledge its involvement in sin, in broken structures, and in broken relationships. Opportunity is appropriately given in worship for special services of acknowledgment and recognition of failure in relationships, of grieving together over the loss of relationship, and of mutual forgiveness and reconciliation within the believing community. (W-2.6001; W-3.3301; W-3.5400; W-6.3007–.3008; W-6.3011; W-7.4004)

W-4.8000:   2 Cor. 5:18–20; Jas. 5:16; West.Conf. 6.086; Conf.1967 9.07, 9.22

W-4.8003
Form of a Service

These services include

a.   readings from Scripture which reveal the grace of God,

b.   prayers of confession, intercession, and supplication,

c.   declarations of forgiveness and freedom from guilt and shame,

d.   expressions of praise and thanksgiving for forgiveness and reconciliation,

e.   enactments of mutual commitment and reconciliation.

W-4.9000

9. Marriage

W-4.9001
Christian
Marriage

Marriage is a gift God has given to all humankind for the well-being of the entire human family. Marriage is a civil contract between a woman and a man. For Christians marriage is a covenant through which a man and a woman are called to live out together before God their lives of discipleship. In a service of Christian marriage a lifelong commitment is made by a woman and a man to each other, publicly witnessed and acknowledged by the community of faith.

W-4.9002
Preparing for
Marriage

a.   In preparation for the marriage service, the teaching elder† shall provide for a discussion with the man and the woman concerning

(1) the nature of their Christian commitment, assuring that at least one is a professing Christian,

(2) the legal requirements of the state,

(3) the privileges and responsibilities of Christian marriage,

(4) the nature and form of the marriage service,

(5) the vows and commitments they will be asked to make,

(6) the relationship of these commitments to their lives of discipleship,

(7) the resources of the faith and the Christian community to assist them in fulfilling their marriage commitments.
This discussion is equally important in the case of a first marriage, a marriage after the death of a spouse, and a marriage following divorce.

W-4.9000:   2 Helv.Conf. 5.245–5.251; West.Conf. 6.131–6.139

| If the Marriage Is Unwise | b.   If the teaching elder is convinced after discussion with the couple that commitment, responsibility, maturity, or Christian understanding are so lacking that the marriage is unwise, the teaching elder shall assure the couple of the church's continuing concern for them and not conduct the ceremony. In making this decision the teaching elder may seek the counsel of the session. |

W-4.9003
Time and Place
of the Service

Christian marriage should be celebrated in the place where the community gathers for worship. As a service of Christian worship, the marriage service is under the direction of the teaching elder† and the supervision of the session. (W-1.4004–.4006) The marriage ordinarily takes place in a special service which focuses upon marriage as a gift of God and as an expression of the Christian life. Others may be invited to participate as leaders in the service at the discretion of the pastor. Celebration of the Lord's Supper at the marriage service requires the approval of the session, and care shall be taken that the invitation to the Table is extended to all baptized present. The marriage service may take place during the Service for the Lord's Day upon authorization by the session. It should be placed in the order as a response to the proclamation of the Word. It may then be followed by the Sacrament of the Lord's Supper. (W-2.4010; W-3.3503)

W-4.9004
Form and Order
of Service

The service begins with scriptural sentences and a brief statement of purpose. The man and the woman shall declare their intention to enter into Christian marriage and shall exchange vows of love and faithfulness. The service includes appropriate passages of Scripture, which may be interpreted in various forms of proclamation. Prayers shall be offered for the couple, for the communities which support them in this new dimension of discipleship, and for all who seek to live in faithfulness. In the name of the triune God the teaching elder† shall declare publicly that the woman and the man are now joined in marriage. A charge may be given. Other actions common to the community and its cultures may appropriately be observed when these actions do not diminish the Christian understanding of marriage. The service concludes with a benediction.

W-4.9005
Music and
Appointments

Music suitable for the marriage service directs attention to God and expresses the faith of the church. (W-2.1004) The congregation may join in hymns and other musical forms of praise and prayer. Flowers, decorations, and other appointments should be appropriate to the place of worship, enhance the worshipers' consciousness of the reality of God, and reflect the integrity and simplicity of Christian life. (W-1.3034; W-1.4004–.4005; W-5.5005)

W-4.9006
Recognizing
Civil Marriage

A service of worship recognizing a civil marriage and confirming it in the community of faith may be appropriate when requested by the couple. The service will be similar to the marriage service except that the opening statement, the declaration of intention, the exchange of the vows by the husband and wife, and the public declaration by the teaching elder† reflect the fact that the woman and man are already married to one another according to the laws of the state.

W-4.10000

10. Services on the Occasion of Death

W-4.10001
Christians
and Death

The resurrection is a central doctrine of the Christian faith and shapes Christians' attitudes and responses to the event of death. Death brings loss, sorrow, and grief to all. In the face of death Christians affirm with tears and joy the hope of the gospel. Christians do not bear bereavement in isolation but are sustained by the power of the Spirit and the community of faith. The church offers a ministry of love and hope to all who grieve. (W-6.3006)

W-4.10002
Planning
Arrangements

Because it is difficult under emotional stress to plan wisely, the session should encourage members to discuss and plan in advance the arrangements which will be necessary at the time of death, including decisions about the Christian options of burial, cremation, or donation for medical purposes. These plans should provide for arrangements which are simple, which bear witness to resurrection hope, and in which the Christian community is central. The session is responsible for establishing general policies concerning the observance of services on the occasion of death. (W-1.4004)

W-4.10003
Setting of
the Service

The service on the occasion of death ordinarily should be held in the usual place of worship in order to join this service to the community's continuing life and witness to the resurrection. The service shall be under the direction of the pastor. Others may be invited to participate as leaders in the service at the discretion of the pastor. This service may be observed on any day. A request to observe such a service as a part of the Lord's Day service or to celebrate the Lord's Supper as a part of a service on the occasion of death requires the approval of the session.

W-4.10000:   2 Helv.Conf. 5.235–5.236

W-4.10004
Form and Order

The service begins with scriptural sentences. It is appropriate for worshipers to sing hymns, psalms, spirituals, or spiritual songs which affirm God's power over death, a belief in the resurrection to life everlasting, and the assurance of the communion of the saints. Scripture shall be read; a sermon or other exposition of the Word may be proclaimed; an affirmation of faith may be made by the people. Aspects of the life of the one who has died may be recalled. Prayers shall be offered, giving thanks to God

    (1) for life in Jesus Christ and the promise of the gospel,

    (2) for the gift of the life of the one who has died,

    (3) for the comfort of the Holy Spirit,

    (4) for the community of faith;

making intercessions

    (5) for family members and loved ones who grieve,

    (6) for those who minister to and support the bereaved,

    (7) for all who suffer loss;

lifting supplications

    (8) for faith and grace for all who are present;

concluding with the Lord's Prayer.

The service ends by commending the one who has died to the care of the eternal God and sending the people forth with a benediction.

W-4.10005
Alternatives
and Options

This service may be observed before or after the committal of the body. In order that attention in the service be directed to God, when a casket is present it ordinarily is closed. It may be covered with a funeral pall. The service may include other actions common to the community of faith and its cultures when these actions do not detract from or diminish the Christian understanding of death and resurrection. The service shall be complete in itself, and any fraternal, civic, or military rites should be conducted separately. When there are important reasons not to hold the service in the usual place of worship, it may be held in another suitable place such as a home, a funeral home, a crematorium, or at graveside.

W-4.10006
Service of
Committal

Members and friends of the family of the one who has died should gather at the graveside or crematorium for a service of farewell, which is to be conducted with simplicity, dignity, and brevity. The service includes readings from Scripture, prayers, words of committal, and a blessing, reflecting the reality of death, entrusting the one who has died to the care of God, and bearing witness to faith in the resurrection from the dead.

CHAPTER V

W-5.0000

WORSHIP AND PERSONAL DISCIPLESHIP

W-5.1000

1. Personal Worship, Discipleship, and the Community of Faith

W-5.1001
Personal and
Communal
Worship

Christians respond to God both in communal worship and service and in personal acts of worship and discipleship. The life of the Christian flows from the worship of the church, where identity as a believer is confirmed and where one is commissioned to a life of discipleship and of personal response to God. The believer's life of response and discipleship flows into the church's life of worship and service. (W-1.1005b; W-2.1001)

W-5.1002
Worship
and Life

Through worship people attend to the presence of God in their life. From a Christian's life in the world comes the need for worship; in worship one sees the world in light of God's grace; from worship come vision and power for living in the world.

W-5.1003
Worship and
Ministry

The Word of God proclaimed and received in worship calls each believer to faithful discipleship in the world. From such service the disciple turns to give thanks, to confess, to intercede, and to hear Christ's call anew. The rhythm of the life of the believer moves from worship to ministry, from ministry to worship.

W-5.1004
Worship and
Discipline

The life of a Christian is empowered by grace, is expressed in obedience, and is shaped by discipline. God has given as means of grace the elements of worship to be used by households and by individuals as well as by congregations. (W-2.0000) The session should encourage people to use the disciplines described in this directory as expressions of their obedience and discipleship and as means for living and growing in the grace of God. (W-5.2000–.5000)

W-5.2000

2. The Discipline of Daily Personal Worship

W-5.2001
Daily Personal
Worship

Daily personal worship is a discipline for attending to God and accepting God's grace. The daily challenge of discipleship requires the daily nurture of worship. Daily personal worship may occur in a gathered community of faith (W-1.1005; W-1.3012; W-3.4000), in households and families (W-5.7000), or in private. Scripture, prayer, self-offering, and commitments to service are elements of daily personal worship. Baptism and the Lord's Supper are by their nature communal, but preparing for and remembering these Sacraments are important in daily personal worship. An aspect of the discipline of daily personal worship is finding the times and places where one can focus on God's presence, hear God's Word, and respond to God's grace in prayer, self-offering, and commitment to service.

W-5.3000

3. Scripture in Personal Worship

W-5.3001
Scripture

Scripture is the record of God's self-revelation through which the Holy Spirit speaks to bear witness to Jesus Christ and to give authoritative direction for the life of faith. Personal worship centers upon Scripture as one reads and listens for God's Spirit to speak. (W-2.2000)

W-5.3002
Uses of Scripture

a.   One may read Scripture for the guidance, support, comfort, encouragement, and challenge which the Word of God presents.

Study of
Scripture

b.   One may study the Scriptures to understand them in their literary forms and in their historical and cultural contexts in order to hear the Word of God more clearly and to obey more faithfully.

Meditate On

c.   One may meditate upon the Word,

(1)   committing passages of Scripture to memory,

(2)   recalling and reflecting upon the revelation of God,

(3)   analyzing and comparing biblical themes, images, and forms,

(4)   finding touchpoints and exploring relationships between Scripture and life,

(5)   entering imaginatively into the world and events portrayed in the Bible to participate in what God does and promises there,

(6)   wrestling with the challenges and demands of the gospel,

(7)   offering one's self afresh for life in response to God.

W-5.3003
Helps in Using
Scripture

It is often helpful to keep a record of one's insights and personal responses to reading, studying, and meditating upon the Word, or to share them with others. Writing paraphrases, summaries, and brief reflections, making creative responses, and keeping journals are all disciplines which assist in responding to the Word of God in Scripture. It is especially important in personal worship to read widely in Scripture. Using lectionaries and various translations and paraphrases is helpful in seeking to hear the full message of God's Word. (W-2.2004)

W-5.4000   **4.   Prayer in Personal Worship**

W-5.4001   Prayer is a conscious opening of the self to God, who initi-
Prayer   ates communion and communication with us. Prayer is receiving
and responding, speaking and listening, waiting and acting in the
presence of God. In prayer we respond to God in adoration, in
thanksgiving, in confession, in supplication, in intercession, and
in self-dedication. (W-2.1000)

W-5.4002   Prayer in personal worship may be expressed in various
Expressing Prayer   ways.

One may engage in conscious conversation with God, putting
into words one's joys and concerns, fears and hopes, needs and
longings in life.

One may wait upon God in attentive and expectant silence.

One may meditate upon God's gifts, God's actions, God's
Word, and God's character.

One may contemplate God, moving beyond words and
thoughts to communion of one's spirit with the Spirit of God.

One may draw near to God in solitude.

One may pray in tongues as a personal and private discipline.

One may take on an individual discipline of enacted prayer
through dance, physical exercise, music, or other expressive activity as a response to grace.

One may enact prayer as a public witness through keeping a
vigil, through deeds of social responsibility or protest, or through
symbolic acts of disciplined service.

One may take on the discipline of holding before God the
people, transactions, and events of daily life in the world.

One may enter into prayer covenants or engage in the regular
discipline of shared prayer.

The Christian is called to a life of constant prayer, of "prayer
without ceasing." (Rom. 12:12; 1 Thess. 5:17)

W-5.4003   In exercising the discipline of prayer in personal worship one
Helps in Prayer   may find help for shaping the form and content of one's prayers

a.   in Scripture, especially the Lord's Prayer and other
prayers, the psalms and other biblical songs;

b.   in hymns, spirituals, and other songs;

W-5.4002:   Ps. 119, 130; Matt. 6:6; Luke 11:1–4; Rom. 8:26 f.; 1 Cor. 12–14

c.   in service books, prayer books, and worship aids;

d.   in the heritages of prayer and devotion expressed in literature and visual arts.

Such resources may also help one see the occasions and subjects of prayer, as may the daily news and church program interpretation materials and guides to personal worship.

W-5.5000

5.   Other Disciplines in Personal Worship and Discipleship

W-5.5001
The Lord's Day

a.   God has given means of grace beyond Scripture, Sacraments, and prayer.

Disciplined
Observance of

b.   Christians have received the Lord's Day to be kept holy to the Lord. (W-1.3011, W-3.2001) It is the beginning of the believer's week and gives shape to the life of discipleship. Disciplined observance of this day includes preparation of one's self for

(1) participation in public worship,

(2) engagement in ministries of witness, service, and compassion,

(3) activities that contribute to spiritual re-creation and rest from daily occupation.

In observing this discipline, Christians whose work takes place on Sunday should set aside another day of the week for these observances.

W-5.5002
Seasons

The seasons of the Christian year provide a rhythm and content for personal worship and discipleship. (W-1.3013; W-3.2002) Special seasons, occasions, and transitions in one's own life also inform personal worship and discipleship.

W-5.5003
Disciplines of
Fasting and
Enacted Prayer

Christians observe special times and seasons for the disciplines of fasting, keeping vigil, and other forms of enacted prayer. It is also appropriate to observe these disciplines at any time, especially in preparation for specific acts of discipleship or as acts of penitence, reconciliation, peacemaking, social protest, and compassion.

W-5.5004
Christian Giving

Giving has always been a mark of Christian commitment and discipleship. The ways in which a believer uses God's gifts of material goods, personal abilities, and time should reflect a faithful response to God's self-giving in Jesus Christ and Christ's call to minister to and share with others in the world. Tithing is a primary expression of the Christian discipline of stewardship. (W-1.3030; W-2.5000)

W-5.5001:   Heid.Cat. 4.103; West.Conf. 6.119; S.Cat. 7.061; L.Cat. 7.227
W-5.5004:   2 Helv.Conf. 5.227–5.231

W-5.5005
Stewardship
of Life

Those who follow the discipline of Christian stewardship will find themselves called to lives of simplicity, generosity, honesty, hospitality, compassion, receptivity, and concern for the earth and God's creatures. (W-7.5000)

W-5.6000

6. Christian Vocation

W-5.6001
God's Call

God calls a people

    a.   to believe in Jesus Christ as Lord and Savior;

    b.   to follow Jesus Christ in obedient discipleship;

    c.   to use the gifts and abilities God has given, honoring and serving God

        (1) in personal life,

        (2) in household and families,

        (3) in daily occupations,

        (4) in community, nation, and the world.

W-5.6002
Our Response

A person responds to God's call to faith in Jesus Christ through Baptism and through life and worship in the community of faith.

Persons respond to God's call to discipleship through the ministries of God's people in and for the world.

Persons respond to God's call to honor and serve God in every aspect of human life

    a.   in their work and in their play,

    b.   in their thought and in their action,

    c.   in their private and in their public relationships.

W-5.6003
Worship and
Work

God hallows daily life, and daily life provides opportunity for holy living. As Christians honor and serve God in daily life, they worship God. For Christians, work and worship cannot be separated.

W-5.7000

7. Worship in Families and Households

W-5.7001
Household
Worship

When Christians live together in a family or in a household they should observe times of worship together. When it is possible to worship together daily, households may engage in

    a.   table prayer, which may be accompanied by the use of Scripture and song;

    b.   morning and evening prayer;

    c.   Bible reading, study, reflection, and memorization;

d.   singing psalms, hymns, spirituals, and other songs;

e.   expressions of giving and sharing.

Given the complexity of schedules and the separations incurred in daily occupations, it is especially important to cultivate the discipline of regular household worship. When members of a household are not able to come together for worship, they may nevertheless observe a common time of personal worship with common readings and prayer concerns.

**W-5.7002
Children in
Household
Worship**

The parent(s) or the one(s) exercising parental responsibility should teach their children about Christian worship by example, by providing for household worship, and by discussion and instruction. Children join in household worship

a.   praying and singing,

b.   listening to and telling Bible stories,

c.   reading and memorizing,

d.   leading and sharing,

e.   enacting and responding.

Children should be taught appropriate elements of worship used regularly in the Service for the Lord's Day. (W-2.3012–.3013; W-3.1004; W-3.3100; W-3.5202; W-6.2000)

**W-5.7003
Special Occasions
and Seasons**

Household worship should reflect those occasions of special recognition and celebration which occur in the life of the church and in the lives of those in the household. Birthdays, baptismal days, and other anniversaries are all appropriate occasions for special observance. It is also important in household worship to anticipate and remember the Lord's Day and the celebration of the Sacraments of Baptism and the Lord's Supper. Seasons of the Christian year provide direction and content for household worship, with the seasons of Advent and Lent and the celebration of Christmas and Easter being particularly appropriate to observe in worship in households. Worship in this setting will also recognize the cycle of seasons in nature and the rhythm of community, national, and world life, as well as those events and needs which remind believers of their call to live as disciples of Jesus Christ in the world. (W-2.3014; W-3.2000; W-3.3600)

CHAPTER VI

W-6.0000

WORSHIP AND MINISTRY
WITHIN THE COMMUNITY OF FAITH

W-6.1000

1. Mutual Ministries in the Church

W-6.1001
Responding
to God in
Ministries

In communal and personal worship God calls people to faith and discipleship. Those responding to this call offer themselves and the gifts which God has given them to be used in the life of the community of faith for ministries to the world and to one another. (W-1.1000; W-5.1000; F-1.0301; F-1.0302a; F-1.0403)

W-6.1002
Mutual
Ministries in
the Church

Mutual ministries to one another in the church spring from and are nourished by the Word proclaimed and heard, by the Sacraments celebrated and received, and by prayer offered and shared in worship.

W-6.1003
Nurture and
Pastoral Care

Nurture and pastoral care are ways in which Christians minister to one another. The nurture of believers and their children in the Christian community is a process of bringing them to full maturity in Jesus Christ. Pastoral care is the support which Christians offer one another in daily living and at times of need and of crisis in personal and communal life. Often nurture involves pastoral care and pastoral care furthers Christian nurture.

W-6.2000

2. Christian Nurture

W-6.2001
Entering the
Community

The Christian community provides nurture for its members through all of life and life's transitions. The church offers nurture to those entering the community of faith,

    a.   preparing for Baptism,

    b.   including them in the life of the community,

    c.   welcoming them to participate in its worship and to come to the Lord's Table,

    d.   assisting them to claim their identity as believers in Jesus Christ,

    e.   equipping them to live as commissioned disciples in the world. (W-2.3012; W-2.3013; W-4.2002; W-4.2003)

W-6.2002
Assuming
Responsibility

The church offers nurture to people assuming responsibility in the world, assisting them

---

W-6.1003:   Rom. 12:15; Gal. 6:2; Eph. 4:12b–16; 2 Helv.Conf. 5.233–5.234; West.Conf. 6.147

a.   with self-discovery and world awareness,

b.   with self-discipline and discipleship,

c.   with developing commitment to moral and ethical values,

d.   with making informed choices about education and occupations,

e.   with making wise commitments in personal relationships and marriage.

W-6.2003
Living Out
Vocation

As the church ministers to people who are discovering Christian vocation, so it offers nurture to those who are living out Christian vocation in public, active life. (W-5.6000) It guides and supports them in their discipleship

a.   as ministers to one another in the community of faith,

b.   as stewards of material resources, time, and talents,

c.   as members of families, especially in their own role of sharing the faith with others of their households,

d.   as responsible citizens,

e.   as servants of God for the world.

W-6.2004
Responding
to Change

The church provides nurture to guide and support people as they continue their discipleship in circumstances offering new limitations and new freedoms.

W-6.2005
Providers of
Nurture in
the Church

In the service of Baptism the congregation, trusting in the power of the Holy Spirit, and on behalf of the universal Church, pledges responsibility for Christian nurture. (W-2.3013; W-3.3603) The session and the ruling elders are responsible for providing for the development and supervision of the educational program of the church, for instructing ruling elders and deacons, and for developing discipleship among members. (G-2.0301; G-3.0201) The pastor nurtures the community through the ministries of Word and Sacrament, by praying with and for the congregation, through formal and informal teaching, and by example. (G-2.0104; G-2.0504) Some in the community of faith whose special gifts and training have prepared them for a ministry of education are called to the task of leadership in nurture. Teachers, advisers, and others appointed by the session guide, instruct, and equip those for whose education and nurture they are responsible. (W-3.3503) Parents or those exercising parental responsibility share the faith of the church with children. (W-4.3002; W-5.7000)

W-6.2006
Resources and
Occasions for
Nurture

The primary standard and resource for the nurture of the church is the Word of God in Scripture. The central occasion for nurture in the church is the Service for the Lord's Day, when the Word is proclaimed and the Sacraments are celebrated. All members of the community, from oldest to youngest, are encouraged to be present and to participate. Educational activities should not be scheduled which prevent regular participation in this service. (W-3.1004) An important and continuing context for Christian nurture is the home, where faith is shared through worship, teaching, and example. The church provides other occasions for nurture

    a.   in the classes of the church school,

    b.   in other groups and fellowships organized for education and nurture,

    c.   in groups and associations gathered for service and mission,

    d.   in committees, boards, and councils,

    e.   in retreats, camps, and conferences.

The confessional documents of the church provide guidance in nurture. (F-2.00) Shape and content for study and instruction are provided by the rich resources of the liturgical, cultural, and ethnic heritages of the church. Educational materials developed for various approaches to Christian nurture are appropriate for use as approved by the session. (G-3.0201)

W-6.3000

W-6.3001
Pastoral Care

W-6.3002
Care by All
Christians

W-6.3003
Pastoral
Counseling

3. Pastoral Care

The Christian community offers pastoral care to its members in their personal and communal life. The church may provide different levels of this mutual ministry of care.

All Christians are called to care for one another in daily living, sharing joys and sorrows, supporting in times of stress and need, offering mutual forgiveness and reconciliation. This care is primarily offered as the community of faith worships together. It is also provided as people interact in community and as they come together in groups for nurture or to carry on ministries of the church. Ruling elders, deacons, and pastors are called to special responsibility for this common pastoral care. (G-2.0501; G-2.0301; G-2.0201)

Some in the community of faith who have special gifts and appropriate training are called in the church to the particular ministry of pastoral counseling with individuals and with groups formed for this purpose.

W-6.3004
Referral

In certain circumstances the ministry of pastoral care may call for referral to teaching elders in specialized ministries or others qualified by credentials and faith-perspective to provide appropriate counseling or therapy.

W-6.3005
Care in
Illness

The church offers pastoral care to people in the special needs and crises of their lives. When people are ill, Christians respond with prayer, visits, and other acts which express love and support for those who are sick and for their households, their families, and their friends. When illness is critical or is prolonged, those offering pastoral care will give special attention to the needs and stresses experienced by everyone involved. Terminal illness calls for particular care which mediates trust in God, support in suffering, comfort for distress, and hope in the face of death.

W-6.3006
Care at
Death

When death comes, the church in its pastoral care immediately offers the ministry of presence, of shared loss and pain, of faith and hope in the power of the resurrection, and of ordinary acts of care and love. The church continues special pastoral care during the time of grieving and adjusting. (W-4.10000)

W-6.3007
Care in Loss

Other occasions of loss in life, such as

    a.   the loss of power,

    b.   the fading away of a once-important relationship,

    c.   the departure of children from the home,

    d.   the loss of meaningful employment, means of livelihood, or financial security,

    e.   the ending of a marriage in separation or divorce, call for pastoral care which provides opportunities to grieve and offers practical help and support in the process of renewal and adjustment.

W-6.3008
Care in Broken
Relationships

The church provides pastoral care which calls people to healing and seeks to support those caught up in the hurts, hostilities, and conflicts of daily living which lead to broken relationships in families and households, in the school and the workplace, in neighborhoods and communities, and in the church. (W-4.8000)

W-6.3009
Care in Sin and
Forgiveness

The call to healing in pastoral care involves the recognition in each one's life of the reality of sin, which is the source of all human brokenness. The believing community announces the good news of God whose love gives people grace

    a.   to confess their sin and complicity in brokenness,

    b.   to repent, expressing sorrow and intention to change,

c. to accept God's forgiveness and extend that forgiveness to another,

d. to forgive the other and accept the other's forgiveness,

e. to work toward reconciliation in brokenness,

f. to trust the power of God to bring healing and peace. (W-4.8000)

Receiving confession and declaring God's forgiveness, calling for repentance and supporting in the struggle toward new life, encouraging people to forgive and receive forgiveness, and mediating reconciliation are appropriate acts of pastoral care.

**W-6.3010
Care in the
Transitions
of Life**

The church recognizes transitions which bring joy and sorrow in human life:

a. children are born, grow up, become independent, find their aging parents becoming dependent upon them;

b. people begin work, change jobs, retire;

c. households are established, move to new locations, gain and lose members;

d. people are empowered, restored, make new commitments.

The ministries of pastoral care support people in recognizing, accepting, and celebrating these and other such times of adjustment, assisting them in working toward a new role in life and affirming their identity through transition.

**W-6.3011
Resources of
Worship for
Pastoral Care**

The community of faith engages in the ministries of mutual care in its worship, and its members draw upon the resources of worship in giving pastoral care.

a. Scripture is central as a resource for support, comfort, and guidance. The proclamation of the Word in sermon and song may lead to recognizing need and may provide care. (W-2.2000; W-3.3400)

b. Prayers—silent, spoken, and sung—give thanks, intercede, make supplication, and acknowledge God's presence and power. Prayer enacted by the laying on of hands and anointing calls upon God to heal, empower, and sustain. (W-2.1000; W-3.3506; W-3.5400)

c. Offering the Sacraments in hospital or household celebrates the presence of Christ, and extends the community of faith beyond the sanctuary. (W-2.3000–.4000; W-3.3600)

d.   The Lord's Prayer, psalms, doxologies, benedictions, and other familiar portions of a congregation's worship may extend the support and care of the community of faith to those whose special needs or circumstances have placed them in isolation and remind them of their place in that community.

e.   Times of remembrance, concerns of the people, prayers of intercession, and other such occasions in corporate worship will bring into the worship of the community of faith those who are absent. (W-3.3500; W-3.3700)

W-6.4000
Worship and
Ministry

The worship of God in the Christian community is the foundation and context for the ministry of pastoral care as well as for the ministry of nurture in the faith.

CHAPTER VII

W-7.0000

WORSHIP AND THE MINISTRY
OF THE CHURCH IN THE WORLD

W-7.1000

1. Worship and Mission

W-7.1001
Worship and
Ministry

The church participates in God's mission to the world through its ministry and worship. Worship presents the reality of the divine rule which God has promised in Jesus Christ as the final renewal of creation. The worshiping community in its integrity before the Word and its unity in prayer and Sacraments is a sign of the presence of the reign of God. The church in its ministry bears witness to God's reign through the proclamation of the gospel, through works of compassion and reconciliation, and through the stewardship of creation and of life. Signs of God's reign are also manifest in the world wherever the Holy Spirit leads people to seek justice and to make peace. (F-1.01)

W-7.1002
Worship and
Mission

God calls the church in worship to join the mission of Jesus Christ in service to the world. As it participates in that mission the church is called to worship God in Jesus Christ, who reigns over the world. (F-1.0304)

W-7.2000

2. Proclamation and Evangelism

W-7.2001
The Scope of
Evangelism

God sends the church in the power of the Holy Spirit

a. to announce the good news that in Christ Jesus the world is reconciled to God,

b. to tell all nations and peoples of Christ's call to repentance, faith, and obedience,

c. to proclaim in deed and word that Jesus gave himself to set people free,

d. to offer in Christ's name fullness of life now and forever,

e. to call people everywhere to believe in and follow Jesus Christ as Lord and Savior,

f. to invite them into the community of faith to worship and serve the triune God. (F-1.03; F-1.0304)

W-7.2002
Contexts of
Evangelism

Worship is the primary context in which people regularly hear the proclamation of the gospel, are presented with God's promise, are given the opportunity to respond with faith and acts

---

W-7.2001:   2 Cor. 5:19–20; West.Conf. 6.055–6.058, 6.187–6.190

of commitment, and receive the nurture and support of the community. (W-2.2000; W-2.5001; W-3.3501–.3503; W-3.5500) In the life of the church, the transforming power of the Holy Spirit is manifest in mutual love and service, in self-giving and acceptance, drawing people from their separateness into the community of shared faith in Jesus Christ. As Christians daily live out their vocation in the world, they invite those they meet to come and share the life of the people of God and join in their worship.

W-7.3000

3. Compassion

W-7.3001
A Ministry of
Compassion

God sends the church in the power of the Holy Spirit to exercise compassion in the world,

    a.   feeding the hungry,

    b.   comforting the grieving,

    c.   caring for the sick,

    d.   visiting the prisoners,

    e.   freeing the captives,

    f.   sheltering the homeless,

    g.   befriending the lonely.

W-7.3002
Compassion
and Worship

God's call to compassion is proclaimed in worship. Those called are equipped and strengthened for the ministry of compassion by the proclamation of the Word and by the celebration of the Sacraments. The call is accepted as the faithful respond in prayers of confession and intercession, in acts of self-offering, and in offering material goods to be shared in ministries of compassion. (W-2.1002; W-2.5000; W-3.3505–.3507) Those called are commissioned and sent by the church to do acts of compassion on Christ's behalf. (W-2.6000; W-3.3701; W-4.3000)

W-7.3003
Compassion
and Advocacy

Such acts of compassion, done corporately and individually, are the work of the church as the body of Christ. The church is called to minister to the immediate needs and hurts of people. The church is also called to engage those structures and systems which create or foster brokenness and distortion. Christians respond to these calls through acts of advocacy and compassion, through service in common ministries of the church, and through cooperation with agencies and organizations committed to these ends. (F-1.03)

W-7.3001:   Matt. 25:31–46; Luke 4:18–21; Rom. 12:6–8; Gal. 6:9–10; Jas. 1:27, 2:14–17

W-7.3004 Faithful Compassion	Following the example of Jesus Christ, faithful disciples to-day express compassion

    a.   with respect for the dignity of those in need,

    b.   with openness to help even those judged undeserving,

    c.   with willingness to risk their own comfort and safety,

    d.   with readiness to receive as well as to give,

    e.   with constant prayer in the midst of ministering, always in communion with the renewing power of the worshiping community. (F-1.02)

W-7.4000   **4.   Reconciliation: Justice and Peace**

W-7.4001
Reconciliation
in Christ

God sends the church in the power of the Holy Spirit to share with Christ in establishing God's just, peaceable, and loving rule in the world. (F-1.02) God's reconciliation in Jesus Christ is the ground of justice and peace. (Conf. 1967 9.45) The church in worship proclaims, receives, and enacts reconciliation in Jesus Christ and commits itself to strive for justice and peace in its own life and in the world.

W-7.4002
Doing Justice

Justice is the order God sets in human life for fair and honest dealing and for giving rights to those who have no power to claim rights for themselves. The biblical vision of doing justice calls for

    a.   dealing honestly in personal and public business,

    b.   exercising power for the common good,

    c.   supporting people who seek the dignity, freedom, and respect that they have been denied,

    d.   working for fair laws and just administration of the law,

    e.   welcoming the stranger in the land,

    f.   seeking to overcome the disparity between rich and poor,

    g.   bearing witness against political oppression and exploitation,

    h.   redressing wrongs against individuals, groups, and peoples in the church, in this nation, and in the whole world.

W-7.3004:   Mark 1:32–38; Luke 6:12
W-7.4000:   Conf.1967 9.43–9.47
W-7.4002:   Ex. 22:21–27; Lev. 19:33, 34; Ps. 34, 82; Isa. 2:1–5; 32:1–8, 16, 17; Amos 5:6–15; Mic. 6:8; Matt. 23:23–24; Luke 4:16–21; West.Conf. 6.127–6.128; L.Cat. 7.246, 7.251, 7.252, 7.254, 7.255; Conf.1967 9.43–9.47

W-7.4003
Making Peace

There is no peace without justice. Wherever there is broken-ness, violence, and injustice the people of God are called to peacemaking

a.   in the Church universal fragmented and separated by histories and cultures, in denominations internally polarized by mutual distrust, and in congregations plagued by dissension and conflict;

b.   in the world where nations place national security above all else, where the zealotry of religion, race, or ideology explodes in violence, and where the lust for getting and keeping economic or political power erupts in rioting or war;

c.   in communities racked by crime and fear, in schools and workplaces marked by vicious competition and rebellion against order, and in households and families divided against themselves, scarred by violence and paralyzed by fear.

W-7.4004
Reconciliation
in Worship

The ministries of reconciliation, justice, and peace are initiat-ed and nurtured in the church's worship of God. In the proclama-tion of God's Word people are given assurance of freedom from the guilt and fear which keep them from fulfilling these minis-tries. In Baptism and the Lord's Supper believers are united in Christ, are made one in the church through the Holy Spirit, and recognize one another across all boundaries and divisions as sis-ters and brothers in the faith. (W-2.3000–.4000) In prayer the faithful lift intercessions for all who experience brokenness, vio-lence, and injustice; give thanks to God for reconciliation, peace, and justice in Jesus Christ; and commit themselves to be recon-cilers seeking justice and pursuing peace. (W-2.1000; W-2.6000; W-3.3506; W-3.3700)

W-7.5000

5.   Caring for Creation and Life

W-7.5001
God's Mandate

God calls the Church in the power of the Holy Spirit to partic-ipate in God's work of creation and preservation. God has given humankind awesome power and perilous responsibility to rule and tame the earth, to sustain and reshape it, to replenish and renew it.

W-7.4003:   Isa. 2:1–5; 32:16, 17; Mic. 6:8; Jas. 3:13–18; West.Conf. 6.128; L.Cat. 7.245, 7.246;
              Conf.1967 9.43–9.47, 9.53–9.56
W-7.5001:   Gen. 1:26–28; 2:15–20; Ps. 8

W-7.5002
Worship and the
Use of Creation

In worship Christians rejoice and give thanks to God, who gives and sustains the created universe, the earth, all life, and all goods. They acknowledge God's command to be stewards. They confess their own failures in caring for creation and life. They rejoice in the promise of the redemption and renewal of the creation in Jesus Christ, proclaimed in the Word and sealed in the Sacraments. They commit themselves to live as God's stewards until the day when God will make all things new. (W-1.0000)

W-7.5003
Stewardship
of Creation

As stewards of God's creation who hold the earth in trust, the people of God are called to

a.   use the earth's resources responsibly without plundering, polluting, or destroying,

b.   develop technological methods and processes that work together with the earth's environment to preserve and enhance life,

c.   produce and consume in ways that make available to all people what is sufficient for life,

d.   work for responsible attitudes and practices in procreation and reproduction,

e.   use and shape earth's goods to create beauty, order, health, and peace in ways that reflect God's love for all creatures.

In gratitude for the gifts of creation, the faithful bring material goods to God in worship as a means of expressing praise, as a symbol of their self-offering, and as a token of their commitment to share earth's goods. (W-2.5000; W-3.3507; W-5.5005; W-5.6000)

W-7.6000

6.   The Church and the Reign of God

W-7.6001
The Church and
the Kingdom

The church in its worship and ministry is a sign of the reign of God, which is both a present reality and a promise of the future. The church's worship and service do not make the Kingdom of God come. In an age hostile to the reign of God, the church worships and serves, with confidence that God's rule has been established and with firm hope in the ultimate manifestation of the triumph of God.

W-7.6002
Confidence
and Hope

In the present age the church's ministries of evangelism and caring for creation, of compassion and reconciliation are signs of God's reign and offer hope in the midst of life-denying situations. That hope is not dependent on the success of the church's ministries or the effectiveness of its worship, but is sustained by the power of God present with the church as it ministers and worships.

W-7.7000   **7. Worship as Praise**

W-7.7001   In worship the church is transformed and renewed, equipped
Ascription   and sent to serve God's reign in the world. The church looks for
of Praise   the day

> when every knee shall bow,
> in heaven and on earth and under the earth
> and every tongue confess
> that Jesus Christ is Lord,
> to the glory of God the Father.
>
> (Phil. 2:9–11)
>
> Now to the One who is able to keep us from falling
> and to present us without blemish
> before the presence of God's glory with rejoicing,
> to the only God, our Savior
> through Jesus Christ our Lord,
> be glory, majesty, dominion, and authority,
> before all time, now, and forever.
>
> (Jude 24)
>
> Amen!
> Blessing and glory and wisdom and thanksgiving
> and honor and power and might
> be to our God
> for ever and ever!
> Amen.
>
> (Rev. 7:12)

THE
RULES OF
DISCIPLINE

[TEXT]

[Approved 1996, Effective July 6, 1996.]

Note 1:

In light of the addition of the Foundations of Presbyterian Polity and the revision of the Form of Government (2011), the following terms in use in the Directory for Worship have been replaced with terms employed in the new and revised documents:

- "Minister" or "minister of the Word and Sacrament" = "teaching elder"
- "Elder" = "ruling elder"
- "Governing body" = "council"
- "Commissioned Lay Pastor" = "ruling elder commissioned to particular pastoral service" or "ruling elder commissioned to pastoral service"
- "Office" or "Ordained Office" = "ordered ministry"
- "Officer/s," "Church Officer/s," or "Ordained Officer/s" = "[person/those in] ordered ministry"

CHAPTER I

D-1.0000

PRINCIPLES OF CHURCH DISCIPLINE

PREAMBLE

D-1.0101
Church
Discipline

Church discipline is the church's exercise of authority given by Christ, both in the direction of guidance, control, and nurture of its members and in the direction of constructive criticism of offenders. The church's disciplinary process exists not as a substitute for the secular judicial system, but to do what the secular judicial system cannot do. The purpose of discipline is to honor God by making clear the significance of membership in the body of Christ; to preserve the purity of the church by nourishing the individual within the life of the believing community; to achieve justice and compassion for all participants involved; to correct or restrain wrongdoing in order to bring members to repentance and restoration; to uphold the dignity of those who have been harmed by disciplinary offenses; to restore the unity of the church by removing the causes of discord and division; and to secure the just, speedy, and economical determination of proceedings. In all respects, all participants are to be accorded procedural safeguards and due process, and it is the intention of these rules so to provide.

D-1.0102
Power Vested in
Christ's Church

The power that Jesus Christ has vested in his Church, a power manifested in the exercise of church discipline, is one for building up the body of Christ, not for destroying it, for redeeming, not for punishing. It should be exercised as a dispensation of mercy and not of wrath so that the great ends of the Church may be achieved, that all children of God may be presented faultless in the day of Christ.

D-1.0103
Conciliate and
Mediate

The traditional biblical obligation to conciliate, mediate, and adjust differences without strife is not diminished by these Rules of Discipline. Although the Rules of Discipline describe the way in which judicial process within the church, when necessary, shall be conducted, it is not their intent or purpose to encourage judicial process of any kind or to make it more expensive or difficult. The biblical duty of church people to "come to terms quickly with your accuser while you are on the way to court ..." (Matthew 5:25) is not abated or diminished. It remains the duty of every church member to try (prayerfully and seriously) to bring about an adjustment or settlement of the quarrel, complaint, delinquency, or irregularity asserted, and to avoid formal proceedings under the Rules of Discipline unless, after prayerful deliberation, they are determined to be necessary to preserve the purity and purposes of the church.

CHAPTER II

D-2.0000　　　　　**JUDICIAL PROCESS DEFINED**

D-2.0100　　　**1.　Judicial Process**

D-2.0101
Church
Discipline

Judicial process is the means by which church discipline is implemented within the context of pastoral care and oversight. It is the exercise of authority by the councils of the church for

a.　the prevention and correction of irregularities and delinquencies by councils, the Presbyterian Mission Agency, or an entity of the General Assembly (Remedial Cases, D-6.0000);

b.　the prevention and correction of offenses by persons (Disciplinary Cases, D-10.0000).

D-2.0102
Councils of
the Church

The councils of the church for judicial process are the session, the presbytery, the synod, and the General Assembly. The session itself conducts trials. The presbytery, the synod, and the General Assembly conduct trials and hearings through permanent judicial commissions.

D-2.0103
Alternative
Forms of
Resolution

To meet the goals of D-1.0103, the investigating committee may initiate if it deems appropriate, and with the written consent of the accused, alternative forms of resolution conducted by professionally trained and certified mediators and arbitrators. The purpose of this process is to achieve justice and compassion for all persons involved through mediation and settlement.

No statements, written or oral, made at or in connection with this process, shall be themselves admissible in evidence at a subsequent investigation or trial.

D-2.0200　　　**2.　Types of Cases**

D-2.0201
Remedial or
Disciplinary

Judicial process consists of two types of cases: remedial and disciplinary.

D-2.0202
Remedial

A remedial case is one in which an irregularity or a delinquency of a lower council, the Presbyterian Mission Agency, or an entity of the General Assembly may be corrected by a higher council.

Irregularity

a.　An irregularity is an erroneous decision or action.

Delinquency

b.　A delinquency is an omission or failure to act.

D-2.0203
Disciplinary

Persons in
Ordered
Ministries
Offense

A disciplinary case is one in which a church member or a person in an ordered ministry may be censured for an offense.

a.   Persons in ordered ministries are teaching elders, ruling elders, and deacons.

b.   An offense is any act or omission by a member or a person in an ordered ministry of the church that is contrary to the Scriptures or the Constitution of the Presbyterian Church (U.S.A.).

CHAPTER III

D-3.0000

JURISDICTION IN JUDICIAL PROCESS

D-3.0101
Jurisdiction

In judicial process, each of the councils has jurisdiction as follows:

Session

a. The session of a church has original jurisdiction in disciplinary cases involving members of that church.

Presbytery

b. (1) The presbytery has original jurisdiction in disciplinary cases involving teaching elder members of that presbytery and ruling elders commissioned to pastoral service in congregations in the presbytery. (G-3.0307)

(2) A teaching elder engaged in work within the **geographic** bounds of a presbytery other than the presbytery of membership, whether that work is under the jurisdiction of the presbytery or not, does, by engaging in that work, submit to the jurisdiction of that presbytery for the purposes of discipline. Should disciplinary process be initiated against a teaching elder under this provision, the presbytery of membership shall be notified. **The presbytery within whose bounds the teaching elder is engaged in work may, alternatively, choose to cede jurisdiction to the presbytery of membership, or choose to cooperate with the presbytery of membership in any disciplinary inquiry, alternative form of resolution, or trial.** This paragraph shall not apply if the teaching elder is working in a validated ministry **in other service of this church such as a staff member of a council beyond the session, or of an organization related to one of these councils; or in an organization sponsored by two or more denominations, one of which is this church, such as a joint congregational witness church, a specialized ministry, an administrative office, an interdenominational agency; or as a partner in mission in connection with a church outside the United States of America.**

Presbytery, Synod,
General Assembly

c. The presbytery, the synod, and the General Assembly have jurisdiction in remedial cases (D-6.0000) and in appeals (D-8.0000 and D-13.0000).

Church Is
Dissolved

d. When a church is dissolved, the presbytery shall determine any case of discipline begun by the session and not concluded.

D-3.0102
No Further
Judicial Action

When a case, either remedial or disciplinary, has been transmitted to a permanent judicial commission, the electing council shall take no further judicial action on the case.

D-3.0103
Lower Council
Fails to Act

When a lower council fails to act in a particular remedial or disciplinary case for a period of ninety days after the filing of a complaint in a remedial case or charges in a disciplinary case, the higher council, on the request of any party, may assume jurisdiction in the case. It may either issue specific instructions to the lower council as to its disposition or conclude the matter itself.

D-3.0104
Jurisdiction Over
Transferred
Teaching Elders

A teaching elder transferred from one presbytery to another presbytery shall be subject to the jurisdiction of the first until received by the second. A teaching elder transferred by a presbytery to another denomination shall be subject to the jurisdiction of the presbytery until received by that denomination.

D-3.0105
Enforce and
Recognize
Judgments and
Decisions

Each council shall enforce and recognize the judgments, decisions, and orders of every other council acting under the provisions of the Rules of Discipline.

D-3.0106
When
Jurisdiction Ends

Jurisdiction in judicial process ends when a person in an ordered ministry or a member renounces the jurisdiction of the church. Should the accused in a disciplinary case renounce the jurisdiction of the church as provided in G-2.0407 or G-2.0509, the clerk or stated clerk shall report to the council both the renunciation and the status of the matter at that time, including the name of the accused, the date and fact of renunciation during an investigation or trial, and the charges filed.

CHAPTER IV

D-4.0000   **REFERENCE**

D-4.0100   1.   **Reference**

D-4.0101   A reference is a written request, made by a session or a per-
Definition   manent judicial commission of a presbytery or synod to the per-
                    manent judicial commission of the next higher council, for trial
                    and decision or a hearing on appeal in a remedial or disciplinary
                    case not yet decided.

D-4.0102   A proper subject of reference involves matters or questions
Proper   for which it is desirable or necessary that a higher council decide
Subject   the case.

D-4.0103   With its written request for reference to a higher council, the
Duty of Lower   lower council shall specify its reasons for the request and transmit
Council   the whole record of proceedings in the case and shall take no fur-
                    ther action thereon. If the reference is accepted, all proceedings,
                    including the trial or hearing on appeal, shall thereafter be held in
                    the higher council.

D-4.0200   2.   **Action on Reference**

D-4.0201   Upon receipt of a request for reference, the stated clerk of the
Duty of Higher   higher council shall transmit the request to the permanent judicial
Council   commission for a decision whether or not to accept the case.

D-4.0202   If the permanent judicial commission decides to accept the
Acceptance   reference, it shall proceed to trial and decision or to a hearing on
                    appeal.

D-4.0203   The permanent judicial commission may refuse to accept the
Refusal   case for reference and return it to the lower council, stating its
                    reasons for refusal. The lower council shall then conduct the trial
                    or hearing on appeal and proceed to a decision.

CHAPTER V

D-5.0000

PERMANENT JUDICIAL COMMISSIONS

D-5.0100

1. Service on Permanent Judicial Commissions

D-5.0101
Election

The General Assembly, each synod **or cooperating synods**, and each presbytery shall elect a permanent judicial commission from the teaching elders and ruling elders subject to its jurisdiction. Each commission shall be composed of teaching elders and ruling elders in numbers as nearly equal as possible. When the commission consists of an odd number of members, the additional member may be either a teaching elder or a ruling elder. The General Assembly commission shall be composed of one member from each of its constituent synods. The synod commission shall be composed of no fewer than eleven members distributed equally, insofar as possible, among the constituent presbyteries. In those synods with fewer than eleven presbyteries, each presbytery shall have at least one member. **When two or more synods form a shared permanent judicial commission, the commission shall be composed of no fewer than twelve members, with each synod electing members proportional to the number of the presbyteries in each synod, insofar as possible. The cooperating synods shall designate between them one stated clerk to process the cases filed with the shared permanent judicial commission**. The presbytery commission shall be composed of no fewer than seven members, with no more than one of its ruling elder members from any one of its constituent churches. Two of the members of the presbytery commission shall be designated to review any petition for review of the procedures of the investigating committee while the investigation in a disciplinary case is in process (D-10.0204) and to review any petition for review of the decision not to file charges (D-10.0303). These two members shall not take part in any subsequent trial. A session shall refer either form of petition to the presbytery commission.

D-5.0102
Term

The term of each member of a permanent judicial commission shall be six years, with the exception that membership on the Permanent Judicial Commission of the General Assembly shall end when that member transfers membership to a church or presbytery outside the synod from which nominated. In each even-numbered year, the General Assembly shall elect members for a term of six years to fill the vacancies then occurring. Their terms of office will begin with the dissolution of the General Assembly at which they are elected.

D-5.0103
Classes

In synods and presbyteries, commissioners shall be elected in three classes, with no more than one half of the members to be in one class. When established for the first time, one class shall serve for two years, the second class for four years, and the third class for six years.

D-5.0104
Vacancy

Any vacancy due to resignation, death, or any other cause may be filled by the electing council, which may elect a person to fill the unexpired term at any meeting thereof.

D-5.0105
Eligibility

No person who has served on a permanent judicial commission for a full term of six years shall be eligible for reelection until four years have elapsed after the expired six-year term. No person shall serve on more than one permanent judicial commission at the same time. No person shall serve on the Permanent Judicial Commission of the General Assembly who is a member of any other entity elected by the General Assembly until that person shall have resigned such membership. The moderator, stated clerk, or any member of the staff of a council or the staff of any of its entities shall not serve on its permanent judicial commission.

D-5.0106
Commission
Expenses

All necessary expenses of a permanent judicial commission shall be paid by the electing council **or councils. Cooperating synods shall pay the necessary expenses of a shared permanent judicial commission equally; however, each synod shall pay the necessary expenses for processing a particular judicial case arising within its bounds**.

D-5.0200   2. **Meetings**

D-5.0201
Officers

Each permanent judicial commission shall meet and elect from its members a moderator and a clerk.

D-5.0202
Bases of Power

In the cases transmitted to it, the permanent judicial commission shall have only the powers prescribed by and conduct its proceedings according to the Constitution of the Presbyterian Church (U.S.A.).

D-5.0203
Meetings

The meetings of the permanent judicial commission shall be held at such times and places as the electing council **or councils** shall direct, or, if no directions are given, at such times and places as the commission shall determine.

D-5.0204
Quorum

The quorum of a permanent judicial commission shall be a majority of the members, except that the quorum of a presbytery commission for a disciplinary case shall be a majority of the membership other than the two members assigned responsibilities under D-10.0204 or D-10.0303. The quorum of a session for judicial process shall be the moderator of the session and a majority of the ruling elder members.

D-5.0205
Who Shall Not
Participate

When a church or lower council is a party to a case, members of a permanent judicial commission who are members of that church, or of that lower council, or of churches within that lower council shall not participate in the trial or appeal of that case.

D-5.0206
Lack of Quorum

If, through absence, disqualification, or disability, a sufficient number of the members of a permanent judicial commission are not present to constitute a quorum, the permanent judicial commission shall recess until a quorum can be obtained.

Inability to Reach
a Quorum

a.   The permanent judicial commission shall report its inability to reach a quorum to the stated clerk **designated for processing the cases**.

Roster of Former
Members

b.   The **designated** stated clerk shall keep a current roster of those members of the permanent judicial commission whose terms have expired within the past six years. The names shall be arranged alphabetically within classes beginning with the most recent class. Whenever the permanent judicial commission reports its inability to obtain a quorum, the stated clerk shall immediately select, by rotation from that roster, a sufficient number of former members of the permanent judicial commission to constitute a quorum. The stated clerk shall report the roster annually to the council **or councils**.

Participant
Expenses

c.   If a permanent judicial commission is unable to try a case for lack of a quorum, the council **in whose geographic boundary the case arose** shall reimburse the expenses reasonably incurred by those persons required to be present.

CHAPTER VI

D-6.0000   REMEDIAL CASES

D-6.0100   1.   **Initiating a Remedial Case and Obtaining a**
                          Stay of Enforcement

D-6.0101   A remedial case is initiated by the filing of a complaint with the
Method of   stated clerk of the council having jurisdiction. **If a different clerk has**
Initiation   **been designated to process judicial cases for a shared judicial**
                     commission, the stated clerk having jurisdiction shall immediately
                     transmit the complaint to the clerk.

D-6.0102   A complaint is a written statement alleging an irregularity in a
Definition of   particular decision or action, or alleging a delinquency. (D-2.0202)
Complaint   The filing of a complaint does not, by itself, stay enforcement of the
                     decision or action.

D-6.0103   A stay of enforcement is a written instruction from the perma-
Stay of   nent judicial commission having jurisdiction that orders the suspen-
Enforcement   sion of a decision or an action until a complaint or appeal is finally
                     determined.

Time Limit to   a.   No later than thirty (30) days after the alleged irregular ac-
File a Request   tion of the council or the remedial decision of a permanent judicial
for a Stay   commission being appealed, a person having standing to file a com-
                     plaint or appeal may simultaneously file either a complaint or an ap-
                     peal, and a request for a stay of enforcement with the stated clerk of
                     the council having jurisdiction to hear the case. The request may be
                     made in the following manner:

                          (1)   A request signed by one third of the members recorded
                     as present when the decision or action was made by the council;

                          (2)   A request signed by one third of the members of the
                     permanent judicial commission that decided the remedial case; or

                          (3)   A request signed by the complainant or appellant re-
                     questing that at least three members of the permanent judicial com-
                     mission having jurisdiction to hear the complaint or appeal sign the
                     stay of enforcement.

Request Given   b.   The complaint or appeal shall be promptly transmitted by the
to Moderator   most expeditious means available by the stated clerk along with the
and Clerk   request for a stay of enforcement to the permanent judicial commission
                     moderator and clerk for their determination as to:

                          (1)   whether the complaint or appeal meets the preliminary is-
                     sues in D-6.0305 or D- 8.0301, and

(2) if the request is made under D-6.0103a(1) or D-6.0103a(2), either:

(a) whether the request made under D-6.0103a(1) is complete and timely, including validation of the signatures and intent of those who signed; or

(b) whether the request made under D-6.0103a(2) is complete and timely.

Time Line for
Preliminary
Questions

c. The moderator and clerk of the permanent judicial commission within seven (7) days after their receipt of the request shall report their findings to the permanent judicial commission and the parties.

Time Line for
Entering a Stay
of Enforcement

d. The permanent judicial commission may enter a stay of enforcement within ten (10) days of the moderator and clerk's findings in the following manner:

(1) By the moderator and the clerk in determining that the request made under D-6.0103a(1) or D-6.0103a(2) is complete and timely and the preliminary issues are met for the complaint or appeal.

(2) If the request is made under D-6.0103(a)(3), by three members of the permanent judicial commission filing with the stated clerk of the council that has jurisdiction to hear the case a statement that in his or her judgment substantial harm will occur if the action or decision is not stayed and that in her or his judgment probable grounds exist for finding the decision or action erroneous. Each permanent judicial commission member must include a summary of the specific council action or decision being stayed.

Distribution
of Stay

e. The stated clerk shall send a copy of the stay of enforcement to the parties and to the permanent judicial commission members.

Effective Time

f. The stay of enforcement shall be effective until the time for filing a complaint or notice of appeal shall have expired or, if timely filed, until the decision of the permanent judicial commission having jurisdiction over the case, except as hereafter provided.

Objection to Stay
of Enforcement

g. The respondent may, within forty-five days of the filing of a stay of enforcement, file with the permanent judicial commission having jurisdiction over the case an objection to the stay of enforcement, whereupon no fewer than three members of such permanent judicial commission shall conduct a hearing on all of the issues relating to the stay of enforcement. The parties may be present or represented at such hearing. At such hearing, the stay of enforcement may be modified, terminated, or continued until the decision on the merits of the case by the permanent judicial commission.

D-6.0200   2.   **Filing a Complaint in a Remedial Case**

D-6.0201   In a remedial case the party or parties filing the complaint shall
Parties   be known as the complainant or complainants and the party or parties
                     against whom the complaint is made shall be known as the respond-
                     ent or respondents.

D-6.0202   A complaint of an irregularity or a complaint of a delinquency
Who May File   may be filed by one or more persons or councils subject to and sub-
Complaint   mitting to the jurisdiction of a council.

Against   a.   In the instance of a complaint against a presbytery, a synod,
Presbytery,   or by a council against another council at the same level, a complaint
Synod, or   of an irregularity shall be filed within ninety days after the alleged
Council at   irregularity has occurred; and a complaint of a delinquency shall be
Same Level   filed within ninety days after failure or refusal of respondent to cure
                     the alleged delinquency at its next meeting, provided that a written
                     request to do so has been made prior to said meeting. Those eligible
                     to file such a complaint are

                          (1) a teaching elder or a ruling elder enrolled as a member
                     of a presbytery concerning an irregularity or a delinquency during
                     that period of enrollment, against the presbytery, with the synod;

                          (2) a commissioner to a synod, concerning an irregularity or
                     a delinquency during that commissioner's period of enrollment,
                     against the synod, with the General Assembly;

                          (3) a session against the presbytery, with the synod;

                          (4) a presbytery against the synod, with the General Assembly;

                          (5) any council against any other council of the same level,
                     with the council immediately higher than the council complained
                     against and to which the latter council is subject;

                          (6) a person who is an employee of a presbytery, a synod
                     or cooperating synod, or an entity of a presbytery or synod, claim-
                     ing to have sustained injury or damage to person or property by the
                     council or entity, against the presbytery, with the synod, or against
                     the synod **or cooperating synod**, with the General Assembly.

Against Session or   b.   In the instance of a complaint against a session, the Presby-
Presbyterian   terian Mission Agency, or an entity of the General Assembly, a com-
Mission Agency or   plaint of an irregularity shall be filed within ninety days after the al-
Entity   leged irregularity has occurred; and a complaint of a delinquency
                     shall be filed within ninety days after failure or refusal of respondent
                     to cure the alleged delinquency at its next meeting, provided that a
                     written request to do so has been made prior to said meeting. Those
                     eligible to file such a complaint are

(1) a member of a particular church against the session of that church, with the presbytery;

(2) a session, a presbytery, or a synod against the Presbyterian Mission Agency or an entity of the General Assembly, with the General Assembly;

(3) a person who is an employee of the Presbyterian Mission Agency or an entity of the General Assembly, claiming to have sustained injury or damage to person or property by the Presbyterian Mission Agency or an entity of the General Assembly, with the General Assembly;

(4) a person who is an employee of a particular church claiming to have sustained injury or damage to person or property by the session or an entity of the session against the session of the church, with the presbytery.

D-6.0300   3. **Pretrial Procedures**

D-6.0301   A complaint shall state the following:
Statements in
Complaint   a.   The name of the complainant and the name of the respondent.

b.   The particular irregularity including the date, place, and circumstances thereof; or the particular delinquency including the dates of the written request to cure the delinquency and of the next meeting at which the respondent failed to do so.

c.   The reasons for complaint of the irregularity or delinquency.

d.   The interest or relationship of the complainant, showing why that party has a right to file the complaint.

e.   The relief requested.

f.   That a copy of the complaint has been delivered to the respondent by certified delivery or personal service. The complainant shall file with the stated clerk of the higher council a receipt signed by the addressee or an affidavit of personal service.

D-6.0302   When a council, the Presbyterian Mission Agency, or an entity
Committee   of the General Assembly becomes either a complainant or a respond-
of Counsel   ent, it shall designate no more than three persons to be a committee of
                      counsel. This committee shall represent that complainant or respond-
                      ent in the case until final decision is reached in the highest council to
                      which the case is appealed.

Provide by Rule   a.   A council, the Presbyterian Mission Agency, or an entity of the General Assembly may provide by rule for the appointment of a committee of counsel.

Shall Not Serve	b. The clerk of session, the stated clerk, or executive of presbytery or synod shall not serve on a committee of counsel of the council served.
D-6.0303 Answer to Complaint	The committee of counsel of the respondent shall file with the stated clerk of the higher council a concise answer within forty-five days after receipt of the complaint, and shall furnish a copy of the answer to the complainant. The answer shall admit those facts alleged in the complaint that are true, deny those allegations that are not true or are mistakenly stated, and present other facts that may explain the situation identified as an irregularity or delinquency. The answer may also raise any issues mentioned in D-6.0305 and may include a motion to dismiss the complaint.
D-6.0304 Procedure Prior to Trial	When the complaint and answer have been filed with the stated clerk of the higher council, the stated clerk shall transmit them at once to the officers of the permanent judicial commission of the council and shall give notice to the parties that the case has been received.
D-6.0305 Examination of Papers	Upon receiving the papers specified in D-6.0304, the moderator and the clerk of the permanent judicial commission of the body that will try the case shall promptly examine the papers to determine whether

  a. the council has jurisdiction;

  b. the complainant has standing to file the case;

  c. the complaint was timely filed; and

  d. the complaint states a claim upon which relief can be granted.

D-6.0306 Preliminary Questions Determined	The moderator and clerk shall report their findings to the parties and to the permanent judicial commission.

  a. If a challenge is made to the findings of the moderator and clerk within thirty days after receipt of those findings, either by a party to the case or by a member of the permanent judicial commission, opportunity shall be provided to present evidence and argument on the finding in question. Parties shall be invited to submit briefs prior to the hearing on the jurisdictional questions.

  b. If a hearing is necessary to decide the finding in question, that hearing shall be scheduled at least thirty days prior to the trial on the complaint, unless the circumstances, including monetary considerations, render advisable the disposition of the preliminary questions immediately before the trial on the complaint.

  c. If the permanent judicial commission determines that any point listed in D-6.0305 has been answered in the negative, the permanent judicial commission shall dismiss the case.

d.   If no challenge is made to a finding of the moderator and clerk that one or more points listed in D-6.0305 (or D-8.0301, or D-13.0106, as applicable) has been answered in the negative, the case shall be dismissed without further action or order of the permanent judicial commission.

D-6.0307
Duty of
Respondent Clerk
of Session or
Stated Clerk

a.   Within forty-five days after the receipt of a complaint, the clerk of session or stated clerk of the respondent council or the respondent entity or council shall list in writing to the parties all of the papers and other materials pertaining to the case.

Minutes and
Papers

b.   Within fifteen days thereafter, the complainant may request in writing that the respondent file additional minutes or papers pertaining to the case.

c.   Upon notification by the stated clerk of the higher council of jurisdiction that the case has been accepted, the clerk of session or stated clerk of the respondent shall transmit to the stated clerk of the higher council without delay the minutes and papers pertaining to the case, along with the list of the record and any requests for additional papers which, if available, shall be included.

D-6.0308
Procedure
for Records

When the minutes and papers have been filed with the stated clerk of the higher council, the stated clerk shall transmit them to the permanent judicial commission and give notice to the parties of an estimated date for trial.

D-6.0309
Trial Briefs

The permanent judicial commission may require either party in an original proceeding to file a trial brief outlining the evidence to be produced and the theory upon which the evidence is considered to be relevant.

D-6.0310
Pretrial
Conference

At any time after a case is received by a permanent judicial commission, the commission may provide by rule for the parties or their counsel, if any, to explore settlement possibilities; or, in a pretrial conference, to seek agreement on a statement of facts and disputed issues, to exchange documents and other evidence, and to take other action which might reasonably and impartially narrow the dispute and expedite its resolution.

CHAPTER VII

D-7.0000

TRIAL IN A REMEDIAL CASE

D-7.0100

1. **Conduct of Trial**

D-7.0101
Trial—Remedial

The trial of a remedial case shall be conducted by a permanent judicial commission.

D-7.0102
Conducted
Formally

The trial shall be conducted formally with full decorum in a neutral place suitable to the occasion.

D-7.0200

2. **Citations and Testimony**

D-7.0201
Citation of Parties
and Witnesses

Citations to appear at trial for parties or such witnesses as either party may request shall be signed by the moderator or clerk of the permanent judicial commission, who shall cause them to be served.

Members Cited

a. Only members of the Presbyterian Church (U.S.A.) may be cited to appear.

Others Requested

b. Other persons can only be requested to attend.

Witnesses
from Another
Council

c. When it is necessary in the trial to summon witnesses who are under the jurisdiction of another council of the church, the clerk or stated clerk of the other council shall, on the application of the permanent judicial commission trying the case, issue a citation to the witnesses to appear at the place of trial and give evidence as may be required.

Expenses

d. Any witness shall be entitled to receive from the party calling the witness reimbursement for expenses incurred in attendance at the trial.

D-7.0202
Service of
Citation

A citation shall be delivered by personal service or by certified delivery. The moderator or clerk of the permanent judicial commission trying the case shall certify the fact and date of service or delivery.

D-7.0203
Second Citation

If a party or a witness who is a member of the Presbyterian Church (U.S.A.) fails to obey a citation, a second citation shall be issued accompanied by a notice that if the party or witness does not appear at the time appointed, unless excused for good cause, the party or witness shall be considered guilty of disobedience and contempt, and for such offense may be subject to disciplinary action.

D-7.0204
Refusal of
Witness to
Testify

A member of the Presbyterian Church (U.S.A.) who, having been summoned as a witness and having appeared, refuses without good cause to testify, and, after warning, continues to refuse may be subject to disciplinary action.

D-7.0205
Deposition

Testimony by deposition may be taken and received in accordance with the provisions of D-14.0304.

D-7.0300

3. Procedures in Trial

D-7.0301
Counsel

Each of the parties in a remedial case shall be entitled to appear and may be represented by counsel, provided, however, that no person shall act as counsel who is not a member of the Presbyterian Church (U.S.A.). No member of a permanent judicial commission shall appear as counsel before that commission while a member.

D-7.0302
Circulation
of Materials

No party to a remedial case or any other person shall circulate or cause to be circulated among the members of the permanent judicial commission any written, printed, or visual materials of any kind upon any matter pertaining to the case before the final disposition thereof. Notwithstanding this prohibition, the permanent judicial commission may request, or grant leave to file, additional materials.

D-7.0303
Control Conduct
of Trial

The permanent judicial commission shall have full authority and power to control the conduct of the trial and of all parties, witnesses, counsel, and the public, including removal of them, to the end that proper dignity and decorum shall be maintained.

Questions as
to Procedure

a.   Questions as to procedure or the admissibility of evidence arising in the course of a trial shall be decided by the moderator after the parties have had an opportunity to be heard. A party or a member of the permanent judicial commission may appeal from the decision of the moderator to the commission, which shall decide the question by majority vote.

Absences

b.   The absence of any member of the permanent judicial commission after a trial has commenced shall be recorded. That person shall not thereafter participate in that case.

D-7.0304
Loss of
Quorum

Loss of a quorum shall result in a mistrial and the case shall be tried again from the beginning.

D-7.0400

4. Trial

D-7.0401
Procedure in a
Remedial Case

The trial of a remedial case shall proceed as follows:

Announcement by
the Moderator

a.   The moderator shall read aloud sections D-1.0101 and D-1.0102, shall announce that the council is about to proceed to trial, and shall enjoin the members to recollect and regard their high character as judges of a council of the Church of Jesus Christ and the solemn duties they are about to undertake.

Eligibility of
Commission
Members

b. The parties or their counsel may object and be heard on the organization and jurisdiction of the permanent judicial commission.

Disqualification

(1) A member of a permanent judicial commission is disqualified if the member is personally interested in the case, is related by blood or marriage to any party, has been active for or against any party, or is ineligible under the provisions of D-5.0205.

Challenges

(2) Any member of a permanent judicial commission may be challenged by any party, and the validity of the challenge shall be determined by the remaining members of the permanent judicial commission.

Procedural
Objections

c. The permanent judicial commission shall determine all preliminary objections, and any other objections affecting the order or regularity of the proceedings.

Amend
Complaint

d. The complainant shall be permitted to amend the complaint at the time of the trial, provided that the amendment does not change the substance of the complaint or prejudice the respondent.

Opening
Statements

e. The parties shall be given an opportunity to make opening statements.

Rules of Evidence

f. The rules of evidence in D-14.0000 shall be followed.

Evidence

g. Evidence as is deemed necessary or proper, if any, shall be presented on behalf of the complainant and the respondent.

Final Statements

h. The parties shall be given an opportunity to make final statements, the complainant having the right of opening and closing the argument.

D-7.0402
Decision

The permanent judicial commission shall then meet privately. All persons not members of the commission shall be excluded.

Deliberation

a. No complaint in a remedial case shall be sustained unless it has been proved by a preponderance of the evidence. Preponderance means such evidence as, when weighed with that opposed to it, has more convincing force and the greater probability of truth. After careful deliberation the commission shall vote on each irregularity or delinquency assigned in the complaint and record the vote in its minutes.

Decision

b. The permanent judicial commission shall then decide the case. If the complaint is sustained either in whole or in part, the commission shall either order such action as is appropriate or direct the lower council to conduct further proceedings in the matter.

Written Decision   c.   A written decision shall be prepared while in session, and shall become the final decision when a copy of the written decision is signed by the moderator and clerk of the permanent judicial commission. A copy of the written decision shall immediately be delivered to the parties to the case by personal service or by certified delivery.

Filed Promptly   d.   Within thirty days of the conclusion of the trial, the decision shall be filed with the stated clerk of the council that appointed the permanent judicial commission.

Further Publicity   e.   The moderator or clerk of the permanent judicial commission shall disseminate the decision as the permanent judicial commission may direct.

D-7.0500   **5.   Provisions for Appeal**

D-7.0501   For each party, the time for filing an appeal shall run from the date the decision is delivered to, or refused by, that party.
Appeal Time

D-7.0502   An appeal may be initiated only by one or more of the original parties. Rules of appeal are found in D-8.0000.
Appeals

D-7.0600   **6.   Record of Proceedings**

D-7.0601   The clerk of the permanent judicial commission shall do the following:
Record of
Proceedings

Verbatim   a.   Arrange in advance for the accurate verbatim recording of all testimony and oral proceedings.
Recording

Exhibits   b.   Identify and maintain all exhibits offered in evidence (noting whether or not they were accepted as evidence) and keep a list of all exhibits;

Minutes   c.   Record minutes of the proceedings, which shall include any actions or orders of the permanent judicial commission relating to the case with the vote thereon.

Record   d.   Prepare the record of the case, which shall consist of

(1) the complaint and the answer thereto;

(2) all minutes and papers filed in the case;

(3) a certified transcript, if requested;

(4) all properly marked exhibits, records, documents, and other papers;

(5) the written decision; and

(6) any actions or orders of the permanent judicial commission relating to the case with the vote thereon.

Preservation
e.   Within fourteen days after the decision becomes final, certi-fy and transmit the record of the case to the stated clerk of the elect-ing council, who shall preserve it for at least two years.

Transcript
f.   Upon the request, and at the expense of any requesting party, cause to be prepared, as promptly as circumstances permit, a true and complete transcript of all the testimony and oral proceedings during the course of the trial. A copy of this transcript, when certified by the person making the same to be true and complete, shall be delivered to each party requesting the same upon satisfactory arrangement for payment, and one additional copy shall be made for inclusion in the record to be sent forward upon any appeal pursuant to D-8.0000.

D-7.0602
Additions to
the Record

No person may supplement or add to the record in a case except for good cause as determined by the moderator and clerk of the per-manent judicial commission responsible for conducting the trial. No request to supplement the record shall be considered until received in writing by the stated clerk of the lower council, who shall transmit it to the moderator and clerk of the permanent judicial commission. A copy of the request shall be delivered to all parties and every party shall have ten days to respond in writing.

D-7.0700   **7.   Duty of Stated Clerk**

D-7.0701
Reporting
the Decision

If the council is meeting when the decision is received from the clerk of the permanent judicial commission, the stated clerk shall report the decision immediately and enter the full decision upon the minutes of the council. If the council is not meeting, the stated clerk shall report the decision to the council at its first stated or adjourned meeting thereafter, or at a meeting called for that purpose, and enter the full decision upon the minutes of the council.

CHAPTER VIII

D-8.0000   **APPEAL IN A REMEDIAL CASE**

D-8.0100   **1. Initiation of an Appeal**

D-8.0101   An appeal of a remedial case is the transfer to the next higher
Definition   council of a case in which a decision has been rendered in a lower
                    council, for the purpose of obtaining a review of the proceedings and
                    decision to correct, modify, set aside, or reverse the decision.

D-8.0102   An appeal may be initiated only by one or more of the original
Initiation   parties in the case, and is accomplished by the filing of a written no-
of Appeal   tice of appeal.

D-8.0103   The notice of appeal shall not suspend any further action imple-
Effect of   menting the decision being appealed unless a stay of enforcement has
Appeal   been obtained in accordance with the provisions of D-6.0103.

D-8.0104   On application, the permanent judicial commission of the higher
Withdrawal   council may grant a petition for withdrawal of an appeal. The perma-
of Appeal   nent judicial commission shall deny a petition if its approval would
                    defeat the ends of justice.

D-8.0105   The grounds for appeal are
Grounds for
Appeal   a.   irregularity in the proceedings;

                    b.   refusing a party reasonable opportunity to be heard or to ob-
                    tain or present evidence;

                    c.   receiving improper, or declining to receive proper, evidence
                    or testimony;

                    d.   hastening to a decision before the evidence or testimony is
                    fully received;

                    e.   manifestation of prejudice in the conduct of the case;

                    f.   injustice in the process or decision; and

                    g.   error in constitutional interpretation.

D-8.0200   **2. Filings in Appeal Process**

D-8.0201   A written notice of appeal shall be filed within forty-five days af-
Time for Filing   ter a copy of the judgment has been delivered by certified delivery or
Written Notice   personal service to the party appealing.
of Appeal

                    a.   The written notice of appeal shall be filed with the stated
                    clerk of the lower council which elected the permanent judicial com-
                    mission from whose judgment the appeal is taken.

b.   The party appealing shall provide a copy of the notice of appeal to each of the other parties and to the stated clerk of the council which will hear the appeal.

D-8.0202
Content of
Written Notice
of Appeal

The written notice of appeal shall state and include

a.   the name of the party or parties filing the appeal, called the appellant or appellants, and their counsel if any;

b.   the name of the other party or parties, called the appellee or appellees, and their counsel if any;

c.   the council from whose judgment the appeal is taken;

d.   the judgment or decision, and date and place thereof, from which the appeal is taken (enclose a copy of the judgment or decision with the notice of appeal);

e.   a statement of the errors of the permanent judicial commission which conducted the trial or hearing on appeal that are the grounds for the appeal (D-8.0105); and

f.   a certification that a copy of the notice of appeal was provided by certified delivery or by personal service to each of the other parties and to the stated clerk of the council that will hear the appeal.

D-8.0203
Transmittal of
Notice of Appeal
to Officers

Upon receipt of the notice of appeal and the decision being appealed, the stated clerk of the higher council shall transmit them to the officers of the permanent judicial commission.

D-8.0300   3.   **Prehearing Proceedings**

D-8.0301
Examination
of Papers

Upon receiving the papers specified in D-8.0203, the moderator and the clerk of the permanent judicial commission of the council that will hear the case shall promptly examine the papers to determine whether

a.   the council has jurisdiction;

b.   the appellant has standing to file the appeal;

c.   the appeal papers were properly and timely filed; and

d.   the appeal states one or more of the grounds for appeal set forth in D-8.0105.

D-8.0302
Preliminary
Questions
Determined

The moderator and clerk shall report their findings to the parties and to the permanent judicial commission.

a.   If a challenge is made to the findings of the moderator and clerk within thirty days after receipt of those findings, either by a party to the case or by a member of the permanent judicial commission, opportunity shall be provided to present evidence and argument on the finding in question.

b.   If a hearing is necessary to decide the item in question, that hearing shall be scheduled at least thirty days prior to the hearing on the appeal unless the circumstances, including monetary considerations, render advisable the disposition of the preliminary questions immediately before the hearing on the appeal.

c.   If the permanent judicial commission determines that any point listed in D-8.0301 has been answered in the negative, the permanent judicial commission shall dismiss the appeal.

d.   If no challenge is made to a finding of the moderator and clerk that one or more points listed in D-6.0305 (or D-8.0301, or D-13.0106, as applicable) has been answered in the negative, the case shall be dismissed without further action or order of the permanent judicial commission.

D-8.0303
Record on Appeal

The record on appeal shall be formed as follows:

List of Record

a.   Within forty-five days after the receipt of a written notice of appeal, the stated clerk of the lower council shall list in writing to the parties all of the papers and other materials that constitute the record of the case. (D-7.0601d)

Additional
Records

b.   Within fifteen days thereafter, any party may file with the stated clerk of the lower council a written statement challenging the accuracy or completeness of the record of the case as listed by the stated clerk. The written challenge shall state specifically the item or items listed in D-7.0601d which are claimed to be omitted from the record of the case.

Filing of Record
on Appeal

c.   Upon notification by the stated clerk of the higher council of jurisdiction that the case has been accepted, the stated clerk of the lower council shall certify and file the record of the case, which may include authenticated copies of parts of the record, and shall include any written challenges disputing the completeness or accuracy of the record, with the stated clerk of the higher council.

Correction of
the Record

d.   If anything material to either party is omitted from the record by error or accident, or is misstated therein, the omission or misstatement may be corrected. The parties may stipulate to the correction, or the session or permanent judicial commission of the lower council may certify and transmit a supplemental record, or the permanent judicial commission of the higher council may direct that the omission or misstatement be corrected. All other questions as to the form and content of the record shall be presented to the permanent judicial commission of the higher council.

Notice of Date
of Reception

e.   The stated clerk of the higher council shall notify the parties of the date the record on appeal was received.

Copy Furnished
at Cost

f.   Upon written request, the stated clerk of the higher council shall furnish any party to the appeal, at cost to that party, a copy of the record on appeal.

Extension

g.   For good cause shown, the stated clerk of the higher council may extend the time limits in D-8.0303 for a reasonable period.

D-8.0304
Filing of
Appellant's
Brief

Within thirty days after the date of the filing of the record on appeal, the appellant shall file with the stated clerk of the higher council a written brief containing specifications of the errors alleged in the notice of appeal and arguments, reasons, and citations of authorities in support of the appellant's contentions as to the alleged errors specified.

Copy to
Other Party

a.   The brief shall be accompanied by a certification that a copy has been furnished to the other party or parties.

Extension

b.   For good cause shown, the stated clerk of the higher council may extend this time limit for a reasonable period.

Failure to
File Brief

c.   Failure of appellant to file a brief within the time allowed, without good cause, shall be deemed by the permanent judicial commission an abandonment of the appeal.

D-8.0305
Filing of
Appellee's Brief

Within thirty days after the filing of appellant's brief, the appellee shall file with the stated clerk of the higher council a written brief responding thereto.

Copy to
Other Party

a.   The brief shall be accompanied by a certification that a copy has been furnished to the other party or parties.

Extension

b.   For good cause shown, the stated clerk of the higher council may extend this time limit for a reasonable period.

Failure to
File Brief

c.   Failure of appellee to file a brief within the time allowed, without good cause, shall constitute waiver of the rights to file a brief, to appear, and to be heard.

D-8.0306 Transmittal of Record and Briefs	Upon receipt of the record and the briefs, or upon the expiration of the time for filing, the stated clerk of the higher council shall transmit the record and briefs to the clerk of the permanent judicial commission.
D-8.0307 Prehearing Conference	At any time after an appeal is received by a permanent judicial commission, the commission may provide by rule for the parties or their counsel, if any, in a prehearing conference, to seek agreement on any of the disputed issues in the appeal, and to take other action which might reasonably and impartially narrow the dispute and expedite its resolution.

D-8.0400   4. Hearing of Appeal

D-8.0401 Notice of Hearing	The moderator or clerk of the permanent judicial commission shall notify the parties of the date when they may appear in person or by counsel before the permanent judicial commission to present the appeal.
D-8.0402 Failure to Appear	Failure of a party to appear in person or by counsel shall constitute a waiver of participation in the hearing on appeal.
D-8.0403 Hearing	At the hearing the permanent judicial commission shall
New Evidence	a. determine whether to receive newly discovered evidence, under the provisions of D-14.0502, providing for the verbatim recording of such new evidence; and
Hearing	b. give opportunity to be heard on the grounds of the appeal to those parties who have not waived that right, the appellant having the right of opening and closing argument.
D-8.0404 Decision of Permanent Judicial Commission	After the hearing and after deliberation, the permanent judicial commission shall vote separately on each specification of error alleged. The vote shall be on the question, "Shall the specification of error be sustained?" The minutes shall record the numerical vote on each specification of error.
If No Errors Are Found	a. If not one of the specifications of error is sustained, and no other error is found, the decision of the lower council shall be affirmed.
If Errors Are Found	b. If one or more errors are found, the permanent judicial commission shall determine whether the decision of the lower council shall be affirmed, modified, set aside, reversed, or the case remanded for a new trial.

Written Decision

    c.   A written decision shall be prepared while in session, and shall become the final decision when a copy of the written decision is signed by the moderator and clerk of the permanent judicial commission. A copy of the decision shall immediately be delivered to the parties to the case by personal service or by certified delivery.

Determination
of Each Error

    d.   The decision shall include the determination of errors specified, and state the remedy as provided in D-8.0101. The permanent judicial commission may prepare its decision in a manner that will dispose of all substantive questions without redundancy. It may include an explanation of its determination.

Filed Promptly

    e.   Within thirty days of the conclusion of the hearing, the decision shall be filed with the stated clerk of the council that appointed the permanent judicial commission.

Further Publicity

    f.   The moderator or clerk of the permanent judicial commission shall disseminate the decision as the permanent judicial commission may direct.

CHAPTER IX

D-9.0000

REQUEST FOR VINDICATION

D-9.0101
Request for
Vindication

A member of the Presbyterian Church (U.S.A.) who feels injured by rumor or gossip may request an inquiry for vindication by submitting to the clerk of session or stated clerk of the presbytery a clear narrative and statement of alleged facts.

Review by
Council

a.   If a council, through its appropriate committee, finds it proper to grant the request, it shall proceed with an investigating committee as provided in D-10.0201.

Investigating
Committee

b.   The investigating committee shall conduct an inquiry to ascertain the facts and circumstances and report in writing to the council.

D-9.0102
Concludes Matter
Unless Charges
Filed

The report shall conclude the matter, unless the investigating committee reports that charges are being filed against the person requesting vindication. If charges are to be filed, the matter shall proceed with appropriate judicial process beginning with D-10.0402.

CHAPTER X

D-10.0000

DISCIPLINARY CASES

D-10.0100

1. Procedure Preliminary to a Disciplinary Case

D-10.0101
Initiation of
Preliminary
Procedures

Procedure preliminary to a disciplinary case is initiated by submitting to the clerk of session or the stated clerk of the presbytery having jurisdiction over the member (D-3.0101) a written statement of an alleged offense, together with any supporting information. The statement shall give a clear narrative and allege facts that, if proven true, would likely result in disciplinary action. Such allegations shall be referred to an investigating committee. (D-10.0201)

D-10.0102
Statement of
Offense

The written statement may be submitted by

Accusation

a. a person under jurisdiction of a council of the Presbyterian Church (U.S.A.) making an accusation against another;

Council

b. a member of a council receiving information from any source that an offense may have occurred which should be investigated for the purpose of discipline; or

Self-Accusation

c. a person under jurisdiction of a council of the Presbyterian Church (U.S.A.) coming forward in self-accusation.

D-10.0103
Referral to
Investigating
Committee

Upon receipt of a written statement of an alleged offense, the clerk of session or the stated clerk of presbytery, without undertaking further inquiry, shall then report to the council only that an offense has been alleged without naming the accused or the nature of the alleged offense, and refer the statement immediately to an investigating committee.

D-10.0104
Accusation from
Other Council

When a member is accused of an offense by a written statement presented to a council other than the one having jurisdiction over the member, it shall be the duty of the clerk of that session or the stated clerk of that presbytery to submit the written statement to the clerk of session or the stated clerk of the presbytery having jurisdiction over the member. The involved councils shall proceed cooperatively with judicial process.

D-10.0105
Transfer
Prohibited

A session shall not grant a certificate of transfer to a member, nor shall a presbytery grant a certificate of transfer to a teaching elder, while an inquiry or charges are pending. The reasons for not granting transfer may be communicated by the clerk of session or the stated clerk of the presbytery to the appropriate persons.

D-10.0106
Administrative
Leave

When a written statement of an alleged offense of sexual abuse toward any person has been received against a teaching elder, the stated clerk receiving the allegation shall immediately communicate the allegation to the permanent judicial commission. The moderator of the permanent judicial commission shall within three days designate two members, who may be from the roster of former members of the permanent judicial commission, to determine whether the accused shall be placed on a paid administrative leave during the resolution of the matter. The cost of such shall be borne by the employing entity whenever possible or be shared by the presbytery as necessary. While administrative leave is in effect, a teaching elder may not perform any pastoral, administrative, educational, or supervisory duties, and may not officiate at any functions such as Baptism, funerals, or weddings.

a.   The designated members of the permanent judicial commission, after giving the accused the opportunity to be heard, shall determine whether the risk to the congregation and to potential victims of abuse, when considered in light of the nature and probable truth of the allegations, requires administrative leave or other restrictions upon the teaching elder's service. Such administrative leave or restrictions will continue until resolution of the matter in one of the ways prescribed in the Rules of Discipline or the leave or restrictions are altered or removed by the designated members of the commission.

b.   If the designated members of the commission determine that no administrative leave or restriction is required, the investigating committee appointed to investigate the allegations shall be free at any point in its investigation to present additional evidence to the designated members supporting the imposition of administrative leave or other restrictions.

D-10.0200   **2.   Investigation**

D-10.0201
Investigating
Committee

An inquiry shall be made by an investigating committee designated by the council having jurisdiction over the member to determine whether charges should be filed.

Membership

a.   An investigating committee shall have no more than five but no less than three members, and may include members from another council, if appropriate, in accordance with D-10.0104. A session shall not appoint members of the session as members of the investigating committee.

Appointment
by Rule

b.   A presbytery may provide by rule for appointment of an investigating committee.

Expenses

c. The expenses of an investigating committee shall normally be paid by the council having designated it. If, however, the written statement results from information presented to a council other than the one having jurisdiction over a member, the council within whose bounds the alleged offense occurred shall pay for the expenses of investigating within its bounds.

D-10.0202
Investigating
Committee
Responsibilities

The investigating committee shall

a. review the statement of alleged offense to determine whether it alleges any facts that, if true, constitute an offense as defined in D-2.0203b. If no offense as defined in D-2.0203b is alleged, the investigating committee shall end its inquiry and report that to the clerk of the body. If an offense as defined in D-2.0203 is alleged, it shall proceed to the steps below.

b. provide the accused with a copy of the statement of alleged offense described in D-10.0101;

c. provide the person making the accusation with a statement of the investigating committee's procedures;

d. determine whether the accusation repeats allegations previously made against the accused, and if so, report to the council having jurisdiction over the accused that it will not file charges (D-10.0202k) unless the accusation contains new information warranting investigation or is the subject of an investigation that has not been concluded.

e. make a thorough inquiry into the facts and circumstances of the alleged offense;

f. examine all relevant papers, documents, and records available to it;

g. ascertain all available witnesses and inquire of them;

h. determine, in accordance with G-3.0102 and D-2.0203b, whether there are probable grounds or cause to believe that an offense was committed by the accused;

i. decide whether the charge(s) filed—on the basis of the papers, documents, records, testimony, or other evidence—can reasonably be proved, having due regard for the character, availability, and credibility of the witnesses and evidence available;

j. initiate, if it deems appropriate, alternative forms of resolution, ordinarily after the investigation has been completed, probable cause has been determined, but before the charges have been filed.

The purpose of alternative forms of resolution will be to determine if agreement can be reached between the investigating committee and the accused concerning any charges which may be filed.

(1) Any mediation shall be completed within 120 days unless a continuance is allowed by the session or permanent judicial commission.

(2) The investigating committee shall report any settlement agreement to the session or permanent judicial commission for its approval.

(3) The session or permanent judicial commission shall convene to receive the settlement agreement; vote to approve it by at least two-thirds of the members eligible to vote; make a record of its proceedings according to the provisions of D-11.0601d, including the name of the accused, the substance of the charge(s), and censure; and transmit its decision to the clerk of session or the stated clerk, who shall report it according to the provisions of D-11.0701.

(4) The investigating committee shall provide an advocate for the accused throughout settlement negotiations, and may provide an advocate for other interested persons at its own discretion.

(5) If a settlement satisfactory to both the investigating committee and the accused in the alternative form of resolution is not reached, the investigating committee shall designate a prosecuting committee per D-10.0202l, and the case shall proceed on the charges filed.

k. report to the council having jurisdiction over the accused only whether or not it will file charges; and

Designate Prosecuting Committee

l. if charges are to be filed, prepare and file them in accordance with the provisions of D-10.0401–.0404, and designate one or more persons (to be known as the prosecuting committee) from among its membership to prosecute the case.

D-10.0203 Rights of the Accusor

a. The investigating committee shall inform the person making the accusation of the right to be accompanied by an advocate at each and every conference between the person making the accusation and the investigating committee, the prosecuting committee, and the session or permanent judicial commission. The role of the advocate is to provide support and consultation.

Rights of the Person Alleging Harm

b. If the statement of accusation is submitted on behalf of another person who is alleged to have been harmed by the offense, the investigating committee shall notify that person of the right to be accompanied by an advocate at each and every conference with the investigating committee, the prosecuting committee, and the session or permanent judicial commission.

Rights of the
Person Alleged
Against

c.   At the beginning of each and every conference with an investigating committee or any of its members, the person against whom an allegation has been made shall be informed by the investigating committee or its members of the right to remain silent, to be represented by counsel, and, if charges are later filed, to have counsel appointed if unable to secure counsel. (D-11.0301–.0302)

D-10.0204
Petition
Commission
to Review
Procedures

During the course of the investigation, the person against whom an allegation has been made may petition the commission to review procedures of the investigating committee. Proper subjects for such a petition shall be limited to whether the committee has followed a proper trail of evidence, whether the evidence being considered is properly in the hands of the investigating committee, and whether the committee has examined relevant evidence proposed by the accused.

a.   The review of the petition shall be done in a hearing conducted by the two members of the commission designated according to D-5.0101, at which both parties may be present and represented by counsel. The hearing shall be conducted within thirty days of receipt of the petition. Decisions shall be communicated to both parties within fifteen days of the hearing.

b.   The results of the review shall be communicated to the moderator of the commission and will inform the review of charges in D-10.0405.

D-10.0300

3.   Communicate Determination

D-10.0301
Communicate
Determination

If the investigating committee initiates an alternative form of resolution, it shall notify the council through its clerk of session or stated clerk.

D-10.0302
If Charges Are
to Be Filed

If the investigating committee has decided to file charges, it shall promptly inform the accused in writing of the charges it will make, including a summary of the facts it expects to prove at trial to support those charges. It shall ask the accused if that person wishes to plead guilty to the charges to avoid full trial and indicate the censure it will recommend to the session or permanent judicial commission.

D-10.0303
Petition for
Review

If no charges are filed, the investigating committee shall file a written report of that fact alone with the clerk of session or stated clerk of the presbytery, and notify the person who submitted the written statement.

a.   Within 30 days of receipt of the report, that person may petition the session or the permanent judicial commission to review the decision of the investigating committee not to file charges. The petition shall allege those instances in which the investigating committee has not fulfilled the duties specified in D-10.0202.

b.   The investigating committee shall submit a written response to the facts alleged in the petition.

c.   The designated members of the permanent judicial commission shall consider the petition and the response, giving attention to the duties specified in D-10.0202 and to the question of whether the principles of church discipline will be preserved by the decision of the investigating committee not to file charges. The decision of the designated members of the commission upon the petition and response shall be rendered within ninety days.

d.   If they sustain the petition, a new investigating committee shall be appointed by the session or presbytery.

e.   If once again no charges are filed, the matter is concluded.

f.   If charges are filed, consideration shall be given to the possibility of reference. (D-4.0000)

**D-10.0304
Disposition
of Records**

If no charges are filed, the disposition of the investigating committee's records shall be in accordance with session or presbytery policy.

D-10.0400

4.   Charges

**D-10.0401
Time Limit**

No charges shall be filed later than five years from the time of the commission of the alleged offense, nor later than one year from the date the investigating committee was formed, whichever occurs first, except as noted below.

a.   In those situations where civil proceedings have commenced, the investigating committee may request of its permanent judicial commission or session and receive an extension of its time for filing charges of up to six months from the conclusion of any investigation or resulting trial undertaken by the civil authorities. The investigating committee shall maintain contact with civil authorities to determine when such civil proceedings have concluded.

b.   For instances of sexual abuse of another person, the five-year time limit shall not apply. Charges may be brought regardless of the date on which an offense is alleged to have occurred.

c.   Sexual abuse of another person is any offense involving sexual conduct in relation to

(1) any person under the age of eighteen years or anyone over the age of eighteen years without the mental capacity to consent; or

(2) any person when the conduct includes force, threat, coercion, intimidation, or misuse of ordered ministry or position.

[*Historical Note*: The original text of D-10.0401c was stricken by action of the 214th General Assembly (2002).]

D-10.0402 Prosecution of Case	If charges are filed, the prosecuting committee shall prosecute the case and represent the church during any appeals. (D-10.0202h)
Parties	a.　All disciplinary cases shall be filed and prosecuted by a council through an investigating committee and a prosecuting committee in the name of the Presbyterian Church (U.S.A.). The prosecuting committee is the representative of the church and, as such, has all of the rights of the appropriate council in the case.
Only Two Parties	b.　The only parties in a disciplinary case are the prosecuting council and the accused.
D-10.0403 Form of Charge	Each charge shall allege only one offense. (D-2.0203b)
Several Together	a.　Several charges against the same person may be filed with the council at the same time.
Details of the Charge	b.　Each charge shall be numbered and set forth the conduct that constituted the offense. Each charge shall state (as far as possible) the time, place, and circumstances of the commission of the alleged conduct. Each charge shall also be accompanied by a list of the names and addresses of the witnesses for the prosecution and a description of the records and documents to be cited for its support.
Tried Together	c.　Several charges against the same person may, in the discretion of the session or permanent judicial commission, be tried together.
D-10.0404 Filing of Charge	Every charge shall be prepared in writing and filed with the clerk of session or stated clerk of the presbytery.
Session	a.　Upon receipt of a charge, the clerk of a session shall present the charge to the session at its next meeting. The session shall determine whether it will try the case or refer it to the presbytery. (D-4.0000)
Presbytery	b.　Upon receipt of a charge, the stated clerk of the presbytery shall immediately forward it to the moderator or clerk of the permanent judicial commission of that presbytery.
D-10.0405 Pretrial Conference	The session or permanent judicial commission, which is to try the case, shall hold a pretrial conference not later than thirty days after receipt of the charge(s).
Time and Place	a.　The moderator and clerk of the session or of the permanent judicial commission shall notify the accused, the counsel for the accused, if any, and the prosecuting committee of the time and place of the pretrial conference, and shall furnish the accused with a copy of the charge(s).

Those Present   b.   At the time set for the pretrial conference, the moderator and clerk of session or of the permanent judicial commission, the prosecuting committee, the accused, counsel for the accused, if any, and other appropriate persons at the discretion of the moderator and clerk shall ordinarily be present. The moderator shall

(1) read the charges to the accused;

(2) inform the accused of the right to counsel (D-11.0301);

(3) furnish the accused with the names and addresses of all the witnesses then known, and a description of the records and documents that may be offered to support each charge;

(4) determine with the accused and the prosecuting committee those charges that are not in dispute and discuss alternatives to a full trial;

(5) review any reports of petitions for review of the work of the investigating committee, hear any additional challenges to the appropriateness of charges, taking preliminary actions to dismiss some or all of the charges, dismiss the case, or permit amendments to the charges. Such preliminary determinations shall be reviewed by the session or permanent judicial commission in accord with D-11.0402c.

(6) schedule a trial to be held no sooner than thirty days following the pretrial conference, or, if all parties agree on those facts contained in the charges that are true and on a recommended degree of censure, schedule a censure hearing;

(7) order all parties to appear.

Nothing More   c.   Nothing more shall be done at that meeting.

D-10.0406   The accused shall provide a list of anticipated witnesses, includ-
Witnesses   ing addresses, to the clerk of session or permanent judicial commis-
Disclosed   sion and the prosecuting committee at least twenty days prior to the trial date. The prosecuting committee and the accused shall each provide the session or permanent judicial commission and the other party with an updated list of witnesses no less than ten days prior to the trial date.

CHAPTER XI

D-11.0000   **TRIAL IN A DISCIPLINARY CASE**

D-11.0100   1. **Conduct of Trial**

D-11.0101   The trial of a disciplinary case shall be conducted by a session or
Trial—Disciplinary   by a permanent judicial commission.

D-11.0102   The trial shall be conducted formally with full decorum in a neu-
Conducted   tral place suitable to the occasion.
Formally

D-11.0200   2. **Citations and Testimony**

D-11.0201   Citations to appear at trial for parties or such witnesses as either
Citation of Parties   party may request shall be signed by the moderator or clerk of the
and Witnesses   session or permanent judicial commission.

Members Cited   a.   Only members of the Presbyterian Church (U.S.A.) may be
                      cited to appear.

Others Requested   b.   Other persons can only be requested to attend.

Witnesses from   c.   When it is necessary in the trial to summon witnesses who
Another   are under the jurisdiction of another council of the church, the clerk
Council   or stated clerk of the other council shall, on the application of the
                      session or permanent judicial commission trying the case, issue a
                      citation to the witnesses to appear at the place of trial and give evi-
                      dence as may be required.

Expenses   d.   Any witness shall be entitled to receive from the party call-
                      ing the witness reimbursement for expenses incurred in attendance at
                      the trial.

D-11.0202   A citation shall be delivered by personal service or by certified
Service of   delivery. The moderator or clerk of the session or permanent judi-
Citation   cial commission trying the case shall certify the fact and date of
                      service or delivery.

Second Citation   a.   If a party or a witness who is a member of the Presbyterian
                      Church (U.S.A.) fails to obey a citation, a second citation shall be
                      issued accompanied by a notice that if the party or witness does not
                      appear at the time appointed, unless excused for good cause shown,
                      the party or witness shall be considered guilty of disobedience and
                      contempt, and for such offense may be subject to disciplinary action.

Accused Does   b.   If an accused in a disciplinary case does not appear after a
Not Appear   second citation, the session or permanent judicial commission, after

having appointed some person or persons to represent the accused as counsel, may proceed to trial and judgment in the absence of the accused.

D-11.0203
Refusal of Witness
to Testify

A member of the Presbyterian Church (U.S.A.) who, having been summoned as a witness and having appeared, refuses without good cause to testify, and, after warning, continues to refuse may be subject to disciplinary action.

D-11.0204
Deposition

Testimony by deposition may be taken and received in accordance with the provisions of D-14.0304.

D-11.0300

3. Procedures in Trial

D-11.0301
Counsel

Each of the parties in a disciplinary case shall be entitled to appear and may be represented by counsel, provided, however, that no person shall act as counsel who is not a member of the Presbyterian Church (U.S.A.). No member of a permanent judicial commission shall appear as counsel before that commission while a member. Counsel need not be a paid representative or attorney-at-law.

D-11.0302
Unable to
Secure Counsel

If the accused in a disciplinary case is unable to secure counsel, the session or permanent judicial commission shall appoint counsel for the accused. Reasonable expenses for defense shall be authorized and reimbursed by the council in which the case originated.

D-11.0303
Circulation
of Materials

No party to a disciplinary case or any other person shall circulate or cause to be circulated among the members of the session or permanent judicial commission any written, printed, or visual materials of any kind upon any matter pertaining to the case before the final disposition thereof. Notwithstanding this prohibition, the session or permanent judicial commission may request, or grant leave to file, additional materials.

D-11.0304
Control Conduct
of Trial

The session or permanent judicial commission shall have full authority and power to control the conduct of the trial and of all parties, witnesses, counsel, and the public, including removal of them, to the end that proper dignity and decorum shall be maintained.

Questions as to Procedure

a.   Questions as to procedure or the admissibility of evidence arising in the course of a trial shall be decided by the moderator after the parties have had an opportunity to be heard. A party or a member of the session or permanent judicial commission may appeal from the decision of the moderator to the session or commission, which shall decide the question by majority vote.

Absences

b.   The absence of any member of the session or permanent judicial commission after a trial has commenced shall be recorded. That person shall not thereafter participate in that case.

D-11.0305
Loss of Quorum

Loss of a quorum shall result in a mistrial and the case shall be tried again from the beginning.

D-11.0306
Closed
Proceedings

The proceedings shall ordinarily be conducted in open session; however, at the request of any party, or on its own initiative, the session or permanent judicial commission may determine at any stage of the proceedings, by a vote of two thirds of the members present, to exclude persons other than the parties and their counsel.

D-11.0400

4.   Trial

D-11.0401
Presumption
of Innocence

The accused in a disciplinary case is presumed to be innocent until the contrary is proved, and unless guilt is established beyond a reasonable doubt, the accused is entitled to be found not guilty.

D-11.0402
Procedure in a
Disciplinary Case

The trial of a disciplinary case shall proceed as follows:

Announcement by
the Moderator

a.   The moderator shall read aloud sections D-1.0101 and D-1.0102, shall announce that the council is about to proceed to trial, and shall enjoin the members to recollect and regard their high character as judges of a council of the Church of Jesus Christ and the solemn duties they are council about to undertake.

Eligibility of
Commission
Members

b.   The parties or their counsel may object and be heard on the organization and jurisdiction of the session or permanent judicial commission.

Disqualification

(1)   A member of a session or permanent judicial commission is disqualified if the member is personally interested in the case, is related by blood or marriage to any party, has been active for or against any party, or is ineligible under the provisions of D-5.0205.

Challenges

(2)   Any member of a session or permanent judicial commission may be challenged by any party, and the validity of the challenge shall be determined by the remaining members of the session or permanent judicial commission.

Preliminary
Objections

c.   The session or permanent judicial commission shall determine all preliminary objections and any other objection affecting the order or regularity of the proceedings. It may dismiss the case or permit amendments to the charges in the furtherance of justice, provided that such amendments do not change the substance of the charges or prejudice the accused.

Plea

     d.   If the proceedings are found to be in order, and the charges are considered sufficient, the accused shall be called upon to plead "guilty" or "not guilty" to each charge. The plea shall be entered on the record. If the accused declines to answer or pleads "not guilty," a plea of "not guilty" shall be entered on the record and the trial shall proceed. If the accused pleads "guilty," the council shall proceed in accordance with D-11.0403.

Opening
Statements

     e.   The parties shall be given an opportunity to make opening statements.

Rules of Evidence

     f.   The rules of evidence in D-14.0000 shall be followed.

Prosecution

     g.   The prosecuting committee shall present its evidence in support of the charges, subject to objection and cross-examination by the accused.

Defense

     h.   The accused shall have the opportunity to present evidence, subject to objection and cross-examination by the prosecuting committee.

Rebuttal

     i.   The prosecuting committee then may introduce additional evidence, but only to rebut evidence introduced on behalf of the accused. This additional evidence is subject to objection and cross-examination by the accused.

Final Statements

     j.   The parties shall be given an opportunity to make final statements. The prosecuting committee shall have the right of opening and closing the argument.

D-11.0403
Decision

The session or permanent judicial commission shall then meet privately. All persons not members of the session or permanent judicial commission shall be excluded.

Beyond a
Reasonable
Doubt

     a.   After careful deliberation, the session or permanent judicial commission shall vote on each charge separately and record the vote in its minutes. In order to find the accused guilty of a charge, the session or permanent judicial commission must find that the pertinent facts within that charge have been proven beyond a reasonable doubt. Proof beyond a reasonable doubt occurs when the comparison and consideration of all the evidence compels an abiding conviction that the material facts necessary to prove the charge are true.

Judgment of
Guilt by a
Two-thirds Vote

     b.   No judgment of guilt may be found on a charge unless at least two thirds of the members of the session or permanent judicial commission eligible to vote agree on the judgment.

Written Decision

     c.   A written decision stating the judgment on each charge and the determination of the degree of censure, if any, shall be prepared while in session. It shall become the final decision when signed by the moderator and clerk of the session or of the permanent judicial commission.

Announcement in Open Meeting

d. When a session or permanent judicial commission has arrived at a decision, the moderator shall, in open meeting, announce the verdict for each charge separately.

Degree of Censure

e. If the accused is found guilty or after the guilty plea, the session or permanent judicial commission should hear evidence as to the extent of the injury suffered, mitigation, rehabilitation, and redemption. This evidence may be offered by either party, or the original accuser, or that person's representative. The person who was directly harmed by the offense may submit a victim impact statement. The statement shall not be subject to cross-examination. The session or permanent judicial commission shall then meet privately to determine the degree of censure to be imposed. (D-12.0000) Following such determination and in an open meeting, the moderator of the session or permanent judicial commission shall then pronounce the censure.

Filed Promptly

f. The decision shall be filed promptly with the clerk or stated clerk of the council.

Notification of Parties

g. The clerk of session or clerk of the permanent judicial commission shall deliver a copy of the decision to each party named in the decision either by personal service or by certified delivery.

Further Publicity

h. The moderator or clerk of session or of the permanent judicial commission shall disseminate the decision as the session or permanent judicial commission may direct.

D-11.0500

5. Provisions for Appeal

D-11.0501 Appeal Time

The time for filing an appeal shall run from the date the decision is delivered to, or refused by, the person found guilty.

D-11.0502 Appeals

Either party may initiate the first level of appeal. Either party may initiate an appeal of the appellate decision. Rules of appeal are found in D-13.0000.

D-11.0600

6. Record of Proceedings

D-11.0601 Record of Proceedings

The clerk of session or the clerk of the permanent judicial commission shall do the following:

Verbatim Recording

a. Arrange in advance for the accurate verbatim recording of all testimony and oral proceedings.

Exhibits   b.   Identify and maintain all exhibits offered in evidence (noting whether or not they were accepted as evidence) and keep a list of all exhibits.

Minutes   c.   Record minutes of the proceedings, which shall include any actions or orders of the session or permanent judicial commission relating to the case with the vote thereon.

Record   d.   Prepare the record of the case, which shall consist of

(1) the charges;

(2) a record of the plea entered by the accused on each charge;

(3) a certified transcript, if requested;

(4) all properly marked exhibits, records, documents, and other papers;

(5) the written decision, including the verdict for each charge and the degree of censure, if any, to be imposed by the council; and

(6) any actions or orders of the session or permanent judicial commission relating to the case, with the vote thereon.

Preservation of   e.   Preserve the original of all records in the following manner:
the Record

(1) The clerk of session shall, after the decision becomes final, retain the record of the case for at least two years.

(2) The clerk of the permanent judicial commission shall, within fourteen days after the decision becomes final, certify and transmit the record of the case to the stated clerk of the electing council, who shall preserve it for at least two years.

Transcript   f.   Upon the request, and at the expense of any requesting party, cause to be prepared, as promptly as circumstances permit, a true and complete transcript of all the testimony and oral proceedings during the course of the trial. A copy of this transcript, when certified by the person making the same to be true and complete, shall be delivered to each party requesting the same upon satisfactory arrangement for payment, and one additional copy shall be made for inclusion in the record to be sent forward upon any appeal pursuant to D-13.0000.

D-11.0602   No person may supplement or add to the record in a case except
Additions to   for good cause as determined by the moderator and clerk of the session or of the permanent judicial commission responsible for conducting the trial. No request to supplement the record shall be considered until received in writing by the clerk of session or the stated
the Record

clerk of the lower council who shall transmit it to the moderator of the session or moderator and clerk of the permanent judicial commission. A copy of the request shall be delivered to all parties and every party shall have ten days to respond in writing.

D-11.0700

D-11.0701
Reporting the
Decision

7. Duty of Stated Clerk

If the presbytery is meeting when the decision is received from the clerk of the permanent judicial commission, the stated clerk shall read the decision to the presbytery immediately and enter the full decision upon the minutes of the presbytery. If the presbytery is not meeting, the stated clerk shall read the decision to the presbytery at its first stated or adjourned meeting thereafter, or at a meeting called for that purpose, and enter the full decision upon the minutes of the presbytery.

D-11.0800

D-11.0801
Enforcement by
Council

8. Enforcement

When a session has completed the trial and found the accused guilty and the decision has been pronounced, or when the stated clerk of a higher council has received the decision of its permanent judicial commission in which the accused was found guilty, the session or higher council shall proceed to enforce the decision. The person against whom the decision has been pronounced shall refrain from the exercise of ordered ministry or from participating and voting in meetings, according to the situation, until an appeal has been decided or the time for appeal has expired, unless the session or the presbytery specifically grants a request to allow the person to continue in ordered ministry pending an appeal.

CHAPTER XII

D-12.0000

CENSURE AND RESTORATION
IN A DISCIPLINARY CASE

D-12.0100

1. Censures

D-12.0101
Degrees of
Church Censure

The degrees of church censure are rebuke, rebuke with supervised rehabilitation, temporary exclusion from exercise of ordered ministry or membership, and removal from ordered ministry or membership.

D-12.0102
Rebuke

Rebuke is the lowest degree of censure for an offense and is completed when pronounced. (D-11.0403e) It consists of setting forth publicly the character of the offense, together with reproof, which shall be pronounced in the following or like form:

> Whereas, you, (Name) _____, have been found guilty of the offense(s) of _____
> (here insert the offense), and by such offense(s) you have acted contrary to (the Scriptures and/or the Constitution of the Presbyterian Church (U.S.A.)); now, therefore, the Presbytery (or Session) of _____, in the name and authority of the Presbyterian Church (U.S.A.), expresses its condemnation of this offense, and rebukes you. You are enjoined to be more watchful and avoid such offense in the future. We urge you to use diligently the means of grace to the end that you may be more obedient to our Lord Jesus Christ.

Prayer

This formal rebuke shall be followed by intercessory prayer to Almighty God.

D-12.0103
Rebuke with
Supervised
Rehabilitation

Rebuke with supervised rehabilitation is the next to lowest degree of censure. It consists of setting forth the character of the offense, together with reproof and mandating a period of supervised rehabilitation imposed by the session or the permanent judicial commission (D-11.0403e). This censure shall be pronounced in the following or like form.

> Whereas, you (Name) _____ have been found guilty in the offense(s) of _____
> and by such offense(s) you have acted contrary to the Scriptures and/or the Constitution of the Presbyterian Church (U.S.A.); now, therefore, the Permanent Judicial Commission (or Session) of _____, in the name and authority of the Presbyterian Church (U.S.A.) expresses its condemnation of this offense, rebukes you, and orders you to complete a program of supervised rehabilitation supervised by

_____ as described below:
_____.

You are enjoined to be more watchful and avoid such offense in the future. We urge you to use diligently the means of grace to the end so that you may be more obedient to our Lord Jesus Christ.

a.   The rebuke shall be followed by intercessory prayer to Almighty God.

b.   The session or permanent judicial commission shall formally communicate to the supervising entity and the person censured the goals of the rehabilitation and the specific authority conferred on the supervisor(s).

c.   The description of the rehabilitation program shall include a clear statement of how progress will be evaluated and how it will be determined when and if the supervised rehabilitation has been satisfactorily completed.

d.   In a case in which the offense is sexual abuse of another person, the rehabilitation program may include the advice that the person found guilty complete a voluntary act or acts of repentance. Such acts may include: public acknowledgement of guilt, community service, symbolic restoration of what was lost by the person who was harmed, and/or contributions toward documented medical/psychological expenses incurred by the person who was harmed.

D-12.0104
Temporary
Exclusion

Temporary exclusion from the exercise of ordered ministry or membership is a higher degree of censure for a more aggravated offense and shall be for a definite period of time, or for a period defined by completion of supervised rehabilitation imposed by the session or the permanent judicial commission. (D-11.0403e) This censure shall be pronounced in the following or like form:

Whereas, you, (Name) _____, have been found guilty of the offense(s) of _____, (here insert the offense), and by such offense(s) you have acted contrary to (the Scriptures and/or the Constitution of the Presbyterian Church (U.S.A.)); now, therefore, the Presbytery (or Session) of _____, in the name and by the authority of the Presbyterian Church (U.S.A.), does now declare you temporarily excluded from _____ for a period of _____, or until completion of the following rehabilitation program supervised by _____, as described below:

_____
_____.

Prayer	a. This formal declaration shall be followed by intercessory prayer to Almighty God.
Supervised Rehabilitation	b. If the period of temporary exclusion is defined by completion of supervised rehabilitation, the session or permanent judicial commission shall formally communicate to the supervising entity and the person found guilty the specific authority conferred on the supervisor.
Duty to Report	c. In a case in which the offense is sexual abuse of another person, the rehabilitation program may include the advice that the person found guilty complete a voluntary act or acts of repentance. Such acts may include: public acknowledgement of guilt, community service, symbolic restoration of what was lost by the person harmed, and/or contributions toward documented medical/psychological expenses incurred by the person who was harmed.
Refrain from Exercise of Ordered Ministry	d. During the period of temporary exclusion from ordered ministry, the person found guilty shall refrain from the exercise of any function of ordered ministry.
Cannot Vote or Hold Office	e. During the period of temporary exclusion from membership, the person found guilty shall refrain from participating and voting in meetings and from holding or exercising any office.
Effect of Temporary Exclusion of a Pastor	f. If a pastor is temporarily excluded from the exercise of ordered ministry, the presbytery may, if no appeal from the case is pending, declare the pastoral relationship dissolved.
Notice of Temporary Exclusion	g. When the censure of temporary exclusion has been pronounced with respect to a teaching elder, the stated clerk of the presbytery shall immediately send the information of the action taken to the Stated Clerk of the General Assembly, who shall make a quarterly report of all such information to every presbytery of the church.
Termination of Censure of Temporary Exclusion	h. A person under the censure of temporary exclusion shall apply in writing to the council, through the clerk of session or stated clerk, for restoration upon the expiration of the time of exclusion or completion of the supervised rehabilitation pronounced. The council that imposed the censure shall approve the restoration when the time of exclusion has expired or when the council is fully satisfied that the supervised rehabilitation pronounced has been completed.
Early Restoration	i. A person under the censure of temporary exclusion from the exercise of ordered ministry or from membership may apply in writing to the council that imposed the censure (through its clerk) to be

restored prior to the expiration of the time of exclusion or the completion of the supervised rehabilitation fixed in the censure. The council may approve such a restoration when it is fully satisfied that the action is justified.

**D-12.0105
Removal from
Ordered Ministry
or Membership**

Removal from ordered ministry or membership is the highest degree of censure.

**Removal from
Ordered Ministry**

a.   Removal from ordered ministry is the censure by which the ordination and election of the person found guilty are set aside, and the person is removed from all ordered ministries without removal from membership.

**Removal from
Membership**

b.   Removal from membership is the censure by which the membership of the person found guilty is terminated, the person is removed from all rolls, and the person's ordination and election to all ordered ministries are set aside.

This censure shall be pronounced in the following or like form:

Whereas, you, (Name) _____, have been found guilty of the offense(s) of _____ (here insert the offense), and by such offense(s) you have acted contrary to (the Scriptures and/or the Constitution of the Presbyterian Church (U.S.A.)); now, therefore, the Presbytery (or Session) of _____, acting in the name and under the authority of the Presbyterian Church (U.S.A.), does hereby set aside and remove you from _____ (here state whether removal is from all ordered ministries and elected offices or from membership, which includes removal from all ordered ministries).

Prayer

c.   This formal declaration shall be followed by intercessory prayer to Almighty God.

**Consequences
of Removal
from Ordered
Ministry**

d.   If a teaching elder is removed from ordered ministry without removal from membership, the presbytery shall give the teaching elder a certificate of membership to a Christian church of the teaching elder's choice. If the teaching elder is a pastor, the pastoral relationship is automatically dissolved by the censure.

**Notice of
Removal**

e.   When the censure of removal has been pronounced with respect to a teaching elder, the stated clerk of that presbytery shall immediately send the information of the action taken to the Stated Clerk of the General Assembly, who shall make a quarterly report of all such information to every presbytery of the church.

D-12.0200	**2. Restoration**
D-12.0201 Decision of Council	A person under the censure of removal from ordered ministry or from membership may be restored by the council imposing the censure when the council is fully satisfied that the action is justified and the person makes a reaffirmation of faith for membership restoration or is reordained for restoration to ordered ministry. The forms of the restoration are described in D-12.0202 and D-12.0203.
D-12.0202 Form of Restoration to Ordered Ministry After Removal	The restoration to ordered ministry shall be announced by the moderator in the following or like form:
Form	a. Whereas, you, (Name) _____, have manifested such repentance as satisfies the church, the Presbytery of _____ (or Session of this church) does now restore you to the ordered ministry of _____ and authorize you to perform the functions of that ministry in accordance with the Constitution of this church by this act of ordination.
Restored to Roll	b. Thereafter, a full service of ordination shall take place and the name shall be restored to the appropriate roll. (W-4.4000)
D-12.0203 Form of Restoration to Membership after Removal	The restoration to membership shall be announced by the moderator in a meeting of the council in the following or like form:
Form	a. Whereas, you, (Name) _____, have manifested such repentance as satisfies the church, the Presbytery (or Session) of _____ does now restore you to full membership in the church by this act of reaffirmation.
Restored to Roll	b. Thereafter, the act of reaffirmation shall take place and the name of the person shall be restored to the appropriate roll or a certificate of membership shall be issued to a Christian church of that person's choice.
Restored to Ordered Ministry	c. If the member is also to be restored to an ordered ministry, the procedure prescribed in D-12.0202 shall be followed.

CHAPTER XIII

D-13.0000

APPEAL IN A DISCIPLINARY CASE

D-13.0100

1. Initiation of Appeal

D-13.0101
Definition

An appeal of a disciplinary case is the transfer to the next higher council of a case in which a decision has been rendered in a lower council, for the purpose of obtaining a review of the proceedings and decision to correct, modify, set aside, or reverse the decision.

D-13.0102
Initiation
of Appeal

Only the person found guilty may initiate the first level of appeal by the filing of a written notice of appeal.

D-13.0103
Appeal of
Appellate
Decision

Either party may initiate an appeal of the appellate decision by the filing of a written notice of appeal.

D-13.0104
Effect of
Appeal

The notice of appeal, if properly and timely filed, shall suspend further proceedings by lower councils, except that, in the instance of temporary exclusion from exercise of ordered ministry or membership or removal from ordered ministry or membership, the person against whom the judgment has been pronounced shall refrain from the exercise of ordered ministry or from participating and voting in meetings until the appeal is finally decided.

D-13.0105
Withdrawal
of Appeal

On application, the permanent judicial commission of the higher council may grant a petition for withdrawal of an appeal. The permanent judicial commission shall deny a petition if its approval would defeat the ends of justice.

D-13.0106
Grounds for
Appeal

The grounds for appeal are

a. irregularity in the proceedings;

b. refusing a party reasonable opportunity to be heard or to obtain or present evidence;

c. receiving improper, or declining to receive proper, evidence or testimony;

d. hastening to a decision before the evidence or testimony is fully received;

e. manifestation of prejudice in the conduct of the case;

f. injustice in the process or decision;

g.   error in constitutional interpretation; and

h.   undue severity of censure.

D-13.0200   **2.   Filings in Appeal Process**

D-13.0201   A written notice of appeal shall be filed within forty-five days af-
Time for Filing   ter a copy of the judgment has been delivered by certified delivery or
Written Notice   personal service to the party appealing.
of Appeal

a.   The written notice of appeal shall be filed with the clerk of
session or stated clerk of the lower council that elected the permanent
judicial commission from whose judgment the appeal is taken.

b.   The party appealing shall provide a copy of the notice of appeal to each of the other parties and to the stated clerk of the council
that will hear the appeal.

D-13.0202   The written notice of appeal shall state and include
Content of Written
Notice of Appeal   a.   the name of the party or parties filing the appeal, called the
appellant or appellants, and their counsel if any;

b.   the name of the other party or parties, called the appellee or
appellees, and their counsel if any;

c.   the council from whose judgment the appeal is taken;

d.   the judgment or decision, and date and place thereof, from
which the appeal is taken (enclose a copy of the judgment or decision
with the notice of appeal);

e.   a statement of the errors of session or permanent judicial
commission which conducted the trial or hearing on appeal that are
the grounds for the appeal (D-13.0106); and

f.   a certification that a copy of the notice of appeal was provided by certified delivery or by personal service to each of the other
parties and to the stated clerk of the council that will hear the appeal.

D-13.0203   Upon receipt of the notice of appeal and the decision being ap-
Transmittal of   pealed, the stated clerk of the higher council shall transmit them to
Notice of Appeal   the officers of the permanent judicial commission.
to Officers

D-13.0300

D-13.0301
Examination
of Papers

3. Prehearing Proceedings

Upon receiving the papers specified in D-13.0203, the moderator and the clerk of the permanent judicial commission of the council that will hear the case shall promptly examine the papers to determine whether

 a. the council has jurisdiction;

 b. the appellant has standing to file the appeal;

 c. the appeal papers were properly and timely filed; and

 d. the appeal states one or more of the grounds for appeal set forth in D-13.0106.

D-13.0302
Preliminary
Questions
Determined

The moderator and clerk shall report their findings to the parties and to the permanent judicial commission.

 a. If a challenge is made to the findings of the moderator and clerk within thirty days after receipt of those findings, either by a party to the case or by a member of the permanent judicial commission, opportunity shall be provided to present evidence and argument on the finding in question.

 b. If a hearing is necessary to decide the item in question, that hearing shall be scheduled at least thirty days prior to the hearing on the appeal, unless the circumstances, including monetary considerations, render advisable the disposition of the preliminary questions immediately before the hearing on the appeal.

 c. If the permanent judicial commission determines that any point listed in D-13.0301 has been answered in the negative, the permanent judicial commission shall dismiss the appeal.

 d. If no challenge is made to a finding of the moderator and clerk that one or more points listed in D-6.0305 (or D-8.0301, or D-13.0106, as applicable) has been answered in the negative, the case shall be dismissed without further action or order of the permanent judicial commission.

D-13.0303
Record on Appeal

The record on appeal shall be formed as follows:

List of Record

 a. Within forty-five days after the receipt of a written notice of appeal, the clerk of session or stated clerk of the lower council shall list in writing to the parties all of the papers and other materials that constitute the record of the case. (D-11.0601d)

Additional
Records

b.   Within fifteen days thereafter, any party may file with the stated clerk of the lower council a written statement challenging the accuracy or completeness of the record of the case as listed by the stated clerk. The written challenge shall state specifically the item or items listed in D-11.0601d which are claimed to be omitted from the record of the case.

Filing of Record
on Appeal

c.   Upon notification by the stated clerk of the higher council of jurisdiction that the case has been accepted, the stated clerk of the lower council shall certify and file the record of the case, which may include authenticated copies of parts of the record, and shall include any written challenges disputing the completeness or accuracy of the record, with the stated clerk of the higher council.

Correction of
the Record

d.   If anything material to either party is omitted from the record by error or accident or is misstated therein, the omission or misstatement may be corrected. The parties may stipulate to the correction, or the session or permanent judicial commission of the lower council may certify and transmit a supplemental record, or the permanent judicial commission of the higher council may direct that the omission or misstatement be corrected. All other questions as to the form and content of the record shall be presented to the permanent judicial commission of the higher council.

Notice of Date
of Reception

e.   The stated clerk of the higher council shall notify the parties of the date the record on appeal was received.

Copy Furnished
at Cost

f.   Upon written request, the stated clerk of the higher council shall furnish any party to the appeal, at cost to that party, a copy of the record on appeal.

Extension

g.   For good cause shown, the stated clerk of the higher council may extend the time limits in D-13.0303 for a reasonable period.

D-13.0304
Filing of
Appellant's Brief

Within thirty days after the date of the filing of the record on appeal, the appellant shall file with the stated clerk of the higher council a written brief containing specifications of the errors alleged in the notice of appeal and arguments, reasons, and citations of authorities in support of the appellant's contentions as to the alleged errors specified.

Copy to
Other Party

a.   The brief shall be accompanied by a certification that a copy has been furnished to the other party or parties.

Extension

b.   For good cause shown, the stated clerk of the higher council may extend this time limit for a reasonable period.

Failure to File Brief	c. Failure of appellant to file a brief within the time allowed, without good cause, shall be deemed by the permanent judicial commission an abandonment of the appeal.

D-13.0305
Filing of
Appellee's Brief

Within thirty days after the filing of appellant's brief, the appellee shall file with the stated clerk of the higher council a written brief responding thereto.

Copy to
Other Party

a.   The brief shall be accompanied by a certification that a copy has been furnished to the other party or parties.

Extension

b.   For good cause shown, the stated clerk of the higher council may extend this time limit for a reasonable period.

Failure to
File Brief

c.   Failure by appellee to file a brief within the time allowed, without good cause, shall constitute waiver of the rights to file a brief, to appear, and to be heard.

D-13.0306
Transmittal of
Record and Briefs

Upon receipt of the record and the briefs, or upon the expiration of the time for filing them, the stated clerk of the higher council shall transmit the record and briefs to the clerk of the permanent judicial commission.

D-13.0307
Prehearing
Conference

At any time after an appeal is received by a permanent judicial commission, the commission may provide by rule for the parties or their counsel, if any, in a prehearing conference, to seek agreement on any of the disputed issues in the appeal, and to take other action which might reasonably and impartially narrow the dispute and expedite its resolution.

D-13.0400   4.   **Hearing of Appeal**

D-13.0401
Notice of
Hearing

The moderator or clerk of the permanent judicial commission shall notify the parties of the date when they may appear in person or by counsel before the permanent judicial commission to present the appeal.

D-13.0402
Failure to Appear

Failure of a party to appear in person or by counsel shall constitute a waiver of participation in the hearing on appeal.

D-13.0403
Hearing

At the hearing, the permanent judicial commission shall

New Evidence

a.   determine whether to receive newly discovered evidence, under the provisions of D-14.0502, providing for the verbatim recording of such new evidence; and

Hearing

b.   give opportunity to be heard on the grounds of the appeal to those parties who have not waived that right, the appellant having the right of opening and closing the argument.

D-13.0404
Decision of
Permanent Judicial
Commission

After the hearing and after deliberation, the permanent judicial commission shall vote separately on each specification of error alleged. The vote shall be on the question, "Shall the specification of error be sustained?" The minutes shall record the numerical vote on each specification of error. If the appeal was initiated by a prosecuting committee appealing a verdict of not guilty and the permanent judicial commission sustains that portion of the appeal, the permanent judicial commission shall remand the case for a new trial.

If No Errors
Found

a.   If none of the specifications of error is sustained, and no other error is found, the decision of the lower council shall be affirmed.

If Errors
Are Found

b.   If one or more errors are found, the permanent judicial commission shall determine whether the decision of the lower council shall be affirmed, set aside, reversed, modified, or the case remanded for a new trial.

Written Decision

c.   A written decision shall be prepared while in session, and shall become the final decision when a copy of the written decision is signed by the clerk and moderator of the commission.

Determination
of Each Error

d.   The decision shall include the determination of errors specified, and state the remedy as provided in D-13.0101. The permanent judicial commission may prepare its decision in a manner that will dispose of all substantive questions without redundancy. It may include an explanation of its determination.

Filed Promptly

e.   The decision shall be filed promptly with the stated clerk of the council that appointed the permanent judicial commission and the parties to the case by personal service or by certified delivery.

Further Publicity

f.   The moderator or clerk shall disseminate the decision as the commission may direct.

D-13.0405
Effect of Reversal
on Appeal in
Disciplinary Case

When a permanent judicial commission in an appeal in a disciplinary case reverses all findings of guilt, it is in effect an acquittal, and the person is automatically restored to ordered ministry or membership in the church. Declaration to this effect shall be made in the lower council.

CHAPTER XIV

D-14.0000   **EVIDENCE IN REMEDIAL OR DISCIPLINARY CASES**

D-14.0100   1. **Evidence**

D-14.0101
Evidence Defined

Evidence, in addition to oral testimony of witnesses, may include records, writings, material objects, or other things presented to prove the existence or nonexistence of a fact. Evidence must be relevant to be received. No distinction should be made between direct and circumstantial evidence as to the degree of proof required.

D-14.0200   2. **Witnesses**

D-14.0201
Challenge

Any party may challenge the ability of a witness to testify, and the session or permanent judicial commission shall determine the competence of the witness so challenged.

D-14.0202
Husband or Wife

A husband or wife, otherwise competent to testify, may be a witness for or against the other, but neither shall be compelled to testify against the other.

D-14.0203
Counselor

A person duly appointed by a council to provide counseling services for persons within the jurisdiction of the council shall not testify before a session or permanent judicial commission, except that the restriction may be waived by the person about whom the testimony is sought.

D-14.0204
Counsel for
Parties

The counsel for the parties involved in a case may not be compelled to testify about confidential matters, nor may they testify concerning any matters without the express permission of the party they represent.

D-14.0205
Credibility of
Witnesses

Credibility means the degree of belief that may be given to the testimony of a witness. The session or permanent judicial commission may consider, in determining the credibility of a witness, any matter that bears upon the accuracy or truthfulness of the testimony of the witness.

D-14.0300   3. **Testimony**

D-14.0301
Separate
Examination

At the request of either party, no witness shall be present during the examination of another witness. This shall not limit the right of the accused or the committee of counsel of the respondent to be present and to have expert witnesses present.

D-14.0302
Examination
of Witnesses

Witnesses in either disciplinary or remedial cases shall be examined first by the party producing them, and then they may be cross-examined by the opposing party. Thereafter, any member of the session or permanent judicial commission may ask additional questions.

Oath

a. Prior to giving testimony, a witness shall make an oath by answering the following question in the affirmative:

"Do you solemnly swear that the evidence you will give in this matter shall be the truth, the whole truth, and nothing but the truth, so help you God?"

Affirmation

b. If a witness objects to making an oath, the witness shall answer the following question in the affirmative:

"Do you solemnly affirm that you will declare the truth, the whole truth, and nothing but the truth in the matter in which you are called to testify?"

D-14.0303
Record of
Testimony

The testimony of each witness shall be accurately and fully recorded by a qualified reporter or other means.

D-14.0304
Testimony Taken
on Deposition

Any session or permanent judicial commission before which a case may be pending shall have power to appoint, on the application of any party, one or more persons to take and record testimony in the form of a deposition.

Person from
Another
Council

a. When necessary, the person or persons so appointed may be from within the geographical bounds of another council.

Taking of
Testimony

b. Any person so appointed shall take the testimony offered by either party after notice has been given to all parties of the time and place where the witnesses are to be examined. All parties shall be entitled to be present and be permitted to cross-examine.

Offered as
Evidence

c. This testimony, properly authenticated by the signature or signatures of the person or persons so appointed, shall be transmitted promptly to the clerk of the session or permanent judicial commission before which the case is pending and may be offered as evidence by any party.

Questions of
Admissibility

d. All questions concerning the admissibility of statements made in deposition testimony shall be determined by the session or permanent judicial commission when the record of such testimony is offered as evidence.

D-14.0305
Member as
Witness

A member of the session or permanent judicial commission before which the case is pending may testify, but thereafter shall not otherwise participate in the case.

D-14.0400   **4.   Records as Evidence**

D-14.0401   The authenticated written records of a council or permanent judi-
Admissibility   cial commission shall be admissible in evidence in any proceeding.
of Records

D-14.0402   A record or transcript of testimony taken by one council or per-
Admissibility   manent judicial commission and regularly authenticated shall be ad-
of Testimony   missible in any proceeding in another council.

D-14.0500   **5.   New Evidence**

D-14.0501   Prior to filing notice of appeal, but without extending the time
Application for   for appeal, any person convicted of an offense, or any party against
New Trial   whom an order or decision has been entered in a remedial case, may
                   apply for a new trial on the ground of newly discovered evidence.
                   The session or permanent judicial commission—when satisfied that
                   such evidence could reasonably have resulted in a different decision
                   and which, in the exercise of reasonable diligence, could not have
                   been produced at the time of trial—may grant such application.

D-14.0502   If, subsequent to the filing by any party of a notice of appeal,
Consideration   new evidence is discovered, which in the exercise of reasonable dili-
in Appeal   gence could not have been discovered prior to the filing of the notice
                   of appeal, the permanent judicial commission receiving the appeal
                   may, in its discretion, receive the newly discovered evidence and
                   proceed to hear and determine the case. However, no newly discov-
                   ered evidence may be admitted unless the party seeking to introduce
                   it shall have made application, with copies to the adverse party, at
                   least thirty days prior to the hearing. That application shall be accom-
                   panied by a summary of the evidence.

APPENDIXES

The following appendixes have been removed from 2013/2015 version of the *Book of Order*, but can be found at www.pcusa.org/polityresources.

"Form for Judicial Process" (Formerly Appendix A)

"Visible Marks of Churches Uniting in Christ" (Formerly Appendix D)

"About the Presbyterian Church (U.S.A.) Seal" and "About the Use of the Presbyterian Church (U.S.A.) Seal" (Formerly Appendix F)

APPENDIX A

Articles of Agreement Between the Presbyterian Church in the United States and the United Presbyterian Church in the United States of America

ARTICLES OF AGREEMENT

PREAMBLE

The Articles of Agreement embody the contractual commitments of the Presbyterian Church in the United States and The United Presbyterian Church in the United States of America concerning the means by which the confessional documents, members, officers, judicatories, courts, agencies, institutions and property of those Churches shall be and become the confessional documents, members, officers, judicatories, courts, agencies, institutions and property of the Presbyterian Church (U.S.A.). The Articles of Agreement record the details of the reunion. Their contents demonstrate the continuity of the reunited Church with each of its antecedents. The reunited Church will be in all ecclesiastical, judicial, legal and other respects the continuing entity of the Presbyterian Church in the United States and The United Presbyterian Church in the United States of America.

Once the two Churches have approved the plan in accordance with their separate Constitutions and the reunion has been effected, the single reunited Church will come into being and the separate existences of the two Churches will terminate. The two parties to the original agreement will no longer be in existence as separate Churches and hence the agreement cannot thereafter be altered. By the act of reunion, the separate interests of the two parties reflected in the agreement are united in one reunited Church that could not represent the concerns of either predecessor body if some change in the Agreement were proposed.

Immediately upon the formation of the reunited Church, its new Constitution (G-1.0500)[1] will be operative. It, rather than the Articles of Agreement, is the basic document of the single church and is subject to amendment in accordance with its provisions.

---

[1] The following abbreviations are used throughout:
   G - Form of Government
   D - Rules of Discipline
   S - Directory for the Service of God [After 1988 this book is called the Directory for Worship.]

ARTICLE 1. CONTINUITY OF THE PRESBYTERIAN CHURCH (U.S.A.) WITH THE PRESBYTERIAN CHURCH IN THE UNITED STATES AND THE UNITED PRESBYTERIAN CHURCH IN THE UNITED STATES OF AMERICA

1.1   These Articles of Agreement are intended to, and they do, provide for the union of the Presbyterian Church in the United States and The United Presbyterian Church in the United States of America to form one Church which shall be known as the Presbyterian Church (U.S.A.). Whenever it becomes necessary to identify the Presbyterian Church in the United States or The United Presbyterian Church in the United States of American after union, the Presbyterian Church (U.S.A.) is, and shall be, the successor of each and the successor shall have that identity. The history of the Presbyterian Church (U.S.A.) is, and shall embody, the history of the Presbyterian Church in the United States and The United Presbyterian Church in the United States of America. These Articles shall be interpreted consistently with the foregoing. The Presbyterian Church in the United States, The United Presbyterian Church in the United States of America, and the Presbyterian Church (U.S.A.) affirm that it is the intention of each that the Presbyterian Church (U.S.A.), from the time of reunion, shall comprise and be one single ecclesiastical entity which is the continuing Church resulting from the reunion of the Presbyterian Church in the United Sates and The United Presbyterian Church in the United States of America.

1.2   Each and every member of the Presbyterian Church in the United States and of The United Presbyterian Church in the United States of America shall be a member of the Presbyterian Church (U.S.A.)

1.3   Each and every ordained officer, whether minister, ruling elder or deacon, of the Presbyterian Church in the United States and of The United Presbyterian Church in the United States of America shall be the comparable ordained officer of the Presbyterian Church (U.S.A.), minister of the Word, elder or deacon.

1.4   Each and every congregation of the Presbyterian Church in the United States and of The United Presbyterian Church in the United States of America shall be a congregation of the Presbyterian Church (U.S.A.).

1.5   Each and every pastoral relationship between a pastor, co-pastor, associate or assistant pastor and a congregation in the Presbyterian Church in the United States and The United Presbyterian Church in the United States of America shall continue in the Presbyterian Church (U.S.A.). Any existing relationship as lay preacher or commissioned church worker shall be undisturbed by the formation of the Presbyterian Church (U.S.A.), but only for so long as the individual holding such relationship continues that relationship to the same particular church.

1.6   Each and every Session, Presbytery and Synod of the Presbyterian Church in the United States and of The United Presbyterian Church in the United States of America shall be the comparable governing body of the Presbyterian Church (U.S.A.).

1.7   The General Assembly of the Presbyterian Church (U.S.A.) shall be the highest governing body of that Church and the successor to the General Assembly of the Presbyterian Church in the United States and to the General Assembly of The United Presbyterian Church in the United States of America.

1.8   Each and every board, agency, institution and committee of the Presbyterian Church in the United States or of The United Presbyterian Church in the United States of America, or under joint control of the two Churches, shall have the same relationship to the appropriate governing body of the Presbyterian Church (U.S.A.) as it now has to a judicatory of the Presbyterian Church in the United States or of The United Presbyterian Church in the United States of America.

1.9   Each and every policy statement adopted by or issued at the direction of the General Assembly of the Presbyterian Church in the United States or of the General Assembly of The United Presbyterian Church in the United States of America shall have the same force and effect in the Presbyterian Church (U.S.A.) as in the Church which adopted or issued it until rescinded, altered or supplanted by action of the General Assembly of the Presbyterian Church (U.S.A.).

ARTICLE 2. TRUSTEES AND CORPORATE STRUCTURES

2.1   Each and every trustee and corporate structure of the congregations, judicatories, boards, agencies and institutions of the Presbyterian Church in the United States and of The United Presbyterian Church in the United States of America, together with all property, real and personal, held by them shall be the trustees and corporate structures of the congregations, governing bodies, boards, agencies and institutions of the Presbyterian Church (U.S.A.). Such legal procedures shall be undertaken without delay as may be necessary and expedient to assure that such trustees and corporate structures together with all property, real and personal, held by them are clearly identified as trustees, corporate structures and property of the Presbyterian Church (U.S.A.).

2.2   The continuity and integrity of all funds held in trust by such trustees or corporations shall be maintained, and the intention of the settlor or testator as set out in the trust instrument shall be strictly complied with. Wherever necessary, steps shall be taken to demonstrate that the appropriate entity of the Presbyterian Church (U.S.A.) has succeeded to the beneficiary named in such trust instrument.

ARTICLE 3. CONFESSIONAL DOCUMENTS

3.1   The confessional documents of the two preceding Churches shall be the confessional documents of the reunited Church. The interim stated clerks of the Presbyterian Church (U.S.A.) shall prepare the official text of the confessional documents as defined in G-1.0501.

3.2   The General Assembly of the reunited Presbyterian Church shall at an early meeting appoint a committee representing diversities of points of view and of groups within the reunited Church to prepare a Brief Statement of the Reformed Faith for possible inclusion in *The Book of Confessions* as provided in G-18.0201.

3.3   Until the Brief Statement of the Reformed Faith has been incorporated into *The Book of Confessions*, the Presbyterian Church (U.S.A.) accepts *A Brief Statement of Belief* adopted by the 102nd General Assembly of the Presbyterian Church in the United States in 1962, as a summary of the Reformed understanding of historic Christian doctrine set forth in Scripture and contained in the Confessions of the Presbyterian Church (U.S.A.). During that interval, *A Brief Statement of Belief* shall be utilized with the Confessions of the Church in the instruction of Church members and officers, in the orientation and examination of ordinands prior to ordination, and of ministers seeking membership in Presbyteries by transfer from other Presbyteries or other Churches.

ARTICLE 4. THE OFFICE OF THE GENERAL ASSEMBLY

4.1   The work of the Office of the General Assembly immediately following reunion shall be provided for as follows:

The offices of the two highest governing bodies of the uniting Churches shall be continued for a period of one year after the effective date of the reunion in order to assure the orderly transfer of records and functions to an office of the new highest governing body. During such transition period the stated clerk of the Presbyterian Church in the United States and the stated clerk of The United Presbyterian Church in the United States of America shall be titled interim stated clerks of the General Assembly and shall function in consultation with the General Assembly Council. The interim stated clerks shall, following consultation with the General Assembly Council, one year after the effective date of the union, recommend the assignments to and an organizational structure for the Office of the General Assembly.

4.2   Not later than nine months after the effective date of the union, the General Assembly Council shall select a Special Committee on Nominations for Stated Clerk. This committee shall be nine in number and representative of all the geographical areas of the reunited Church. None of its members shall be considered eligible for nomination for the office of stated clerk. The committee shall consider at once the availability and qualifications of all persons whose names may be presented to it by individuals or governing bodies within the reunited Church and shall seek out on its own initiative persons who, in its judgment, should be considered for the office. This committee shall be prepared to present directly to a committee of the next General Assembly the names of not more than three persons whom the Special Committee considers suitable for nomination.

That General Assembly shall establish a General Assembly Committee on Nominations for Stated Clerk to which the Special Committee mentioned in the preceding paragraph shall report with its recommendations. It is understood that the General Assembly Committee need not be limited in its choice to those whose names are suggested by the

Special Committee. After full consideration and consultation with the Special Committee, the General Assembly Committee shall select not more than two candidates, whose names shall be presented to the General Assembly not later than forty-eight hours prior to its adjournment. If there is only one nominee and no further nominations from the floor, election may be by acclamation. If there are two or more candidates, the election shall be in the same manner as for the moderator. The candidate receiving a majority of the votes cast shall be declared elected.

ARTICLE 5. TRANSITIONAL COMPOSITION AND WORK OF THE GENERAL ASSEMBLY COUNCIL AND AGENCIES

5.1   During the period immediately following reunion, the General Assembly Council shall consist of the Moderator of the General Assembly, the Moderators of the two immediately preceding General Assemblies of each Church, and forty-eight members elected by the General Assembly as provided in 5.2 below. In addition to the voting members, the stated clerk of the General Assembly, and such staff persons as the General Assembly on the recommendation of the General Assembly Council may from time to time designate, shall be corresponding members, with the right to speak but not to vote.

5.2   The first General Assembly of the Presbyterian Church (U.S.A.) shall elect forty-eight members of the General Assembly Council. Twenty-four shall be nominated by the last General Assembly of the Presbyterian Church in the United States, twenty-one from the membership of the General Assembly Mission Board and three from the Committee on Assembly Operations upon recommendation of those bodies. Twenty-four shall be nominated by the last General Assembly of The United Presbyterian Church in the United States of America from the membership of the General Assembly Mission Council upon recommendation of this body. Among those elected there shall be at least one resident of each of the Synods of the Church. Among those elected there shall also be persons from the divisions, agencies and councils of the General Assemblies of the reuniting Churches including the Councils on Church and Race, the Council on Women and the Church and the Committee on Women's Concerns. One half of those elected shall be ministers of the Word, one half laypersons. Care shall be taken to comply with the provisions of G-9.0104 and G-9.0105. The members so elected shall serve for five years without change except that vacancies occasioned by resignation or death may be filled through election by the General Assembly upon nomination of its Nominating Committee. At the end of the five years, the General Assembly Council shall assign its members to three classes of equal size, expiring at the end of one additional year, two additional years, and three additional years. Thereafter, members shall be elected in accordance with G-13.0202.

5.3   During the first five years after reunion, the General Assembly Council shall elect its own moderator and vice-moderator and shall designate its own staff, subject to confirmation by the General Assembly. The stated clerk of the General Assembly shall be its recording secretary.

5.4   The General Assembly Council shall have the responsibilities enumerated in G-13.0201, and in addition shall provide the necessary coordination, management and consolidation of the functions, divisions, agencies, councils, commissions and institutions of the General Assemblies of the reuniting Churches. Upon adjournment of the first General Assembly of the Presbyterian Church (U.S.A.), the General Assembly Mission Council of The United Presbyterian Church in the United States of America will cease to exist. The General Assembly Mission Board of the Presbyterian Church in the United States (consisting of the members remaining after election of the General Assembly Council) and the Program Agency, the Support Agency, and the Vocation Agency of The United Presbyterian Church in the United States of America will continue to administer the programs, previously conducted by each of them, for five years unless earlier terminated by action of the General Assembly. During this period the elected membership of the agencies above shall continue to serve without change except that vacancies occasioned by resignation or death may be filled through election by the General Assembly upon nomination of its Nominating Committee.

The General Assembly Council shall develop and propose to subsequent General Assemblies a design for the work of the General Assembly which will effectively relate the functions, divisions, agencies, councils, commissions and institutions of the General Assemblies of the reuniting Churches not otherwise provided for in these Articles of Agreement, except an agency for pensions which is hereinafter provided for in Article 11. Agencies whose functions will be served by other bodies or in other ways in the reunited Church will not be continued.

5.5   The General Assembly Council shall carefully review the continuing mission directions and priorities approved by both General Assemblies prior to reuniting, and prepare means to harmonize the programmatic work of its agencies.

The General Assembly Council shall ensure the continuance of an organized approach in the areas of world mission, evangelism, education, church renewal, church extension and social-economic justice within the context of the unity of Christ's Church throughout the world.

The General Assembly Council shall take particular care to design agencies and to commit major resources, both human and financial, to put into action with other Churches and agencies, in this land and other nations, ministries that serve the purpose of the Presbyterian Church (U.S.A.) to confront men and women, structures and principalities, with the claims of Jesus Christ.

5.6   The General Assembly Council in its development of a design for the work of the General Assembly shall also ensure the continuance of the advocacy and monitoring functions of the existing Councils on Church and Race (both denominations), Committee on Women's Concerns (Presbyterian Church in the United States) and Council on Women and the Church (The United Presbyterian Church in the United States of America). Until such time as the design for work of the General Assembly is completed and these functions are ensured, the existing structures and functions of these bodies shall be maintained.

5.7   As the various boards, agencies, councils and offices of the General Assemblies of the reuniting Churches continue to function within the life of the reunited Church, or as new agencies are created at the time of reunion, and especially as consideration is given to the location or locations of General Assembly offices and agencies, care and sensitivity shall be shown employed personnel. The General Assembly Council shall ensure continuity of employment at comparable levels insofar as possible. As staff vacancies occur, they shall be filled in accordance with the church-wide plan for equal employment opportunity (G-13.0201b) and the principle of full participation (G-4.0403). The General Assembly Council shall provide for an equitable termination policy.

ARTICLE 6. LOCATION OF THE GENERAL ASSEMBLY'S AGENCIES

6.1   The General Assembly Council shall immediately appoint a representative committee to examine with professional consultants the values of establishing a single location or multiple locations for the General Assembly's agencies. The committee shall propose a possible location or locations. The committee shall suggest a timetable for the move, if relocation is involved.

ARTICLE 7. SPECIAL COMMITTEE ON PRESBYTERY AND SYNOD BOUNDARIES

7.1   A Special Committee on Presbytery and Synod Boundaries shall be formed to work with the governing bodies where Presbyteries and Synods of the existing Churches overlap and for other Presbyteries and Synods as necessary. Its work will be done on behalf of the General Assembly and its recommendations made for the General Assembly's action. (G-13.0103, l and m)

7.2   This Special Committee, composed of one person from each Synod of the reuniting Churches, shall be elected by the uniting General Assembly through the regular nominating procedures of the existing Churches. The committee shall elect its own moderator when it is convened by the interim stated clerks immediately upon adjournment of the uniting General Assembly.

7.3   The Special Committee shall set in motion a procedure whereby overlapping Presbyteries and Synods, through negotiation, shall consult in developing a mutually acceptable plan for Presbytery and Synod boundaries which shall become effective within five years following reunion. The governing bodies of affected Presbyteries and Synods shall be encouraged to initiate boundary adjustment by means of overture to the General Assembly. Recognizing that in several areas of the country some Presbyteries and Synods have overlapped and existed side by side for years, care must be taken, in the spirit of fair representation reflected in G-9.0104, that the responsibilities and privileges of governing now enjoyed by members of each Presbytery be honored and enhanced. The Special Committee shall develop guidelines for the governing bodies to use in their negotiations and, when each plan is approved by the governing bodies concerned and the Special Committee, shall forward the plan to the General Assembly recommending approval.

7.4   On the principle that a geographically related area makes possible greater fellowship and ease in the conduct of the business of a governing body, it shall be the further goal of the Special Committee that the resulting governing bodies shall be of sufficient strength and geographical proximity to enhance the total mission of the Church. Care must be taken to protect the rights and privileges of members of each of the uniting governing bodies so that they may exercise the responsibilities of leadership in the newly formed governing body.

7.5   The Special Committee shall report annually to the General Assembly on the progress the governing bodies are making. If realignments are not mutually developed within the five years following reunion to the satisfaction of all parties concerned, application for continuance of the process may be made to the General Assembly. If granted, the efforts shall be reviewed by each General Assembly with the expectation that full geographical consolidation shall be accomplished no later than ten years following the uniting General Assembly.

7.6   In cases involving Presbyteries based on racial ethnic or language considerations, or Presbyteries whose membership consists predominately of racial ethnic persons, plans for realignment shall be completed within ten years or, if that is not accomplished, upon application for continuance of the process, which may be granted by the General Assembly, within fifteen years after the uniting General Assembly.

7.7   At such time as all problems of overlapping boundaries and related problems of other Presbyteries and Synods shall have received General Assembly action, the Special Committee shall be dissolved and future issues of boundaries shall be handled under the provisions of G-13.0103 l and m.

ARTICLE 8. RACIAL ETHNIC REPRESENTATION, PARTICIPATION AND ORGANIZATIONS

8.1   The Presbyterian Church (U.S.A.) shall provide for a Committee on Representation for each governing body above the Session. Its membership shall consist of equal numbers of men and women. A majority of the members shall be selected from the racial ethnic groups within the governing body and the total membership shall include persons from each of the following categories:

a.   majority male membership

b.   majority female membership

c.   racial ethnic male membership

d.   racial ethnic female membership

e.   youth male and female membership

Its main function shall be to guide the governing bodies with respect to their membership and to that of their committees, boards, agencies and other units, in implementation of the principles of participation and inclusiveness, to ensure effective representation in the decision making of the church.

8.2   Governing bodies of the Church shall be responsible for implementing the Church's commitment to inclusiveness and participation which provides for the full expression of the rich diversity within its membership. All governing bodies shall work to become more open and inclusive and to correct past patterns of discrimination on the basis of racial ethnic background.

Racial ethnic members in the United States (Presbyterians of African, Hispanic and Asian descent and Native Americans) shall be guaranteed full participation and access to representation in the decision-making of the Church, and shall be able to form caucuses.

Participation and representation of racial ethnic membership shall be assured by the Committees on Representation (8.1).

8.3   Consistent with the principles of diversity and inclusiveness as set forth in 8.2, the General Assembly Council shall consult with and receive input from the racial caucuses of the Church, and shall make provision for the expenses necessary to such consultations. The purposes of such consultations shall include:

determining the priorities for assisting racial ethnic churches and ministries,

developing a denominational strategy for racial ethnic church development,

finding ways to assure the funding and operational needs of schools and other institutions which historically have served Black Americans and other racial ethnic groups.

8.4   Racial ethnic educational institutions have been the primary source from which racial ethnic church leadership has developed. Consistent with the dire need for racial ethnic church leadership, the General Assembly Council shall propose to the General Assembly ways whereby the General Assembly shall be able to fulfill its responsibility for education through colleges and secondary schools and for meeting the operational and developmental needs of those Presbyterian schools that historically have served Black Americans and those serving other racial ethnic groups.

ARTICLE 9. WOMEN'S REPRESENTATION, PARTICIPATION AND ORGANIZATIONS

9.1   The Committees on Representation required by G-9.0105 for each governing body above the Session shall guide those bodies, with respect to their membership and that of their committees, boards, agencies and other units, in implementing the principles of participation and inclusiveness, to ensure the fair representation of women, both of the majority race and of racial ethnic groups, in the decision making of the Church.

9.2   The General Assembly Council in consultation with elected representatives from each recognized women's group of both Churches shall make provision for the continuation of the women's programs and organizations of the two Churches at all levels, until such time as programs are formulated as described in 9.3.

9.3   A group of representatives elected by each recognized women's group from the two Churches shall meet to develop programs and organizations, these proposals to be approved by the constituent groups. Such approval shall be reported to the General Assembly Council by the Executive Committees of each of the women's groups. The group shall report to the General Assembly annually and is expected to complete its work in six years.

ARTICLE 10. INSTITUTIONS OF THEOLOGICAL EDUCATION

10.1   The reunited church has continuing responsibility for its institutions of theological education. These institutions are charged to prepare women and men for ordained ministries and other vocations of professional church leadership and to provide strong theological resource centers for the leadership of the whole church.

10.2   Theological institutions of the Presbyterian Church in the United States:

Austin Presbyterian Theological Seminary,
Austin, Texas,

Columbia Theological Seminary,
Decatur, Georgia,

Louisville Presbyterian Theological Seminary,
Louisville, Kentucky,[2]

Presbyterian School of Christian Education,
Richmond, Virginia

Union Theological Seminary in Virginia,
Richmond, Virginia,

and of The United Presbyterian Church in the United States of America:

Dubuque Theological Seminary,
Dubuque, Iowa,

Johnson C. Smith Seminary, of the Interdenominational
Theological Center, Atlanta, Georgia

Louisville Presbyterian Theological Seminary,
Louisville, Kentucky,[3]

---

[2] This seminary is operated jointly with the United Presbyterian Church in the United States of America.

McCormick Theological Seminary,
Chicago, Illinois,

Pittsburgh Theological Seminary,
Pittsburgh, Pennsylvania,

Princeton Theological Seminary,
Princeton, New Jersey,

San Francisco Theological Seminary,
San Anselmo, California,

shall continue into the reunited Church with their present boards, charters and plans of governance.

10.3   The present pattern of financial support of these institutions by the courts or judicatories to which they are related at the time of the reunion shall continue in there united Church. Levels of financial support to the theological institutions from Synods and the General Assembly shall continue so that each receives a similar percentage of the total amount allocated by the governing bodies in the year prior to reunion.

10.4   A Special Committee on Theological Institutions shall be established at the first General Assembly of the reunited Church as a committee of the General Assembly. The Special Committee shall consist of twenty-two members. Eleven members shall be elected from the Church at large by the General Assembly (following the procedures for nominating and electing special committees of the General Assembly). The boards of the eleven institutions named above each shall elect one representative from the institution to serve on the committee. The Special Committee shall be convened by the Moderator of the first General Assembly or the Moderator's designee, and shall elect its own moderator. It shall be funded from the budget of the General Assembly Council and assisted by its staff.

10.5   The Special Committee shall review the relationships between theological institutions and the governing bodies of the reunited Church and study the system of funding theological education by the governing bodies. Plans shall be made for the continuation of and financial support for all the present institutions, with particular attention to be given to the developmental needs of Johnson C. Smith Seminary, which uniquely serves the constituency of Black Presbyterians. The Special Committee shall report to the General Assembly annually. At or before the sixth General Assembly of the reunited Church, it shall make a final report with recommendations concerning the way theological institutions are to be funded through the governing bodies.

10.6   The Council of Theological Seminaries of The United Presbyterian Church in the United States of America and the Committee on Theological Education of the Presbyterian Church in the United States shall continue with their present functions and membership. Where vacancies occur, they shall be filled by the procedure appropriate for the category of membership. The Council and the Committee shall work cooperatively on the common concerns of the theological institutions until the General Assembly has acted upon the recommendations of the Special Committee on Theological Institutions.

---

[3] This seminary is operated jointly with the Presbyterian Church in the United States.

ARTICLE 11. PENSION, ANNUITY, INSURANCE, BENEFIT, ASSISTANCE AND RELIEF PROGRAMS

11.1   Following the consummation of the union between the Presbyterian Church in the United States and The United Presbyterian Church in the United States of America, the Board of Annuities and Relief of the Presbyterian Church in the United States and the Board of Pensions of The United Presbyterian Church in the United States of America shall continue to function under their charters as separate corporations until their responsibilities are assumed by the corporate body provided for in 11.3. During the continued existence of these corporations as separate bodies, the membership of their Boards of Directors as constituted at the time of the reunion of the two Churches shall be frozen, except that the General Assembly of the reunited Church may elect new Directors in the event any vacancies occur. There shall be no interruption in the fulfillment of contractual commitments or other procedures in effect at the time of reunion.

11.2   Following the final vote by the two General Assemblies for reunion of the two Churches, the Board of Annuities and Relief of the Presbyterian Church in the United States and the Board of Pensions of The United Presbyterian Church in the United States of America shall, as expeditiously as possible, develop and recommend to the General Assembly of the reunited Church:

a.   new unified plans and programs to replace the present pension and benefit plans and the assistance and relief programs of the Presbyterian Church in the United States and The United Presbyterian Church in the United States of America; and

b.   a program for the equitable application of the present Annuity, Relief and Insurance Funds of the Board of Annuities and Relief and the present Pension, Endowment, Assistance, Homes and Equipment and Specific Trust Funds of the Board of Pensions that assures adherence to the purposes for which such funds were set aside.

11.3   When the new unified plans and programs are approved by the General Assembly of the reunited Church, they shall be administered by a legally responsible corporate body established under a civil charter and having no responsibilities other than to administer these plans and programs and to assume the responsibilities of the former Board of Annuities and Relief of the Presbyterian Church in the United States and the former Board of Pensions of The United Presbyterian Church in the United States of America. The members of the board of this corporate body shall be elected by the General Assembly of the reunited Church.

Following approval by the General Assembly of the reunited Church of the program for equitable application of the existing funds, said funds shall be placed under the administration of the corporate body provided for in the immediately preceding paragraph as soon as the necessary legal requirements are fulfilled.

11.4   Until the new unified plans and programs become effective, the existing plans and programs of the two denominations will be continued without amendment. All members will continue in the plan to which they belonged immediately prior to the reunion except that newly ordained ministers, new lay employees and those changing service among churches or employing organizations may participate in either plan, provided the individual and the employing organization agree on one plan and pay the requisite dues under the plan selected.

The new unified plans and programs shall make appropriate provision for all members of the present plans and programs who are ministers or lay employees of the reunited Church. After the new pension and benefit plans are operating, no new members shall be enrolled in any of the previously existing plans and no dues related to salaries received after the effective date of the new plans shall be collected under any of the previously existing plans.

Each of the annuity and pension funds shall be administered on an actuarially sound basis for the sole and exclusive use of its members, active and retired, and their survivors, with a view to the final distribution of all assets occurring simultaneously with the fulfillment of all contractual commitments consistent with all legal requirements.

ARTICLE 12. ECUMENICAL RELATIONSHIPS

12.1   The General Assembly of the reunited Church shall determine its ecumenical relationships, provided that the reunited Church shall initially continue in relationship to those bodies to which either of the uniting Churches had been related prior to reunion.

ARTICLE 13. PROCEDURES FOR DISMISSAL OF A CONGREGATION WITH ITS PROPERTY

13.1   The provisions of this article are intended to apply only to the reunion of the Presbyterian Church in the United States and The United Presbyterian Church in the United States of America to form the Presbyterian Church (U.S.A.) and shall not alter, abridge or nullify in any way the principles as to the ownership of property in either antecedent Church or in the reunited Church as established by ecclesiastical and civil law.

13.2   Following the consummation of union, no congregation shall be dismissed for a period of eighteen months except with the permission of the General Assembly. Members, officers, or ministers who do not desire to be a part of the union may, at any time, unite with other denominations and particular churches as set forth in G-10.0102r, G-10.0302b(1), G-11.0103n.

13.3   After one year from the consummation of union, a congregation formerly a part of the Presbyterian Church in the United States may be dismissed when the following conditions have been met:

a. That the Session of the church shall call a congregational meeting for the purpose of discussing the question, "Shall the (Name) _____ Presbyterian Church (U.S.A.) request dismissal to another Reformed body of its choice?" Due notice of such meeting shall be given orally from the pulpit of the church at regular church services on two successive Sundays, the first of which shall be at least ten days prior to the meeting. The required quorum shall be as follows:

> If the number of members is one hundred or less, one fourth of the members; or

> If the number of members is more than one hundred, twenty-five members or one tenth of the members, whichever is greater.

b. That the Presbytery of jurisdiction shall appoint a special committee to meet with the congregation at the congregational meeting. Presbytery's committee shall have the privilege of the floor with the right to speak.

c. That no type of vote for any purpose shall be taken at the meeting.

d. That the Session call a special congregational meeting, to be held no sooner than six months and no later than twelve months from the date of the congregational meeting held for consideration of dismissal.

e. That due notice of such meeting shall be mailed to all members of the church at least thirty days prior to the meeting, and given orally from the pulpit of the church at regular church services on two successive Sundays, the first of which shall be at least ten days prior to the meeting. The Presbytery committee shall be present at the meeting and have the privilege of the floor with the right to speak.

The form of the call to the meeting shall be as follows:

> A special meeting of the congregation of the (Name) _____ Presbyterian Church (U.S.A.) is called for (a.m. or p.m.) on the _____ day of _____, 19_____, at _____, to consider and decide whether it shall or shall not request to be dismissed to another Reformed body. Provisions and authority for this special meeting are found in the Articles of Agreement, Article 13, entered into by the Presbyterian Church in the United States and The United Presbyterian Church in the United States of America as a part of the plan of reunion in which both Churches became one Church, the Presbyterian Church (U.S.A.).

A quorum for this purpose shall be no less than one third of the active confirmed members in good and regular standing. It is urged that a decision on so important a matter be made by a group large enough to reflect the true mind of the whole congregation.

After discussion, a secret ballot will be taken on the categorical question: Shall the _____ Presbyterian Church (U.S.A.) request dismissal to, _____ another Reformed body?

Request dismissal ___ Do not request dismissal ___

If two thirds of those present and voting vote to request dismissal, this particular church will be dismissed under the special provisions of Article 13 of the Articles of Agreement, and will retain all of its property, subject to any existing liens and encumbrances, but will surrender its membership as a congregation in the Presbyterian Church (U.S.A.).

f. That within ten days any person of the unsuccessful side may contest the regularity of the call for, or the conduct of, or the vote taken in, the congregational meeting by a written notice to the Presbytery of jurisdiction. The Presbytery shall then review the questions at issue and, if the contest is sustained, it shall direct the calling of a new congregational meeting.

g. That if the contest is filed by those persons voting for dismissal from the Presbyterian Church (U.S.A.) and the contest is not sustained by the Presbytery, such church shall continue to be a member church of the Presbyterian Church (U.S.A.). If the contest is filed by those voting against dismissal, and is not sustained by Presbytery, such church shall be dismissed to another Reformed body and shall be permitted to retain all of its property subject to any liens and encumbrances.

h. That the jurisdiction of the Presbytery shall be final in any contest brought under this Article.

13.4   Any petition for dismissal with property filed later than eight years from the consummation of union shall be handled under the appropriate provisions for such a request in the Form of Government.

ARTICLE 14. PROCEDURES FOR IMPLEMENTING REUNION

14.1   When the General Assemblies of the two reuniting Churches shall have approved the Plan for Reunion by a favorable vote on Formal Question 1, the Presbyteries of both Churches shall consider the matter at a meeting held during February of the following calendar year. Formal Question 1 is:

Resolved: that the General Assembly approve and recommend to the Presbyteries full organic union with the General Assembly of The United Presbyterian Church in the United States of America (with the General Assembly of the Presbyterian Church in the United States) under the proposed Plan for Reunion consisting of the Constitution of the Presbyterian Church (U.S.A.) as defined therein (G-1.0500) and the Articles of Agreement, together with all other documents and procedures incident thereto, all of which are attached to this resolution or by necessary implication are incident thereto, and by this reference are incorporated as a part hereof.

14.2   Each Presbytery shall report its action on Formal Question 2 below to the stated clerk of the General Assembly to which it belongs prior to the end of February. The report of the vote shall be on a ballot provided by the stated clerk of the General Assembly. Union Presbyteries shall report their votes to both General Assembly stated clerks. Formal Question 2 is:

Resolved: that the Presbytery of _____give its advice and consent (give its approval) to full organic union with the General Assembly of The United Presbyterian Church in the United States of America (with the General Assembly of the Presbyterian Church in the United States) under the proposed Plan for Reunion consisting of the Constitution of the Presbyterian Church (U.S.A.) as defined therein (G-1.0500) and the Articles of Agreement, together with all other documents and procedures incident thereto, all of which are attached to this resolution or by necessary implication are incident thereto, and by this reference are incorporated as a part hereof.

14.3   When the General Assemblies of the two uniting Churches, following approval of Formal Question 2 by the requisite number of Presbyteries of the two uniting Churches, shall both approve Formal Question 3:

Resolved: that the General Assembly finally approve full organic union with the General Assembly of The United Presbyterian Church in the United States of America (with the General Assembly of the Presbyterian Church in the United States) under the proposed Plan for Reunion consisting of the Constitution of the Presbyterian Church (U.S.A.) as defined therein (G-1.0500) and the Articles of Agreement, together with all other documents and procedures incident thereto, all of which are attached to this resolution or by necessary implication are incident thereto, and by this reference are incorporated as a part hereof.

then the commissioners of each General Assembly shall gather in a common place of meeting to convene as the General Assembly of the Presbyterian Church (U.S.A.). All the commissioners of the General Assemblies of the reuniting Churches shall be commissioners of the General Assembly of the reunited Church, which shall be empowered to act upon all business properly docketed by both General Assemblies of the uniting Churches, as well as the business which may come before it according to the requirements of the Form of Government of the Plan for Reunion.

14.4   The two stated clerks of the General Assemblies of the uniting Churches, who shall be interim stated clerks of the General Assembly of the reunited Church as set forth in Article 4.1 of the Articles of Agreement of the Plan for Reunion, shall prepare and establish a plan for the designation and membership of the necessary General Assembly committees and for recommending to the General Assembly of the reunited Church the referral of business properly before the General Assembly.

14.5   The first act of the General Assembly shall be to convene in worship of Almighty God and for the celebration of the Lord's Supper. The election of a moderator shall be a nearly item on the docket of the first meeting of the General Assembly which shall follow the celebration of the Lord's Supper.

APPENDIX B

Received Ecumenical Statements of Guidance (see G-5.0203):

Official Text

A Formula of Agreement
Between the

Evangelical Lutheran Church in America
the Presbyterian Church (U.S.A.),
the Reformed Church in America,
and the United Church of Christ

On Entering Into Full Communion
On the Basis of *A Common Calling*

Approved by the 209th General Assembly (1997)
and declared made by the 210th General Assembly (1998)

A FORMULA OF AGREEMENT

Between the
**Evangelical Lutheran Church in America,
the Presbyterian Church (U.S.A.),
the Reformed Church in America,
and the United Church of Christ**

On Entering into Full Communion
On the Basis of *A Common Calling*

Preface

In 1997 four churches of Reformation heritage will act on an ecumenical proposal of historic importance. The timing reflects a doctrinal consensus which has been developing over the past thirty-two years coupled with an increasing urgency for the church to proclaim a gospel of unity in contemporary society. In light of identified doctrinal consensus, desiring to bear visible witness to the unity of the Church, and hearing the call to engage together in God's mission, it is recommended:

That the Evangelical Lutheran Church in America, the Presbyterian Church (U.S.A.), the Reformed Church in America, and the United Church of Christ declare on the basis of *A Common Calling* and their adoption of this *A Formula of Agreement* that they are in full communion with one another. Thus, each church is entering into or affirming full communion with three other churches.

The term "full communion" is understood here to specifically mean that the four churches:

- recognize each other as churches in which the gospel is rightly preached and the sacraments rightly administered according to the Word of God;

- withdraw any historic condemnation by one side or the other as inappropriate for the life and faith of our churches today;

- continue to recognize each other's Baptism and authorize and encourage the sharing of the Lord's Supper among their members;

- recognize each others' various ministries and make provision for the orderly exchange of ordained ministers of Word and Sacrament;

- establish appropriate channels of consultation and decision-making within the existing structures of the churches;

- commit themselves to an ongoing process of theological dialogue in order to clarify further the common understanding of the faith and foster its common expression in evangelism, witness, and service;

- pledge themselves to living together under the Gospel in such a way that the principle of mutual affirmation and admonition becomes the basis of a trusting relationship in which respect and love for the other will have a chance to grow.

This document assumes the doctrinal consensus articulated in *A Common Calling: The Witness of Our Reformation Churches in North America Today*, and is to be viewed in concert with that document. The purpose of *A Formula of Agreement* is to elucidate the complementarity of affirmation and admonition as the basic principle of entering into full communion and the implications of that action as described in *A Common Calling*.

A Common Calling, the report of the Lutheran-Reformed Committee for Theological Conversations (1988–1992) continued a process begun in 1962.[1] Within that report was the "unanimous recommendation that the Evangelical Lutheran Church in America, the Presbyterian Church (U.S.A.), the Reformed Church in America, and the United Church of Christ declare that they are in full communion with one another" (*A Common Calling*, pp. 66–67). There followed a series of seven recommendations under which full communion would be implemented as developed with the study from the theological conversations (*A Common Calling*, p. 67). As a result, the call for full communion has been presented to the four respective church bodies. The vote on a declaration of full communion will take place at the respective churchwide assemblies in 1977.

Mutual Affirmation and Admonition

A concept identified as early as the first Lutheran-Reformed Dialogue became pivotal for the understanding of the theological conversations. Participants in the Dialogue discovered that "efforts to guard against possible distortions of truth have resulted in varying emphases in related doctrines which are not in themselves contradictory and in fact are complementary. . ." (*Marburg Revisited*, Preface). Participants in the theological conversations rediscovered and considered the implications of this insight and saw it as a foundation for the recommendation for full communion among the four churches. This breakthrough concept, a complementarity of mutual affirmation and mutual admonition, points toward new ways of relating traditions of Reformation churches that heretofore have not been able to reconcile their diverse witnesses to the saving grace of God that is bestowed in Jesus Christ, the Lord of the Church.

---

[1]For a summary of the history of Lutheran-Reformed Dialogue in North America, see *A Common Calling*, pp. 10–11. The results of the first round of dialogue, 1962–1966, were published in *Marburg Revisited* (Augsburg, 1966). The second round of dialogue took place in 1972–1974. Its brief report was published in *An Invitation to Action* (Fortress, 1983), pp. 54–60. The third series began in 1981 and concluded in 1983, and was published in the book, *An Invitation to Action*. Following this third dialogue a fourth round of "Theological Conversations" was held from 1988 to 1992, resulting in the report, *A Common Calling: The Witness of Our Reformation Churches in North America Today* (Augsburg, 1993). In addition, the North American participants in the Lutheran-Reformed Dialogue have drawn on the theological work found in the Leuenberg Agreement, a Statement of Concord between Reformation churches in Europe in 1973, published in *An Invitation to Action*, pp. 61–73, as well as the Report of the International Joint Commission of the Lutheran World Federation and the World Alliance of Reformed Churches, 1985–1988, *Toward Church Fellowship* (LWF and WARC, 1989).

This concept provides a basis for acknowledging three essential facets of the Lutheran-Reformed relationship: (1) that each of the churches grounds its life in authentic New Testament traditions of Christ; (2) that the core traditions of these churches belong together within the one, holy, catholic, and apostolic Church; and (3) that the historic give-and-take between these churches has resulted in fundamental mutual criticisms that cannot be glossed over, but need to be understood "as diverse witnesses to the one Gospel that we confess in common" (*A Common Calling*, p. 66). A working awareness emerged, which cast in a new light contemporary perspectives on the sixteenth century debates.

The theological diversity within our common confession provides both the complementarity needed for a full and adequate witness to the gospel (mutual affirmation) and the corrective reminder that every theological approach is a partial and incomplete witness to the Gospel (mutual admonition) (*A Common Calling*, page 66).

The working principle of "mutual affirmation and admonition" allows for the affirmation of agreement while at the same time allowing a process of mutual edification and correction in areas where there is not total agreement. Each tradition brings its "corrective witness" to the other while fostering continuing theological reflection and dialogue to further clarify the unity of faith they share and seek. The principle of "mutual affirmation and admonition" views remaining differences as diverse witnesses to the one Gospel confessed in common. Whereas conventional modes of thought have hidden the bases of unity behind statements of differences, the new concept insists that, while remaining differences must be acknowledged, even to the extent of their irreconcilability, it is the inherent unity in Christ that is determinative. Thus, the remaining differences are not church-dividing.

The concept of mutual affirmation and admonition translates into significant outcomes, both of which inform the relationships of these four churches with one another. The principle of complementarity and its accompanying mode of interpretation make it clear that in entering into full church communion these churches:

- do not consider their own traditional confessional and ecclesiological character to be compromised in the least;

- fully recognize the validity and necessity of the confessional and ecclesiological character of the partner churches;

- intend to allow significant differences to be honestly articulated within the relationship of full communion;

- allow for articulated differences to be opportunities for mutual growth of churchly fullness within each of the partner churches and within the relationship of full communion itself.

A Fundamental Doctrinal Consensus

Members of the theological conversations were charged with determining whether the essential conditions for full communion have been met. They borrowed language of the Lutheran confessions: "For the true unity of the church it is enough to agree (*satis est consentire*) concerning the teaching of the Gospel and the administration of the sacraments" (*Augsburg Confession*, Article 7). The theological consensus that is the basis for the current proposal for full communion includes justification, the sacraments, ministry, and church and world. Continuing areas of diversity, no longer to be seen as "church-dividing," were dealt with by the theological conversations under the headings: The Condemnations, the Presence of Christ, and God's Will to Save.

On Justification, participants in the first dialogue agreed "that each tradition has sought to preserve the wholeness of the Gospel as including forgiveness of sins and renewal of life" (*Marburg Revisited*, p. 152). Members of the third dialogue, in their Joint Statement on Justification, said "both Lutheran and Reformed churches are … rooted in, live by, proclaim, and confess the Gospel of the saving act of God in Jesus Christ" (*An Invitation to Action*, p. 9). They went on to say that "both … traditions confess this Gospel in the language of justification by grace through faith alone," and concluded that "there are no substantive matters concerning justification that divide us" (*An Invitation to Action*, pp. 9–10).

Lutherans and Reformed agree that in Baptism, Jesus Christ receives human beings, fallen prey to sin and death, into his fellowship of salvation so that they may become new creatures. This is experienced as a call into Christ's community, to a new life of faith, to daily repentance, and to discipleship (cf. *Leuenberg Agreement*, III.2.a.). The central doctrine of the presence of Christ in the Lord's Supper received attention in each dialogue and in the theological conversations. The summary statement in *Marburg Revisited*, reflecting agreement, asserts:

> During the Reformation both Reformed and Lutheran Churches exhibited an evangelical intention when they understood the Lord's Supper in the light of the saving act of God in Christ. Despite this common intention, different terms and concepts were employed which … led to mutual misunderstanding and misrepresentation. Properly interpreted, the differing terms and concepts were often complementary rather than contradictory (*Marburg Revisited*, pp. 103–4).

The third dialogue concluded that, while neither Lutheran nor Reformed profess to explain <u>how</u> Christ is present and received in the Supper, both churches affirm that, "Christ himself <u>is</u> the host at his table. . . and that Christ himself <u>is</u> fully present and received in the Supper" [emphasis added] (*An Invitation to Action*, p. 14). This doctrinal consensus became the foundation for work done by the theological conversations.

The theme of ministry was considered only by the third dialogue. Agreeing that there are no substantive matters which should divide Lutherans and Reformed, the dialogue affirmed that:

> Ministry in our heritage derives from and points to Christ who alone is sufficient to save. Centered in the proclamation of the word and the administration of the sacraments, it is built on the affirmation that the benefits of Christ are known only through faith, grace, and Scripture (*An Invitation to Action*, p. 24).

The dialogue went on to speak of the responsibility of all the baptized to participate in Christ's servant ministry, pointed to God's use of "the ordained ministers as instruments to mediate grace through the preaching of the Word and the administration of the sacraments," and asserted the need for proper oversight to "ensure that the word is truly preached and sacraments rightly administered" (*An Invitation to Action*, pp, 26, 28, 31).

The first dialogue considered the theme of church and world a very important inquiry. The dialogue examined differences, noted the need of correctives, and pointed to the essentially changed world in which the church lives today. Agreeing that "there is a common evangelical basis for Christian ethics in the theology of the Reformers," (*Marburg Revisited*, p. 177), the dialogue went on to rehearse the differing "accents" of Calvin and Luther on the relation of church and world, Law and Gospel, the "two kingdoms," and the sovereignty of Christ. The dialogue found that "differing formulations of the relation between Law and Gospel were prompted by a common concern to combat the errors of legalism on the one hand and antinomianism on the other." While differences remain regarding the role of God's Law in the Christian life, the dialogue did "not regard this as a divisive issue" (*Marburg Revisited*, p. 177). Furthermore, in light of the radically changed world of the twentieth century, it was deemed inappropriate to defend or correct positions and choices taken in the sixteenth century, making them determinative for Lutheran-Reformed witness today. Thus, the theological conversations, in a section on "Declaring God's Justice and Mercy," identified Reformed and Lutheran "emphases" as "complementary and stimulating" differences, posing a challenge to the pastoral service and witness of the churches. "The ongoing debate about 'justification and justice' is fundamentally an occasion for hearing the Word of God and doing it. Our traditions need each other in order to discern God's gracious promises and obey God's commands" (*A Common Calling*, p. 61).

Differing Emphases

The Condemnations:

The condemnations of the Reformation era were an attempt to preserve and protect the Word of God; therefore, they are to be taken seriously. Because of the contemporary ecclesial situation today, however, it is necessary to question whether such condemnations should continue to divide the churches. The concept of mutual affirmation and mutual admonition of *A Common Calling* offers a way of overcoming condemnation language while allowing for different emphases with a common understanding of the primacy of the Gospel of Jesus Christ and the gift of the sacraments. *A Common Calling* refers with approval to the *Leuenberg Agreement* where, as a consequence of doctrinal agreement, it is stated that the "condemnations expressed in the confessional documents no longer apply to the contemporary doctrinal position of the assenting churches" (*Leuenberg Agreement*, IV.32.b). The theological conversations stated:

> We have become convinced that the task today is not to mark the point of separation and exclusion but to find a common language which will allow our partners to be heard in their honest concern for the truth of the Gospel, to be taken seriously, and to be integrated into the identity of our own ecumenical community of faith (*A Common Calling*, p. 40).

A major focus of the condemnations was the issue of the presence of Christ in the Lord's Supper. Lutheran and Reformed Christians need to be assured that in their common understanding of the sacraments, the Word of God is not compromised; therefore, they insist on consensus among their churches on certain aspects of doctrine concerning the Lord's Supper. In that regard Lutheran and Reformed Christians, recalling the issues addressed by the conversations, agree that:

In the Lord's Supper the risen Jesus Christ imparts himself in his body and blood, given for all, through his word of promise with bread and wine. He thus gives himself unreservedly to all who receive the bread and wine; faith receives the Lord's Supper for salvation, unfaith for judgment (*Leuenberg Agreement,* III.1.18).

We cannot separate communion with Jesus Christ in his body and blood from the act of eating and drinking. To be concerned about the manner of Christ's presence in the Lord's Supper in abstraction from this act is to run the risk of obscuring the meaning of the Lord's Supper (*Leuenberg Agreement,* III.1.19).

The Presence of Christ:

The third dialogue urged the churches toward a deeper appreciation of the sacramental mystery based on consensus already achieved:

Appreciating what we Reformed and Lutheran Christians already hold in common concerning the Lord's Supper, we nevertheless affirm that both of our communions need to keep on growing into an ever-deeper realization of the fullness and richness of the eucharistic mystery (*An Invitation to Action*, p. 14).

The members of the theological conversations acknowledged that it has not been possible to reconcile the confessional formulations from the sixteenth century with a "common language ... which could do justice to all the insights, convictions, and concerns of our ancestors in the faith" (*A Common Calling*, p. 49). However, the theological conversations recognized these enduring differences as acceptable diversities with regard to the Lord's Supper. Continuing in the tradition of the third dialogue, they respected the different perspectives and convictions from which their ancestors professed their faith, affirming that those differences are not church dividing, but are complementary. Both sides can say together that "the Reformation heritage in the matter of the Lord's Supper draws from the same roots and envisages the same goal: to call the people of God to the table at which Christ himself is present to give himself for us under the word of forgiveness, empowerment, and promise." Lutheran and Reformed Christians agree that:

In the Lord's Supper the risen Christ imparts himself in body and blood, given up for all, through his word of promise with bread and wine. He thereby grants us forgiveness of sins and sets us free for a new life of faith. He enables us to experience anew that we are members of his body. He strengthens us for service to all people. (The official text reads, "*Er starkt uns zum Dienst an den Menschen*," which may be translated "to all human beings") (*Leuenberg, Agreement*, II.2.15).

When we celebrate the Lord's Supper we proclaim the death of Christ through which God has reconciled the world with himself. We proclaim the presence of the risen Lord in our midst. Rejoicing that the Lord has come to us, we await his future coming in glory (*Leuenberg Agreement*, II.2.16).

With a complementarity and theological consensus found in the Lord's Supper, it is recognized that there are implications for sacramental practices as well, which represent the heritage of these Reformation churches.

As churches of the Reformation, we share many important features in our respective practices of Holy Communion. Over the centuries of our separation, however, there have developed characteristic differences in practice, and these still tend to make us uncomfortable at each other's celebration of the Supper. These differences can be discerned in several areas, for example, in liturgical style and liturgical details, in our verbal interpretations of our practices, in the emotional patterns involved in our experience of the Lord's Supper, and in the implications we find in the Lord's Supper for the life and mission of the church and of its individual members. ... We affirm our conviction, however, that these differences should be recognized as acceptable diversities within one Christian faith. Both of our communions, we maintain, need to grow in appreciation of our diverse eucharistic traditions, finding mutual enrichment in them. At the same time both need to grow toward a further deepening of our common experience and expression of the mystery of our Lord's Supper (*An Invitation to Action*, pp. 16–17).

God's Will to Save:

Lutherans and Reformed claim the saving power of God's grace as the center of their faith and life. They believe that salvation depends on God's grace alone and not on human cooperation. In spite of this common belief, the doctrine of predestination has been one of the issues separating the two traditions. Although Lutherans and Reformed have different emphases in the way they live out their belief in the sovereignty of God's love, they agree that "God's unconditional will to save must be preached against all cultural optimism or pessimism" (*A Common Calling*, p. 54). It is noted that "a common language that transcends the polemics of the past and witnesses to the common predestination faith of Lutheran and Reformed Churches has emerged already in theological writings and official or unofficial statements in our churches" (*A Common Calling*, page 55). Rather than insisting on doctrinal uniformity, the two traditions are willing to acknowledge that they have been borne out of controversy, and their present identities, theological and ecclesial, have been shaped by those arguments. To demand more than fundamental doctrinal consensus on those areas that have been church-dividing would be tantamount to denying the faith of those Christians with whom we have shared a common journey toward wholeness in Jesus Christ. An even greater tragedy would occur were we, through our divisiveness, to deprive the world of a common witness to the saving grace of Jesus Christ that has been so freely given to us.

The Binding and Effective Commitment to Full Communion

In the formal adoption at the highest level of this *A Formula of Agreement,* based on *A Common Calling*, the churches acknowledge that they are undertaking an act of strong mutual commitment. They are making pledges and promises to each other. The churches recognize that full commitment to each other involve serious intention, awareness, and dedication. They are binding themselves to far more than merely a formal action; they are entering into a relationship with gifts and changes for all.

The churches know these stated intentions will challenge their self-understandings, their ways of living and acting, their structures, and even their general ecclesial ethos. The churches commit themselves to keep this legitimate concern of their capacity to enter into full communion at the heart of their new relation.

The churches declare, under the guidance of the triune God, that they are fully committed to *A Formula of Agreement*, and are capable of being, and remaining, pledged to the above-described mutual affirmations in faith and doctrine, to joint decision-making, and to exercising and accepting mutual admonition and correction. *A Formula of Agreement* responds to the ecumenical conviction that "there is no turning back, either from the goal of visible unity or from the single ecumenical movement that unites concern of the unity of the Church and concern for engagement in the struggles of the world" ("On the Way to Fuller Koinonia: The Message of the Fifth World Conference on Faith and Order," 1983). And, as St. Paul reminds us all, "The one who calls you is faithful, and he will do this," (1 Thessalonians 5:24, NRSV).[2]

---

[2] **The Evangelical Lutheran Church in America:**

To enter into full communion with these churches [Presbyterian Church (U.S.A.), Reformed Church in America, United Church of Christ], an affirmative two-thirds vote of the 1997 Churchwide Assembly, the highest legislative authority in the ELCA, will be required. Subsequently in the appropriate manner other changes in the constitution and bylaws would be made to conform with this binding decision by an assembly to enter into full communion.

The constitution and bylaws of the Evangelical Lutheran Church in America (ELCA) do not speak specifically of this church entering into full communion with non-Lutheran churches. The closest analogy, in view of the seriousness of the matter, would appear to be an amendment of the ELCA's constitution or bylaws. The constitution provides a process of such amendment (Chapter 22). In both cases a two-thirds vote of members present and voting is required.

The Presbyterian Church (U.S.A.):

Upon an affirmative vote of the General Assembly of the Presbyterian Church (U.S.A.), the declaration of full communion will be effected throughout the church in accordance with the Presbyterian *Book of Order* and this *Formula of Agreement*. This means a majority vote of the General Assembly, a majority vote in the presbyteries, and a majority vote of the presbyteries.

The Presbyterian Church (U.S.A.) orders its life as an institution with a constitution, government, officers, finances, and administrative rules. These are instruments of mission, not ends in themselves. Different orders have served the Gospel, and none can claim exclusive validity. A presbyterian polity recognizes the responsibility of all members for ministry and maintains the organic relation of all congregations in the church. It seeks to protect the church from every exploitation by ecclesiastical or secular power ambition. Every church order must be open to such reformation as may be required to make it a more effective instrument of the mission of reconciliation. ("Confession of 1967," *Book of Confessions*, p. 40).

The Presbyterian Church (U.S.A.) shall be governed by representative bodies composed of presbyters, both elders and ministers of the Word and Sacrament. These governing bodies shall be called session, presbytery, synod, and the General Assembly (*Book of Order*, G-9.0100).

All governing bodies of the Church are united by nature of the Church and share with one another responsibilities, rights, and powers as provided in this Constitution. The governing bodies are separate and independent, but have such mutual relations that the act of one of them is the act of the whole Church performed by it through the appropriate governing body. The jurisdiction of each governing body is limited by the express provisions of the Constitution, with the acts of each subject to review by the next higher governing body. (G-9.0103).

APPENDIX C

Covenant Relationship Between
the Korean Presbyterian Church in America
and the Presbyterian Church (U.S.A.)

Received Ecumenical Statement
Approved by the 218th General Assembly (2008)
Approved by Majority Vote of Presbyteries
(G-5.0203)

COVENANT RELATIONSHIP BETWEEN
THE KOREAN PRESBYTERIAN CHURCH IN AMERICA
AND THE PRESBYTERIAN CHURCH (U.S.A.)

"I therefore, the prisoner in the Lord, beg you to lead a life worthy of the calling to which you have been called, with all humility and gentleness, with patience, bearing with one another in love, making every effort to maintain the unity of the Spirit in the bond of peace. There is one body and one Spirit, just as you were called to the one hope of your calling, one Lord, one faith, one baptism, one God and Father of all, who is above all and through all and in all."

Ephesians 4:1–6(NRSV)

I. History of Relationship

The Presbyterian Church (USA) [PC(USA)] and the Korean Presbyterian Church in America (KPCA) are denominations with common roots and commitments in the Reformed tradition. The emotional ties are the legacy of their mission history. Protestant Christianity in Korea began through the sending of U.S. Presbyterian missionaries to Korea in 1885. Over the past century, Presbyterians in Korea have demonstrated phenomenal growth despite their difficult experiences of suffering. They have become genuine partners in mission and ecumenical engagement not only in Korea and Asia but also throughout the world.

In the middle of the 1960s the U.S. immigration law changed, opening the doors for many Koreans to immigrate to the United States. This started a new page in the history of Korean Presbyterians. Unfortunately, the PC(USA) was unprepared to welcome and accept the large number of Korean Presbyterians into its life. While some Koreans joined the PC(USA), some felt the need to establish an independent Korean Presbyterian Church in the United States. Each of these organized groupings of Korean American Presbyterian churches has contributed to the growth and development of the Presbyterian witness in the United States through its unique gifts and calling.

After many years of informal cooperation between leadership of the two churches, the 204th General Assembly (1992) of the PC(USA) and the 17th General Assembly (1992) of the KPCA authorized the establishment of the Joint Committee on Presbyterian Cooperation between the PC(USA) and the KPCA. Over the past thirty years, the joint committee has focused its work in the areas of ministries and education, global mission, peace, justice, reconciliation, and church polity. Of particular note is the opportunity that Korean Americans born and raised in the United States present for our churches to move from immigrant-focused ministries to ministries directed toward future generations. The work of the joint committee has been important in shaping the relationship between the PC(USA) and the KPCA.

The joint committee believes that God is calling us to move to a deeper relationship between the KPCA and the PC(USA) and to request our General Assemblies to declare covenant relationship between the two churches. Covenant relationship establishes a formal mutual commitment in our ecclesial and missional life together. The nature of covenant relationship is a call to mutuality based upon core theological principles.

II. Mutual Recognition and Reconciliation

A. As churches within the Reformed tradition, each holding membership in the World Alliance of Reformed Churches, we recognize each other as churches in which the gospel is preached, sacraments are rightly administered according to the Word of God, and the mission of Jesus Christ is lived out.

B. Baptism marks us as belonging to Christ and Christ's church. According to scripture, "there is one Lord, one faith, one baptism." To that end, we recognize the baptism of each of our churches and welcome one another's members as brothers and sisters in Christ. We recognize that it is Christ that has showed us the way of self-sacrificing love and given to us the sacrament of the Lord's Supper to remember this love and to be fed with the bread of life and the cup of salvation. We encourage the sharing in the Lord's Supper together in all arenas of the church.

C. Christ has entrusted the ministry of the gospel to all of his disciples, calling us to follow him in the way of love, righteousness, peace, and justice. Ordination is the act by which men and women are set aside for particular ministries of the Church. We identify and name these ministries as deacon, elder, and minister of the Word and Sacrament. We recognize that the calling and setting aside of persons for service in the church and the world is for the sake of the mission of Christ. We recognize the authenticity of one another's ordination of ministers, elders, and deacons.

D. The Church lives to fulfill the mission of God in the world. The Church does not live for its own sake, but seeks to witness to the saving work of Jesus Christ, the transformative power of the gospel, justice, and reconciliation in all areas of its life and witness. God's gift of unity strengthens the witness of the Church. While divisions within the Church cannot destroy the mission of the Church, they do serve as distractions to the message and the mission of the Church. We recognize that the mission of our churches is strengthened by commitment to work cooperatively in the areas of congregational support, resource and leadership development, national and global mission.

III. Covenant Commitments

A. We covenant to support one another through prayer, dialogue, and continued cooperative work. Through mutual affirmation and admonition, we covenant to an honest relationship in which our joys are celebrated, our trials are shared, and disagreements are addressed with the goal of strengthening this covenant. We will seek to affirm the witness of our churches and when necessary speak loving words of correction for the edification of the body of Christ.

B. While we recognize each other's ministries as authentic, we covenant to develop a process of orderly exchange of ministers. This provision will be governed by the principle that the presbyteries decide who shall be members and approves calls for service in churches. This process will allow for ministers to share in the ministry of each other's churches, identify processes for transferring ministers, and the procedures for ministers to be dually affiliated. This process will only apply to ministers who are in good standing and include processes for discipline in accordance with our individual polities.

C. We recognize that we are one family and our congregations have common roots. Many Koreans within the PC(USA) and in the KPCA have shared roots in Korea. We covenant to develop a process of orderly transfer of congregations. This process will encourage, where feasible, congregations to share together in ministry and to be dually affiliated. We covenant to develop a process that seeks to strengthen the witness of our churches and not to contribute to divisions within the body of Christ. This process will be developed in a way that respects our individual polities.

D. We recognize that there is much we share in mission together. We covenant to continue to work together in the following areas of mission and pray that other areas may also emerge—Curriculum Development; Second Generation and Youth and Young Adult Ministry; Congregational Support and Leadership Development; Women's Leadership and Resource Development; Global Mission and Justice and Reconciliation in the world.

IV. Enabling Acts

A. This covenant will be forwarded to our General Assemblies through the appropriate channels in each of our churches for action by 2008.

B. Our assemblies will be asked to enter into covenant relationship, make the necessary constitutional amendments to enable this covenant and to forward it to presbyteries for ratification.

C. Upon the ratification by presbyteries, covenant relationship will be established and a service of worship celebrating and formally entering into covenant relationship will be held by 2010.

D. A covenant implementation committee will be established to shape and support the covenanting process and to make recommendations that enable us to live fully into this covenant.

V. Prayer for the Future

We offer thanksgiving to you O God, Creator of the Universe, Lord of all peoples. You sent the gospel to Korea through the work of Presbyterian missionaries. Through the power of the Holy Spirit, you have nurtured the faith of Koreans in the midst of difficult sufferings and we witnessed the growth of the church in Korea and amongst Korean Presbyterians in the United States. We recognize that while there has been a separation because of human limitations, you have continued to work in and through each of our churches. You have taken our differences in culture, custom, and language and made us one family in Christ. We are grateful that you are bringing us to this time of deeper relationship and seek your guidance and blessing as we make this covenant between the Korean Presbyterian Church in America and the Presbyterian Church (U.S.A.) for now and generations to come.

"Now to him who by the power at work at within us is able to accomplish abundantly far more than all we can ask or imagine, to him be glory in the church and in Christ Jesus to all generations, forever and ever. Amen."

Ephesians 3:20–21 (NRSV)

APPENDIX D

Polity and Church Law Resources

POLITY AND CHURCH LAW RESOURCES

PRINT AND ELECTRONIC RESOURCES AVAILABLE
(Order information and/or links to electronic formats can be found at
www.pcusa.org/polityresources.)

Annotated Book of Order

Articles of Agreement (Current Appendix A of the *Book of Order*)

Book of Confessions
English
Braille
Spanish
Korean
Portuguese

Book of Order
English
Braille
Spanish
Korean
Indonesian
Portuguese

Companion to the Constitution

Forms for Judicial Process (Plus Dissent and Protest) (Formerly Appendix A of the
Book of Order)

Legal Resource Manual for Councils and Churches

Mission Policy Guide

Presbyterian Seal (About and the use of) (formerly Appendix F of the *Book of Order*)

Selected Theological Statements of the Presbyterian Church (U.S.A.)

Visible Marks of Churches Uniting in Christ (formerly Appendix D of the *Book
of Order*)

ECUMENICAL RESOURCES

A Formula of Agreement (Appendix B of the *Book of Order*)

Churches in Correspondence

*Covenant Relationship Between the Korean Presbyterian Church in America and the
Presbyterian Church (U.S.A.)* (Current Appendix C of the Book of Order)

Full Communion Partners

Orderly Exchange with Formula of Agreement Partners (ELCA, RCA, UCC)

Orderly Exchange with Korean Presbyterian Church in America (KPCA)

Constitution of the Presbyterian Church (U.S.A.)
   Book of Confessions
   Book of Order (Annotated)

General Assembly Minutes

Presbyterian Social Witness Policy Compilation

Selected Theological Statements of the Presbyterian Church (U.S.A.)

INDEXES

SCRIPTURAL ALLUSION INDEX[1]

THE FOUNDATIONS OF PRESBYTERIAN POLITY

CHAPTER I

F-1.0201
a. Eph. 1:20, 21; Ps. 68:18
b. Ps. 2:6; Dan. 7:14; Eph. 1:22, 23

F-1.0301
c. Col. 1:18; Eph. 4:16; 1 Cor. 1:18

F-1.0302a
d. Ps. 2:8; Rev. 7:9

F-1.0402
e. Ezek. 43:11, 12

CHAPTER II

F-2.02
a. The Confession of 1967, Preface at 9.03

F-2.03
b. Nicene Creed, 1.3; Theological Declaration of Barmen, 8.01, 8.06

F-2.04
c. Scots Confession, 3.08; Westminster, 6.062, 6.065

d. Second Helvetic, 5.108, 5.109; Heidelberg, 4.061, 4.065; Shorter Catechism, 7.033; Larger Catechism, 7.180

e. Westminster, 6.001, 6.006, 6.007

F-2.05
f. Scots Confession, 3.02, 3.13, 3.14; Heidelberg, 4.011, 4.047, 4.117, 4.121; Second Helvetic, 5.074; Larger Catechism, 7.295, 7.299

g. Heidelberg, 4.006, 4.036; 2nd Helvetic, 5.036; Shorter Catechism, 7.004; Larger Catechism, 7.262

h. Scots Confession, 3.01; Heidelberg, 4.026, 4.027, 4.028; Second Helvetic, 5.029, 5.030, 5.031; Westminster, 6.008, 6.024, 6.025, 6.026, 6.027, 6.030, 6.117; Shorter Catechism, 7.008, 7.011, 7.012; Larger Catechism, 7.124, 7.128, 7.129, 7.130, 7.300, 7.302, 7.303, 7.305; Confession of 1967, 9.03

i. Heidelberg, 4.006; Second Helvetic, 5.015; Westminster 6.024, 6.037, 6.105; Confession of 1967, 9.15, 9.16, 9.17, 9.50; Brief Statement, 10.3

j. Heidelberg, 4.079; Westminster, 6.058, 6.190; Larger Catechism, 7.148, 7.303

k. Heidelberg, 4.027

l. Heidelberg, 4.014, 4.037; Brief Statement, 10.3

m. Confession of 1967, 9.15; Brief Statement, 10.3

n. Scots Confession, Chapter VII; Second Helvetic, 5.058; Westminster, 6.021, 6.095, 6.193

o. Second Helvetic, 5.058; Westminster 6.181, 6.192; Shorter Catechism, 7.20; Larger Catechism, 7.189, 7.191

p. Scots Confession, 3.05, 3.14, 3.25; Heidelberg, 4.094, 4.095; Shorter Catechism, 7.215; Larger Catechism, 7.218, 7.300

q. Scots Confession, 3.14

F-3.0107	a.	See and consult Acts 15:1–32
F-3.0108	b.	Matt. 18:15–18; 1 Cor. 5:4, 5
F-3.02	c.	See Acts 15:1–29; 16:4 (found in Footnote 6)

FORM OF GOVERNMENT

CHAPTER I

G-1.0101	a.	Acts 2:41, 47
G-1.0103	b.	Heb. 8:5
	c.	Gal. 1:21, 22; Rev. 2:1
G-1.0402	d.	Heb. 8:5; Gal. 6:16

CHAPTER II

G-2.0102	a.	1 Tim. 3:1; Eph. 4:11, 12
	b.	1 Tim. 5:17
	c.	Phil. 1:1
	d.	1 Peter 5:1; Titus 1:5; 1 Tim. 5:1, 17, 19
G-2.0201	e.	Phil. 1:1; 1 Tim. 3:8–15
	f.	Acts 6:3, 5, 6
G-2.0301	g.	1 Cor. 12:28
	h.	1 Tim. 5:17; Rom. 12:7, 8; Acts 15:25
G-2.0501	i.	Jer. 3:15
G-2.0604	j.	1 Tim. 4:14; Acts 13:2, 3

CHAPTER III

G-3.0105	a.	1 Cor. 14:40
G-3.0108a	b.	Acts 15:22–24
G-3.0109b(5)	c.	Acts 20:17; 6:2; 15:30
G-3.0201	d.	1 Cor. 5:4
	e.	Heb. 13:17; 1 Thess. 5:12, 13; 1 Tim. 5:17
G-3.0201c	f.	1 Thess. 5:12, 13; 2 Thess. 3:6, 14, 15; 1 Cor. 11:27–33
G-3.0202f	g.	Acts 15:2, 6
G-3.0203	h.	Acts 20:17
G-3.0301	i.	Acts 6:1, 6; 9:31; 21:20; 2:41, 46, 47; 4:4; 15:4; 11:22, 30; 21:17, 18; 6:1–7; 19:18–20; 1 Cor. 16:8, 9, 19; Acts 18:19, 24, 26; 20:17, 18, 25, 28, 30, 36, 37; Rev. 2:1–6
	j.	Acts 15:1–6; 1 Cor. 14:26, 33, 40
	k.	Eph. 6:18; Phil. 4:6
G-3.0301c	l.	Acts 15:28; 1 Cor. 5:3
G-3.0304	m.	Acts 14:26–27; Acts 11:18
G-3.04	n.	As the proofs already adduced in favor of a presbyterian

		assembly in the government of the church, are equally valid in support of a synodical assembly, it is unnecessary to repeat the Scriptures to which the reference has been made under Chap. X [sic XI], or add any other. (1888 Form of Government, Presbyterian Church in the United States of America at X)
G-3.0402	o.	Acts 15:10; Gal. 2:4, 5
G-3.0501	p.	See Acts 15:1–29; 16:4

CHAPTER V

G-5.04	a.	Acts 21:17, 18; Acts 6; Acts 15:2, 3, 4, 6, 22
G-5.05	b.	Acts 15:5, 6

CHAPTER VI

G-6.03	a.	Confession of 1967; Preface at 9.03; see also G-2.0200

DIRECTORY FOR WORSHIP

CHAPTER IV

W-4.4003b	a.	2 Tim. 3:16; Eph. 2:20
W-4.4003c	b.	2 Tim. 1:13
W-4.4003e	c.	1 Peter 5:5
W-4.4004a(1)	d.	Acts 6:5, 6
W-4.4006b(2)	e.	James 1:21; Heb. 13:17
W-4.4006b(3)	f.	1 Cor. 9:7–15
	g.	1 Thess. 5:12, 13
W-4.4006c	h.	Acts 13:2, 3
	i.	1 Tim. 4:14
W-4.4006d	j.	2 Tim. 4:1, 2
W-4.4006e	k.	Gal. 2:9; Acts 1:25
W-4.4006f	l.	Mark 4:24; Heb. 2:1

---

[1]In response to *Overture 01-58*, the Office of the General Assembly reviewed previous editions of the Form of Government, which had included scriptural allusions. A large proportion of our current Form of Government has antecedent provisions in prior editions that are immediately apparent. After that review, the Department of Constitutional Services carefully compared those prior editions with the current text of the Form of Government. That department then inserted the scriptural allusions taken from those prior editions of the Form of Government into the scriptural allusions taken from those prior editions of the Form of Government into the current text. They first appeared in the version released during the 215th General Assembly (2003).

INDEX

The references in this index are to the section numbers.

Acceptance and Reconciliation, Services of W-4.8000
Accountability to Presbytery for Worship W-1.4008
Accused—Rights .... D-10.0203 c
Accuser, Rights to Petition if Charges Not Filed D-10.0303
Active Member: G-1.0402
Acts of Commitment and Recognition W-3.3502–.3504
    W-3.3701
    W-3.5503–.5504
    W-4.2006
Acts of Recognition W-3.3502
    W-3.3504
    W-4.7000
Administration (See also Principles of Administration), Defined G-3.0106
Administrative Commissions .... G-3.0109 b
Administrative Leave When Sexual Abuse Is Alleged D-10.0106
Administrative, Manual of Operations G-3.0106
Administrative Review G-3.0108
Administrative Staff:
    Elected under principles of participation and representation G-3.0110
    Executives of, how elected and how terminated G-3.0110
Administrator, Teaching Elder Called to Labor as G-3.0306
Admission to the Lord's Supper:
    Baptized members G-1.0401
    G-1.0404
    Of baptized children G-1.0404
    W-2.4011 b
    W-4.2002
Advent, Season of .... W-3.2002 a
Advisory Committee on the Constitution G-6.02
Advisory Handbooks G-3.0106
Advocate in Disciplinary Process .... D-10.0203 a, b
Affiliate Member G-1.0403
    G-3.0204 a
Affirmation in Place of Oath .... D-14.0302 b
Affirmation of Faith (See also "Creeds and Confessions") W-3.3500
    W-4.10004
Allegations of Offense D-10.0101
Alternative Forms of Resolution D-2.0103
    D-10.0202 h(1–4)
    D-10.0301
Amending Action of Administrative Commission .... G-3.0109 b
Amending the Constitution:
    Book of Confessions G-6.03
    Book of Order G-6.04

Amending the Constitution: (*continued*)

    Must go through Advisory Committee on Constitution G-6.04

    Provisions not to be amended G-6.05

    Special provisions G-6.06

Annual (or Biennial) Review .... G-3.0108 a

Annual Review of Pastor's Terms of Call G-2.0804

Apostles' Creed a Part of the Constitution F-3.04

Appeals:

    Content of written notice of .... D-8.0202 a–f

        D-13.0202 a–f

    Decision of permanent judicial commission .... D-8.0404 a–f

        D-13.0404 a–f

    Defined D-8.0101

        D-13.0101

    Effect of, in disciplinary and remedial cases D-8.0103

        D-13.0104

    Filings in appeal process for disciplinary case D-13.0200

    Filings in appeal process for remedial case D-8.0200

    Grounds of .... D-8.0105 a–g

        D-13.0106 a, b

    Hearing on D-8.0403

        D-13.0403

    Notice of hearing D-8.0401

        D-13.0401

    Record on .... D-8.0203 a–g

        D-13.0303 a–g

    Time for filing written notice of D-8.0201

        D-13.0201

    Time within which filing of briefs of appellant and

        appellee are to be filed D-8.0304

                through D-8.0305

        D-13.0304

                through D-13.0305

    Who may initiate .... D-8.0102 b

        D-13.0102

    Withdrawal of D-8.0104

        D-13.0105

Appellant:

    Abandon appeal by failure to file within time allowed .... D-8.0304 c

        D-13.0304 c

    Shall give notice of appeal within thirty days D-8.0201

        D-13.0201

Appellee Shall File Response Within Thirty Days D-8.0305

        D-13.0305

Appropriate Language W-1.2002

Approval of Presbyteries on Constitutional Amendment G-6.03

        G-6.04

Architecture W-1.3021–.3024

        W-1.4004 g

"Are to be," as a Term defined in the Preface .... Preface
Art Forms and Worship:
    Dance W-1.2001
                                                     W-1.4004 i, j
                                                     W-1.4005 a (5)
                                                     W-2.1005 b
                                                     W-2.2008
                                                     W-3.4002
    Drama W-1.2001
                                                     W-1.3034 (2)
                                                     W-1.4004 j
                                                     W-1.4005 a(5)
                                                     W-2.2008
                                                     W-3.4002
    General W-1.3034 (2)
                                                     W-1.4004 i, j
                                                     W-1.4005 a(5)
                                                     W-3.5102
                                                     W-3.5302
    Music (See also "Music in Public Worship") W-1.4004
                                                     W-1.4005
Associate Pastor:
    Installed Pastoral Relationship .... G-2.0504 a
    Member of session G-3.0201
    Not eligible to become the next installed pastor, co-pastor .... G-2.0504 a
        With one exception .... G-2.0504 c
    Ordination and installation W-4.4000
                                                     W-4.4006
    Pastoral relationships G-2.0504
    Relationship not dependent on that of pastor .... G-2.0504 a
    Terms of call G-2.0804
Assurance of God's Pardon .... W-3.3301 (d)
                                                     W-3.3507
At-Large Member (See also "Member-at-Large") .... G-2.0503 b
Audit (See "Financial Review")
Authentic Language W-1.2005
Baptism:
    Anointing and W-3.3607
    As a Sacrament W-1.3033 (2)
                                                     W-2.3008
                                                     W-3.3601
    As a response to Great Commission W-2.3001
    Chaplains and other Teaching Elders administering .... W-2.3011 b
    Children and .... W-2.3008 b
                                                     W-2.3014
                                                     W-2.4011
                                                     W-3.3602
                                                     W-3.3603
    Church responsibility W-2.3013
    Creeds and .... W-3.3603 (a), (d)

Baptism: (*continued*)

Font or pool for	W-1.3024
Immersion	W-3.3605
Included in service of	W-3.3603
through	W-3.3608
Infant (See under "Baptism, Children and")	
Jesus and	W-2.3001
Laying on of hands and	W-3.3607
Lord's Supper and	W-2.3009
	W-3.3608
Meanings of	W-2.3002–.3008
	W-3.3601
	W-3.3602
Mode	W-3.3605
Parental responsibility and	W-2.3014
Pouring	W-3.3605
Preaching and	W-3.3602
Preparing for	W-6.2001 a
Profession of faith and	W-2.3008
Reaffirmation of	W-2.3009
Received only once	W-2.3009
Recording of	W-2.3011 a(4)
Register of, to be kept	G-3.0204 b
Roll of baptized members	G-3.0204 a
Scripture and	W-3.3602
Sequence of	W-3.3603
through	W-3.3608
Service for the Lord's Day and	W-3.3502
	W-3.3600
Session's responsibility and	W-2.3011
	W-2.3014
Spirit and	W-2.3001
	W-2.3004 e
Sponsors and	W-2.3013
Sprinkling	W-3.3605
Trinitarian formula and	W-2.3010
	W-3.3606
Use of name of person being baptized	W-3.3606
Water and	W-3.3605
Welcome of the congregation and	W-3.3608
	W-4.2001
Where administered	W-2.3011
Where placed in service	W-3.3602
Which are valid	W-2.3010
Who may present children	G-1.0404
	W-2.3014

Baptized Members:

Defined	G-1.0401

Baptized Members: (*continued*)

    Entitled to participate in the Lord's Supper G-1.0401

                                                       W-2.4011

    Register of baptisms kept by session .... G-3.0204 b

    Roll of .... G-3.0204 a

Benefits Plan of PC(USA)

    Clarification of Participation in G-2.0804

    Teaching Elders' participation in, as stated in call G-2.0804

Bible: Confessions Subordinate to (see also Scripture) F-2.02

Biennial General Assemblies:

    Commissioners G-3.0501

    Proposed amendments to the *Book of Order* G-6.04

    Reporting and review of proceedings and actions .... G-3.0108 a

Body of Christ, Church as the F-1.0301

Book of Confessions, The:

    How amended G-6.03

    Part of Constitution of the Church F-3.04

Book of Order:

    How amended G-6.04

    Part of Constitution of the Church F-3.04

Briefs:

    Appellant D-8.0304

                                                       D-13.0304

    Appellee D-8.0305

                                                        D-13.0305

Broken Relationships, Pastoral Care and W-6.3008

Budget of Council G-3.0113

Budget of Particular Church, Approval of, by Session G-3.0205

Calendar (See also "Church Year") .... W-3.3616e.(1)

Call to Certified Christian Educator G-2.1103

Call to Ordered Ministry G-2.0103

Call, to Pastor:

    Called to beyond the jurisdiction of the church G-2.0503

    Election of Pastor Nominating Committee G-2.0802

    Installation Service G-2.0805

    Minimum requirements G-2.0804

    Of another denomination G-2.0505

    Participation in Benefits Plan of PC(USA) G-2.0804

    Pastoral Vacancy G-2.0801

    Presbytery must be consulted G-3.0307

    Process G-2.0803

    Terms of call G-2.0804

    Viewed as request for installation W-4.4006

Called Meetings (See "Special Meetings")

Calling of the Church F-1.03

Calling to Ordered Ministries in the Church,

    Gifts Bestowed on Those Called G-2.0104

Candidates for the Teaching Elders (See "Preparation

    for Ministry") G-2.06

Cases:

Disciplinary, defined... D-2.0203

Remedial, defined D-2.0102

Catechisms, Larger and Shorter:

Part of the Constitution F-3.04

Censures of Church:

Degrees of... D-11.0403 e

D-12.0101

Notice of temporary exclusion or removal of teaching elder to
be sent to General Assembly Stated Clerk .... D-12.0104 g

Rebuke D-12.0102

Rebuke with D-12.0103

Removal from ordered ministry or membership......................... D-12.0105

Supervised rehabilitation D-12.0104b

Temporary exclusion D-12.0104

Termination of... D-12.0104 h

Certificate:

Affiliate member... G-1.0403

Of transfer... G-1.0303 b

Certification G-2.1101

Certified Church Service.. G-2.11

Christian Educators... G-2.1103

Forms of.. G-2.1101

Presbytery Responsibilities.. G-2.1103 b

Roll of.. G-3.0104

Skills and Training... G-2.1103 a

Voice and Vote G-2.1103

Challenge to Findings of PJC Moderator and Clerk:

Appeal in a disciplinary case .... D-13.0302 a

Appeal in a remedial case .... D-8.0302 a

Remedial case.. D-6.0306 a

Chaplain, Teaching Elder Called to Labor as G-3.0306

Chaplains Authorized to Celebrate the Sacraments:

Baptism.. W-2.3011 b

Lord's Supper .... W-2.4012 b

Charge:

To congregation at ordination and installation .... W-4.4006 f

To pastor or associate pastor at ordination and installation .... W-4.4006 f

Charges, in discipline.. D-10.0101

D-10.0400

Child Abuse—Report Required.. G-4.0302

Children:

Admission to the Lord's Supper of Baptized............................... G-1.0401

Baptism and W-2.3008

W-2.3014

W-3.3602

W-3.3603

Entitled to pastoral care and instruction.................................... G-1.0401

Family worship and W-5.7002

Children: (*continued*)
General... W-3.1004
Lord's Supper and.. W-2.4011
                                                                              W-4.2002
Members of Church G-1.04
Choir (See "Music in Public Worship")
Christ:
Alone rules, calls, teaches, and uses the Church........................... G-2.0101
Head of the Church... F-1.02
Living God in common life, the... W-1.1003 c
Perfect Human Response to God .... W-1.1003 b
Christian Nurture W-6.2000
                                                                              W-6.2005
Christian Year (See also "Church Year") W-5.5002
                                                                              W-5.7003
Christmas, Day and Season of .... W-3.2002 b
Church:
And its confessions F-2.00
And its members G-1.0303
And its mission F-1.01
And its ordered ministries.. G-2.0102
And its unity .... F-1.0302 a
Apostolicity of... F-1.0302 d
As the body of Christ... F-1.0301
Authority of Christ... F-1.0201
Catholicity of.. F-1.0302 c
Christ calls into being F-1.0202
Christ equips F-1.0202
Christ gives its life F-1.0203
Christ is hope F-1.0204
Christ is the foundation.. F-.1.0205
Dissolved or extinct:
Member of .... G-3.0301 c
Property of G-4.0205
Finances G-3.0113
God's mission F-1.01
Great Ends of the Church... F-1.0304
Holiness of.. F-1.0302 b
Incorporation of G-4.0101
Mark of F-1.0302
Membership G-1.04
Mission of... F-1.01
Ordered Ministries of.. G-2.0102
Powers of corporation or trustees G-4.0101
Property G-4.02
Reformed, always reforming F-2.02
Rolls of particular .... G-3.0204 a
Trustees of G-4.0101
Unity of... F-1.0302 a
Universal.. F-.3.0101 b

Church Censures (see also "Censures of Church")............................ D-12.0100
Church Finances:
    Annual financial review required... G-3.0113
    Session's responsibility G-3.0205
    Treasurer elected by session G-3.0205
Church Location .... G-3.0303 b
Church Officers (See "Ordered Ministry"; see also "Deacons,"
    "Ruling Elders," "Teaching Elders")
Church Power:
    Cannot bind conscience F-3.0107
    Ministerial and declarative.. F-3.0107
    Not aided by the civil power.. F-3.0101 b
Church Property:
    As a tool for mission.. G-4.0201
    Congregation in schism G-4.0207
    Decisions concerning property G-4.0202
    Dissolved or extinct congregation G-4.0205
    Exceptions to provisions.. G-4.0208
    Held in trust G-4.0203
    Selling, encumbering, or leasing.. G-4.0206
    Subject to the authority of the session G-4.0101
    Trustees.. G-4.0101
    Used contrary to the Constitution G-4.0204
Church Treasurer:
    Elected by the session.. G-3.0205
    Work supervised by the session... G-3.0205
Church Unions
    Organic union by denomination G-5.03
    Particular churches (see also Joint Congregational Witness)....... G-5.05
Church Year:
    General.. W-1.3013
    W-3.2002
    W-3.2003
    Lectionaries and.. W-2.2003
    Seasons and days of... W-3.2002 a–g
    W-3.2003
    W-3.5301
    W-5.5002
Churches:
    Federated .... G-3.0109 b
    In correspondence... G-5.0201
Citations.. D-11.0201
    If defendant does not appear... D-11.0202 b
    Second .... D-11.0202 a
    Service of... D-11.0202
Civil Marriage, Recognition of.. W-4.9006
Civil Powers and Religion F-3.0101
Civil Proceedings, Concurrent with Investigating
    Committee Work D-10.0401a

Clerk:
Duties in case of process...D-11.0601
Of congregational meeting...G-1.0505
Of session, presbytery, synod, General Assembly.......................G-3.0104
Reporting decisions D-11.0700
Responsibilities of G-3.0104
Commission of Council:
Administrative ....G-3.0109 b
Judicial..G-3.0109 a
D-5.0000
Membership of..G-3.0109
D-5.0101–.0105
Permanent judicial commissions......................................D-5.0000
Presbytery and synod shall appoint
permanent judicial commission..................................D-5.0101
Quorum of...D-5.0204
Size of:
For presbytery, synod, General Assembly............................G-3.0109 b
D-5.0101
For session G-3.0109
Commissioned Lay Pastor: (See "Commissioning Ruling Elders to
Particular Pastoral Service")
Commissioners:
To General Assembly:
Number from each presbytery G-3.0501
Number required for a quorum G-3.0503
To presbytery G-3.0301
To synod G-3.0401
Commissioning (See also "Confirmation and Commissioning"):
Baptism and W-2.3006
Service for the Lord's Day and..W-3.3101 (8)
W-3.3503 (c)
Specific acts of discipleship and....................................W-4.3000
Commissioning Ruling Elders to Particular Pastoral Service:
Commissioning...G-2.1002
Confidentiality G-4.0301
Examination G-2.1002
Functions G-2.1001
May administer baptism...G-2.1001
May administer Lord's Supper G-2.1001
May be engaged in Validated Ministry................................G-2.1001
May perform services of marriage....................................G-2.1001
Period valid...G-2.1001
Questions to be answered W-4.4003
Training, Examination, and Commissioning G-2.1002
Commissioning Service G-2.1003
Supervision G-2.1004
Commitment and Recognition, Acts of..................................W-3.3502–.3504
W-3.3701

		W-4.2006
Committal, Service of		W-4.10006
Committee of Counsel Defined		D-6.0302
Provide for by Rule		D-6.0302 a
Who shall not serve on		D-6.0302 b
Committee on Ministry: (See "Pastor, Counselor, and Advisor to Teaching Elders and Congregations")		
Committee on Preparation for Ministry (See "Pastor, Counselor, and Advisor to Teaching Elders and Congregations"; see also "Preparation for Ministry")		
Committee on Representation		G-3.0103
Committees of Council		G-3.0109
Defined		G-3.0109
Communion:		
Full Communion		G-5.0202
Lord's Supper (See also "Lord's Supper")		W-2.4000
Community:		
Christian worship and		W-1.1005
		W-2.6001
Wider human ministry to		W-1.3012 (2)
		W-3.3505
		W-7.0000
Compassion, Ministry of		W-7.3000
Compensation		G-2.1103 b
		G-3.0303
Complaint:		
Against council at same level		D-6.0202 a
Answer to		D-6.0303
Committee of counsel		D-6.0302
Defined		D-6.0102
Duty of respondent		D-6.0304
Employee may file		D-6.0202 a,b
Filed only after request to correct delinquency		D-6.0102
Motion to dismiss		D-6.0303
Pretrial proceedings		D-6.0307
	through	D-6.0310
Procedure prior to trial		D-6.0305
Statements in		D-6.0301
Stay of enforcement		D-6.0103 a
Time within which to file		D-6.0103 a
Trial briefs, contents of		D-6.0306
Who may file and against whom		D-6.0202
Confessional Statements:		
As Faith of the Church catholic		F-2.03
As Faith of the Protestant Reformation		F-2.04
As Faith of the Reformed tradition		F-2.05
As Subordinate standards		F-2.02
Purpose of		F-2.01

Confidence and Privilege.. G-4.03
    Mandatory reporting   G-4.0302
    Trust and confidentiality   G-4.0301
Confirmation and Commissioning...................................... W-4.2003
Congregation.. G-1.01
    Defined G-1.0101
    Fellowship of... G-1.0102
    Governed by the Constitution..................................... G-1.0103
    Mission of.. G-1.0101
    Organizing of.. G-1.02
    Questions asked at ordination and installation
        of deacons and ruling elders W-4.4003
        of teaching elder W-4.4003
Congregational Meetings:
    Annual and special meetings G-1.0501
    Business Proper to Congregational Meetings G-1.0503
    Calling a Congregational Meeting.............................. G-1.0502
    For calling a pastor G-1.0503
                                                       G-2.0802
    For electing ruling elders, deacons, and trustees........ G-1.0503
                                                       G-2.0102
    For matters related to church property....................... G-1.0503
    For matters related to pastoral relationship................ G-1.0503
    For matters requesting an exemption.......................... G-1.0503
    Minutes G-1.0505
    Moderator G-1.0504
    Nominating and voting requirements........................... G-2.0401
    Parliamentary Procedure, *Robert's Rules of Order,*
       Newly Revised G-3.0105
    Public notice G-1.0502
                                                       G-2.0802
    Questions asked at installation of teaching elder........ W-4.4006 a–b
    Quorum of.. G-1.0501
    Secretary of, is clerk of session.................................. G-1.0505
Conscience:
    Church judicatory can make no laws to bind.............. F-3.0107
    Freedom of.. G-2.0105
    God alone is Lord of.. F-3.0101
Constitution of the Presbyterian Church (U.S.A.):
    Amendments to special provisions G-6.06
    Always to be reformed.. G-6.02
    Book of Confession F-3.04
    Book of Order F-3.04
    Defined F-3.04
    How amended:
        Book of Confessions... G-6.03
        Book of Order G-6.04
            Exceptions G-6.05
    Interpreting G-6.02
    Reform.. G-6.01

Constitutional Questions, Affirmative Answer Required:
    In ordaining and installing deacons and ruling elders W-4.4003
    In ordaining and installing teaching elders W-4.4003
Continuity and Change F-1.0401
Co-Pastors G-2.0504
                                                            G-3.0104
    Associate pastor cannot be called as .... G-2.0504 a
        Exception .... G-2.0504 c
    When one leaves, the other is pastor .... G-2.0504 a
Corporation (See also "Incorporation") G-4.0101
Correspondence:
    Churches in G-5.0201
    Requirement for G-3.0501
Councils G-3.01
    General Assembly G-3.05
    Presbytery G-3.03
    Session G-3.02
    Synod G-3.04
Councils of the Church G-3.01
    Administration of Mission G-3.0106
    Administrative Review G-3.0108
        General Review .... G-3.0108 a
        Directed Response .... G-3.0108 c
        Special Review .... G-3.0108 b
    Administrative staff G-3.0110
    Annual audits required G-3.0113
    As an Expression of Unity of the Church G-3.0101
    Can make no laws to bind conscience F-3.0107
    Clerks G-3.0104
    Commissioning and W-4.3003
    Committee on representation G-3.0103
    Committees and Commissions G-3.0109
    Defined G-3.0101
    Equitable compensation G-3.0106
    Fair employment practices G-3.0106
    Finance G-3.0113
    Have only ecclesiastical jurisdiction G-3.0102
    Inclusiveness F-1.0403
                                                             G-3.0103
    Inquiry by, in disciplinary case .... D-10.0102 b
    Insurance G-3.0112
    Jurisdiction, only ecclesiastical G-3.0102
    Maintain relations and activities with other Churches
        to express unity of the Church G-5.01
    Majority shall govern F-3.0205
    Manual of administrative operations to be developed G-3.0106
    Meetings G-3.0105
    Minutes and records of G-3.0107
    Mission determines the form and structures G-3.0106

Councils of the Church (*continued*)

 Moderators of G-3.0104
 G-3.0105
 Names of.. G-3.0101
 Nominating Process G-3.0111
 Operating expenses G-3.0106
 Participation... G-3.0103
 Per capita funds.. G-3.0106
 Presbytery G-3.03
 Principles, General Administration:........................ G-3.01
  Defined G-3.0106
 Procedure when lower council delinquent or irregular D-2.0202
 Records G-3.0107
 Records of lower council reviewed by next higher...... G-3.0108
 Regular gradation.. F-3.0203
 Robert's Rules of Order, Newly Revised, meetings governed in
  accordance with most recent edition of..................... G-3.0105
 Representation G-3.0103
 Session... G-3.02
 Synod... G-3.04
 Unity of.. G-3.0101
 Worship in W-3.6100
Counsel:
 If accused is unable to employ............................... D-11.0302
 Right to be represented by D-7.0301
 D-10.0203 c
 D-11.0301
Counselor for accused—not testify........................ D-14.0203
Court Reporter .... D-7.0601 a
 D-14.0303
Covenant:
 Community F-3.01
 Constituting, for new church G-1.0201
 Living in F-1.01
Creeds and Confessions:
 Baptism and W-2.2009
 W-3.3502
 W-3.3603(a),(d)
 General.. W-2.2009
 Lord's Supper and.. W-2.2009
 Service of the Lord's Day and W-3.3501
Daily Worship (See also "Service of Daily Prayer"):
 Discipline of W-1.3012
 W-5.2000
 General.. W-3.2001
 Prayer and W-5.4000
 Scripture and... W-5.3000
Deacons:
 Board of... G-2.0202
 Defined G-2.0201

Deacons: (*continued*)

 Dissolution... G-2.0405
 Election G-2.0401
 Examination.. G-2.0402
 Ordination and Installation G-2.0403
 Preparation for Ministry... G-2.0402
 Release from the exercise of the ordered ministry..................... G-2.0406
 Renunciation of Jurisdiction . G-2.0407
 Resignation of.. G-2.0405
 Responsibilities of G-2.0201
 Supervised by session G-2.0202
 Terms of Service... G-2.0404
 Under Authority of the Session G-2.0202

Death (See also "Services on the Occasion of Death"):

 Care at the time of.. W-6.3006
 Delete names from the roll.. G-3.0204

Deletion of Name of:

 Member joining some other church G-3.0204
 Renouncing jurisdiction.. G-2.0407
                            G-2.0509

Delinquency:

 Defined .... D-2.0202 b
 Statement in complaint D-6.0301
 Subject of remedial cases... D-6.0102

Deposition, Testimony Taken by D-7.0205
                             D-14.0304

Designated Pastor G-2.0805

Designated Term for Pastor G-2.0504a

Desire to be Restored to Ordered Ministry G-2.0507

Directory for Worship:

 Its authority... W-Preface
 What it is... W-Preface

Disability:

 Inclusion of persons with.. F-1.0403

Disciplinary Cases:

 Accused, rights of... D-10.0203 c
 Charge, filing of.. D-10.0404
 Charge, form of... D-10.0403
 Council inquiry D-10.0102
 Counsel... D-7.0301
                            D-10.0203
 Defined D-2.0201
 Disciplinary committee inquiry D-10.0103
 Enforcement of judgment D-11.0801
 Individual and self-accusation .... D-10.0102 c
  Written statement regarding .... D-10.0102 c
 Initiation, method of D-10.0101

Disciplinary Cases: (*continued*)

Investigating committee D-9.0101
                                                    D-10.0103
                                                    D-10.0201
                                                    D-10.0402

Designation of, between meetings of presbytery .... D-10.0201 b
Notifying a presbytery other than the teaching elder's D-10.0105
Parties are Presbyterian Church (U.S.A.) and accused D-10.0402
Petition for review D-10.0303
       Quorum D-5.0204
       Scope D-10.0204
                                                  D-10.0405
Prehearing conference D-13.0307
Preliminary procedure D-10.0100
Pretrial challenges D-10.0204
Pretrial conference D-10.0405
Prosecution of case D-10.0402
Referral of allegations to special disciplinary committee D-10.0103
Renunciation, effect of D-3.0106
Temporary exclusion D-12.0103
Time limit for filing charges D-10.0401
Transfer prohibited while pending D-10.0105
Vindication, request for D-9.0101

Discipline (See also entire Rules of Discipline):
Context of pastoral care and oversight D-2.0101
Daily worship and W-1.3012
Defined D-1.0101
                             through   D-1.0102
                                                    D-2.0101
Judicial process D-2.0100
Purpose of D-1.0101

Dismissal:
Church members G-3.0204
Churches G-3.0301

Dissent:
Defined G-3.0105
When made G-3.0105

Dissolution of Pastoral Relations:
Activities following dissolution G-2.0905
By congregation request G-2.0903
By Pastor, Co-Pastor, or Associate Pastor Request G-2.0902
By Presbytery Action G-2.0904

Dissolving Church:
Power of presbytery G-3.0301
Property of G-4.0205

Dissolving Relation of Deacon or Ruling Elder:
By session G-2.0405
When change of residence or disability G-2.0405

Diverse Language W-1.2006

Diversity F-1.0403
Doctrine: System of, received and adopted by all persons in
   ordered ministry W-4.4003
Duties of Presbytery and Session in Inquiry and Candidacy G-2.0605
Easter, Day and Season of .... W-3.2002 f
Ecclesiastical Jurisdiction (See also "Jurisdiction of
   Councils of the Church"): F-3.0102
   A shared power .... F-3.0208·
Ecumenical Commitment G-5.01
   Ecumenicity G-5.0101
   Full Organic Union G-5.03
   Interfaith relations G-5.0102
   Relations with other denominations G-5.02
     Correspondence G-5.0201
     Ecumenical statements G-5.0203
     Full Communion G-5.0202
   Secular organizations G-5.0103
Education (See also "Christian Nurture"):
   Presbytery's responsibility for W-1.4009
   Session's responsibility for W-1.4007
Educator (See also "Teaching Elder") G-2.1103
   Teaching Elder, as Expressive Name for Minister of
     Word and Sacrament G-2.0501
Elders (See "Ruling Elders")
Election of Deacons and Ruling elders:
   By vote of congregation G-2.0102
   Congregational meeting called G-2.0401
   Elected for limited term G-2.0404
   Election provisions G-2.0401
   Examined by session G-2.0402
   Ordination and installation G-2.0403
                                         W-4.4000
   Preparation for ministry G-2.0402
   Procedure in congregational meeting G-2.0401
   Who are entitled to vote in congregational meeting G-1.0501
Election of General Assembly Nominating Committee G-3.0111
Election of Pastor Nominating Committee G-2.0802
Election of Pastors (or Associates):
   Call Process G-2.0803
   Call to teaching elder of another denomination G-2.0505
   Installation service G-2.0805
   Pastor Nominating Committee G-2.0802
   Pastoral relationships G-2.0504
   Temporary pastoral relations .... G-2.0504 b
   Terms of call G-2.0804
Election of Trustees G-4.0101
Employee—Standing to file remedial complaint .... D-6.0202 a, b
Enforcement of Judgment D-11.0801
   Refrain from exercise of ordered ministry pending appeal D-11.0801
Entry to Membership G-1.0303

Epiphany, Day of .... W-3.2002 c
Equitable Compensation G-3.0106
Evangelism:
    Ministry of W-7.2000
    Services for (See also "Services for Evangelism") W-3.5500
Evangelist G-3.0306
Evidence in Remedial or Disciplinary Cases (See also "Testimony
    in Remedial or Disciplinary Cases"):
    Defined D-14.0101
    Kinds of D-14.0101
    Newly discovered evidence D-14.0501
    Proof of charge D-11.0401
    Proof of complaint D-7.0402
Examination:
    Of candidate for ordination G-2.0607
    Of deacon or ruling elder G-2.0402
    Of teaching elder for admission to presbytery G-3.0306
Exceptions:
    To church property provisions G-4.0208
    To serve as the next installed pastor .... G-2.0504 c
    To waive any of the requirements for ordination G-2.0610
Executives:
    Election of G-3.0110
    Termination G-3.0110
Faith and Practice, Connection Between F-3.0104
Faith, Reaffirmation of G-1.0303
Families and Worship W-5.7000
Fasting W-1.2003
                                                                                    W-1.3013
                                                                                    W-5.5003

Federated Congregation G-3.0109
Filing a Complaint (See also "Complaint") D-6.0200
Filing Deadlines:
    Complaint of delinquency D-6.0202
    Complaint of irregularity D-6.0202
    Final judgment in judicial case .... D-7.0402 c
Filing of Charges D-10.0401
Filings in Appeal Process for Disciplinary Case D-13.0200
Filings in Appeal Process for Remedial Case D-8.0200
Final Assessment G-2.0607
Finance, of Councils G-3.0113
Financial Review (Full) Required G-3.0113
Floor Nominations G-2.0401
Forms of Worship (See also "Ordering Worship") W-3.1000
Foundational Statements F-3.03
Freedom of Conscience G-2.0105
Full communion G-5.0202
"Full Faith and Credit" Clause D-3.0105
Full organic union G-5.03
Funerals (See also "Services on the Occasion of Death") W-4.10000

Furnishings (See also "Space for Worship") .... W-1.4004 g
General Assembly:
    Advisory Committee on the Constitution G-6.02
    Basis of representation... G-3.0501
    Budget.. G-3.0113
    Commissioners from presbyteries.. G-3.0501
    Committee on representation G-3.0103
    Composition... G-3.0501
    Defined G-3.0501
    Fair employment practice G-3.0106
    Incorporated.. G-4.0101
    Jurisdiction.. G-3.0501 a
    Meetings G-3.0105
                                G-3.0503
    Minutes and records.. G-3.0107
    Moderator G-3.0501
    Nominating Process... G-3.0111
    Notice of special meetings at least sixty days in advance........... G-3.0503
    Quorum.. G-3.0503
    Relationship with Other Councils... G-3.0502
    Requirements of search committee for executives and
       administrative staff... G-3.0110
    Responsibilities G-3.0501
    Staff G-3.0110
Gifts of the Spirit:
    Manifestation in worship .... W-3.1002 b
    Role in the Church... W-1.1005
Giving, Christian... W-2.5000
                                 W-5.5004
God:
    Encounter with humans .... W-1.1002 b
    Entrance into the human condition .... W-1.1002 c
    Initiative of .... W-1.1002 a
    Spirit of... W-1.1002 a
Governing bodies: (See "Councils of the Church")
Grounds for Appeal
    Disciplinary D-13.0106
    Remedial.. D-8.0105
Harm, Risk of, Knowledge of... G-4.0302
Head of the Church... F-1.02
Healing Services W-3.5402
Higher Council, Reviews Records of Lower Councils G-3.0108
Historic Principles of Church Order F-3.01
Holy Spirit:
    Baptism and W-2.3001
                                   W-2.3004 e
                                   W-2.3010
                                   W-3.3604 (c)
                                   W-3.3606
                                   W-3.3607

Holy Spirit: (*continued*)

Healing and... W-3.5405
Lord's Supper and... W-2.4005
 W-2.4007
Ordering worship and .... W-3.1002 a
Preaching and W-2.2007
Role in worship.. W-1.1002 a
 W-1.1004
 W-2.2010
Scripture and.. W-2.2007
Holy Week... W-3.2002 e
Homebound—Lord's Supper.. W-3.3616 e
"Honorably Retired" Teaching Elder:
Defined .... G-2.0503 c
Membership in a presbytery G-2.0503
Presbytery may so designate... G-2.0503 c
Household Worship W-5.7000
Husband Not Compelled to Testify Against Wife D-14.0202
Hymnals and Song books.. W-1.4006
Illness, Care in W-6.3005
Immigrant Congregations, Mission Needs of,
 and Non-geographic Presbyteries..................................... G-3.0403
Immigrant Pastors G-2.0505
Inclusive Language W-1.2006
Inclusiveness.. F-1.0403
 G-3.0103
In worship:
General W-1.4003
 W-3.1003
Lord's Supper and W-2.4006
Incorporation:
At same congregational meeting.. G-1.0503
Members of... G-4.0102
Power.. G-4.0101
Trustees of G-4.0102
Infants: Membership in Church G-1.04
On membership roll if baptized G-1.0401
 G-3.0204
Initiating Appeal in Disciplinary Case.................................. D-13.0102 a
 D-13.0106 a
Inquirer, Preparation for Ministry:
Authorized to administer Lord's Supper if ordained G-2.0606
Covenant relationship with presbytery G-2.0601
Transfer of.. G-2.0608
Withdrawal from G-2.0609
Enrollment of... G-2.0602
Exemption from some educational requirements................ G-2.0610
Oversight G-2.0605
Purpose of.. G-2.0603
Removal from roll.. G-2.0609

Inquirer, Preparation for Ministry: (*continued*)
    Service to the Church.. G-2.0606
    Session responsibility G-2.0605
    Transfer to another presbytery..................................... G-2.0608
Inquiry by Council .... D-10.0102 b
Installation (See also "Call"):
    Service G-2.0805
    Service for the Lord's Day and...................................... W-3.3101 (8)
                                                 W-3.3503 (b)
                                                 W-4.4000
Installation of Ruling Elders or Deacons W-4.4000
Installation of Teaching Elder:
    Procedure.. W-4.4006
    Questions asked candidate.. W-4.4003
    Questions asked congregation .... W-4.4006 b
    Questions asked teaching elder W-4.4003
Insurance, Property and Liability....................................... G-3.0112
Interim Pastor, Associate: (See "Temporary Pastoral
    Relationships")
Interpreting the Constitution G-6.02
    Authoritative interpretation... G-6.02
Investigating Committee:
    Accusation from other council...................................... D-10.0104
    Appointment of, between meetings of council .... D-10.0201 b
    Conference, term defined.. D-10.0203 a, b
    Expenses .... D-10.0201 c
    Inquiry by D-10.0202
    Membership .... D-10.0201 a
    Petition for review D-10.0303
    Procedures provided to person making accusation .... D-10.0202 b
    Prosecuting Committee.. D-10.0202 j
    Referral of allegations to.. D-10.0103
    Responsibilities of D-10.0202
    Rights of Accused... D-10.0203 c
    When request for vindication.. D-9.0101 a
Irregularity, Defined D-2.0202
"Is to be" as a Term Defined in the.................................... Preface
Jesus Christ as Head of the Church (See also "Christ")..... F-1.02
Joint Congregational Witness G-5.05
Judgment of Court Suspended, Effect of Complaint Stayed.............. D-6.0103
Judicial Case (See also "Appeals," "Cases," "Complaint,"
    and "References"): D-6.0101
                                                   D-10.0101
    Reversed only by appeal or complaint........................... D-8.0100
Judicial Commission... G-3.0109 a
                                                   D-5.0000
Judicial Process:
    Councils for D-2.0102
    Defined D-2.0101
    Jurisdiction in D-3.0101

Judicial Process: (*continued*)

    Notifying a presbytery other than teaching elder's D-10.0105

    Types of cases.. D-2.0201

Jurisdiction in Judicial Process:

    Councils, jurisdiction of... D-3.0101 a–d

    Defined D-3.0101

    Of transferred teaching elder D-3.0104

    Over nonmember teaching elders .... D-3.0101b(2)

    Renunciation of.. G-2.0407

    When church is dissolved .... D-3.0101 d

    When jurisdiction ends D-3.0106

    When lower council fails to act D-3.0103

Jurisdiction of Council of the Church:

    Defined for each Council:

        General Assembly.. G-3.0501

        Presbytery... G-3.0301

        Session.. G-3.0201

        Synod.. G-3.0401

    Ecclesiastical Jurisdiction G-3.0102

    Limited by Constitution.. F-3.0209

    Ministerial and declarative... F-3.0107

    Of presbytery over commissioned ruling elder .... D-3.0101 b

    Of presbytery over teaching elder.. D-3.0101 b

    Of session over members.. D-3.0101 a

    Original: session and presbytery.. G-3.0303

                                                                      D-3.0101 a, b

    Over nonresident teaching elders... D-3.0101 b(2)

    Renunciation of.. G-2.0407

    When jurisdiction ends G-2.0407

                                                                      G-2.0509

                                                                      D-3.0106

Justice W-7.1001

                                                                     W-7.4002

Justice and Compassion for All Parties in Judicial Process D-1.0101

Language in Worship:

    Appropriate and authentic... W-1.2005

    Diverse... W-1.2006

    General... W-1.2001

    Inclusive... W-1.2006

    Symbolic.. W-1.2002

Laying on Hands in Ordination.. W-4.4004 b

                                                                      W-4.4005 b

                                                                      W-4.4006 c

Leadership of Worship:

    Congregational participation and.. W-3.1003

    Session's responsibility for.. W-1.4004

    Who may lead in worship W-1.4003

Lectionary:

    Church year and... W-1.3013

    Scripture readings and W-2.2003

Lent, Season of .... W-3.2002 d
Liturgical Calendar (See "Church Year")
Location of Ordination.. G-2.0702
Lord's Day:
    Description of W-1.3011
                                           W-3.2001
    Hearing of Word and celebrating Sacraments W-1.3011 (2)
    Personal use of.. W-5.5001 b
    Service for the (See "Service for the Lord's Day")
Lord's Supper:
    Administered by a teaching elder .... W-2.4012 c
    As a Sacrament W-1.3033
                                           W-2.4010
                                           W-2.4011
                                           W-3.3601
    Baptism and.. W-2.3009
                                           W-3.3608
    Bread and.. W-3.3610
                                             W-3.3614
                                           W-3.3616
    By ruling elder commissioned to particular pastoral service G-2.1001
                                           W-3.3616 e
    Chaplains and other teaching elders administering...................... W-2.4012 b
    Children and .... W-2.4011 b
    Councils and W-2.4012
                                           W-3.6102
    Creeds and W-2.2009
    Cup and.. W-3.3611
                                             W-3.3615
                                          W-3.3616
    Disciplined observance of.. W-5.5001
    Disposition of the elements.. W-3.3619
    Ecumenical gatherings and.. W-3.6205
    Elements of:
        Disposal of leftover W-3.3619
        When placed on Table W-3.3609
    Homebound receive.. W-3.3616 e
    How often observed.. W-2.4009
                                           W-2.4010
                                           W-2.4012
    Invitation and.. W-3.3612
    Jesus and.. W-2.4001
    Meanings of.. W-2.4003
                                through   W-2.4007
    Music and .... W-3.3617 (a)–(c)
    New Testament Church and.. W-2.4002
    Not a private ceremony.. W-2.4010
    Prayer of Thanksgiving.. W-3.3613
    Preaching and W-2.4008
                                           W-2.4010

Lord's Supper: (*continued*)
    Preparing for W-3.3609
    Presbytery and W-2.4012
    Public notice of W-3.3609
    Retreats/special gatherings and W-3.6204
    Sequence of W-3.3612
                               through   W-3.3618
                                         W-3.3701
                                         W-3.3702
    Services for wholeness and W-3.5404
    Services on the occasion of death and W-4.10003
    Session's responsibility for W-2.4012
                                           W-3.3616
                                           W-3.3619
    Table for W-1.3024
    Visitation of the sick and W-2.4010
    When observed W-2.4009
                                           W-2.4010
    Who is welcomed W-2.4006
    Who may receive the W-2.4011
    Who may serve the elements W-3.3616
    Wine and W-3.3611
    Words of Institution and W-3.3612
                                           W-3.3615
Loss, Care in Times of W-6.3007
Lower Council, When Fails to Act in Judicial Process D-3.0101
Manual of Administrative Operations G-3.0106
Marks of the Church F-1.0302
Marriage:
    Civil marriage, recognition of W-4.9006
    Decorations at weddings W-4.9005
    Former teaching elder officiating at G-2.0905
    General W-4.9000
    If unwise, teaching elder may confer with session .... W-4.9002 b
    Lord's Supper at weddings W-4.9003
    Music at weddings W-4.9005
    Ordering of weddings W-4.9004
    Prayer and W-4.9004
    Proclamation and W-4.9004
    Service for the Lord's Day and .... W-3.3503 (a)
    Session and weddings .... W-4.9002 b
                                            W-4.9003
    Teaching Elder and weddings W-4.9002
                                           W-4.9003
    Time and place of weddings W-4.9003
Matter:
    Jesus and W-1.3032
    Mission and W-1.3040
    Old Testament and W-1.3031

Matter: (*continued*)
 Sacraments and W-1.3033
 Worship and W-1.3034
Mediation D-1.0103
Meetings:
 Of congregation (See "Congregational Meetings") G-1.05
 Of councils G-3.0105
 Of General Assembly G-3.0503
 Of presbyteries (See also "Presbytery: Meetings") G-3.0304
 Of sessions (See also "Session, Meetings") G-3.0203
 Of synods G-3.0405
Member-at-Large .... G-2.0503 b
Members, Church:
 Active members G-1.0402
                                                                                   G-1.0501
 Active members' roll G-3.0204
 Affiliate members G-1.0403
 Baptized members G-1.0401
 Baptized members' roll G-3.0204
 Certificate of transfer G-1.0303
 Delete .... G-3.0204 a
 Entrance into active membership G-1.0303
 Received by profession of faith, reaffirmation of faith,
    transfer of certificate G-1.0303
Membership:
 Categories of G-2.0503
 Of presbytery G-3.0306
Membership in Congregation:
 Active member G-1.0402
 Affiliate member G-1.0403
 Baptized member G-1.0401
 Categories of G-1.04
 Entry into membership G-1.0303
 Meaning of G-1.0301
 Ministry of G-1.0304
 Nonmember participants G-1.0404
 Other Participants G-1.0404
 Removal from .... G-3.0204 a
                                                                                   D-12.0104 b
 Renounced G-3.0204
 Restoration after removal D-12.0200
 Roll of, kept by session G-3.0201
 Welcome and Openness G-1.0302
Membership Roll, Session .... G-3.0204 a
Minimum Compensation:
 Certified Christian Educators .... G-2.1103 b
 Pastors G-3.0303
Minister of the Word and Sacrament: (See Teaching Elders)
Ministry of the Church and Worship W-6.0000
                                                                                   W-7.0000

Ministry, Preparation for:
Candidacy defined G-2.0604
Consultation and guidance... G-2.0605
Covenant relationship G-2.0601
Duties of presbytery.. G-2.0605
Duties of session... G-2.0605
Inquiry defined.. G-2.0603
Service to the Church... G-2.0606

Minutes (See also "Records" of a Council"):
Clerk of permanent judicial commission keeps
  proceedings in trial... D-7.0601
Must be kept by each council G-3.0107
Of presbytery.. G-3.0305
Of proceedings in case of trial D-7.0601
Of session G-3.0204
Of synod G-3.0406

Mission Emphasis, Services.. W-3.5601

Mission of the Church.. F-1.01
And the presbytery.. G-3.0301
And the session.. G-3.0201
And the synod.. G-3.0401
And the general assembly G-3.0501
And worship W-1.1001
                                                                                    W-1.1004
                                                                                    W-1.2006
                                                                                    W-1.3040
                                                                                    W-2.4007
                                                                                    W-2.5002
                                                                                    W-2.6000
                                                                                    W-3.3505
                                                                                    W-4.3000
                                                                                    W-4.5000
                                                                                    W-6.2003
                                                                                    W-7.0000

Mission of the Congregation... G-1.0101

Moderator:
Authority of G-3.0104
Chosen by each council G-3.0104
Commissioned ruling elder may moderate session........................... G-2.1001
Duties of in presbytery, synod, and General Assembly.................... G-3.0104
Of congregation when there is co-pastor G-3.0104
Of congregational meeting... G-1.0504
Of General Assembly G-3.0501
Of session when pastor is absent G-3.0104
Of session when there is no installed pastor G-1.0504
Ruling elder moderator of presbytery enrolled as member
  for term of ordered ministries... G-3.0301

Motion to Dismiss... D-6.0303

Music in Public Worship:
    Anthems.. W-2.2008
                                          W-3.3101 (3)
                                          W-3.3501
    Choir... W-2.1004
                                           W-3.3501
    Congregational singing... W-2.1003
                                           W-3.3501
    Hymnals and song books W-1.4006
    Hymns.. W-2.1003
                                           W-2.2008
    Lord's Supper and.. W-3.3617
                                           W-3.3618
    Marriage and... W-4.9005
    Music leaders, relation to pastor .... W-1.4005 b
    Pastor's responsibility for .... W-1.4005 a(4)
    Proclamation and W-2.2008
    Psalms... W-2.1003
                                           W-2.2002
                                           W-2.2008
    Service for the Lord's Day and................................ W-3.3101 (3)
                                           W-3.3301(b),(c)
                                           W-3.3401 (c)
                                           W-3.3501
    Service of daily prayer and W-3.4003
                                           W-3.4004
    Services on the occasion of death and W-4.10004
    Session's responsibility for..................................... W-1.4004 i
                                           W-1.4005
    Spirituals.. W-2.2008
Mutual Forbearance F-3.0105
New Church Development.. G-3.0301 b
New Evidence D-14.0500
New Immigrant Pastors... G-2.0505
New Members:
    Services for reception of members W-4.2004
    Service for the Lord's Day and reception of.............. W-3.3101 (8)
                                           W-3.3502
Nominating Process G-3.0111
    Of pastor:
        Elected by congregation G-2.0802
        Must consult the presbytery................................. G-2.0803
    Opportunity for nominations from the floor G-2.0401
Non-geographic Presbyteries G-3.0403
Nonmembers Entitled to Care of Church........................... G-1.0404
Notice of Appeal:
    Effect of.. D-8.0103
    Must be given to council within thirty days............... D-8.0201
Notice of Meetings (See "Time Limit for")
Nurture, Christian (See also "Christian Nurture") W-6.2000

Oaths Administered to Witnesses (See also "Affirmation")............... D-14.0302
Offense Defined... D-2.0203 b
Offering:
    Bread and wine .... W-2.4005 b,c
                                          W-3.3507
    Deacons may assist.. G-2.0201
    Material offerings W-1.3034
                                           W-2.5003
                                           W-3.3507
    Prayer gatherings and W-3.5302
    Response to Christ W-2.5001
    Self-offering... W-2.5000
    Service for the Lord's Day and.. W-3.3101 (6)
                                           W-3.3507
    Services for wholeness and.. W-3.5404
    Spiritual gifts W-2.5002
    Tithes W-2.5003
                                           W-3.3507
                                           W-5.5004

One-Third Vote Required to Stay Enforcement of
Action Complained Against .... D-6.0103 a
Openness:
    Called to.. F-1.04
                                           F-1.0302
                                           F-1.0404

Ordered Ministries of the Church G-2.01
Ordered Ministry:
    Adhere to essentials of Reformed faith and polity...................... G-2.0105
                                           W-4.4003 c
    Authority from Christ G-2.0101
    Election by the people F-3.0106
                                           G-2.0102
    Gift of Christ to Church... G-2.0101
    Gifts and Qualification... G-2.0104
    Inalienable right of God's people to elect.................................... G-2.0102
    Live in obedience to Scripture and conformity of confessions.... G-2.0104 b
    Ordination to the ministry of G-2.0102
    Removal from ordered ministry.. D-12.0105
    Renunciation of the jurisdiction... G-2.0407
        Effect on judicial process.. D-3.0106
    Resignation of (Ruling Elder and Deacon)................................... G-2.0405
Restoration:
    After removal.. D-12.0202
    To membership.. D-12.0203
        Form of... D-12.0203
    To ordered ministry D-12.0202
        Form of... D-12.0202
Terms of Ordered Ministry (Ruling Elder and Deacon).............. G-2.0404

Ordered Ministry, Commissioning, and Certification:
Call to G-2.0103
Gifts and Qualifications G-2.0104
Ordered Ministries G-2.0102

Ordering Worship:
Church school worship and W-3.5202
Cultural diversity and W-3.1003
Form and freedom .... W-3.1002 a
Guidance for W-3.1001
                                                                        W-3.1002 b
Marriage and W-4.9004
Ordination and W-4.4000
Other Sunday services and W-3.5103
Retreats, worship at W-3.6201
Service for the Lord's Day and W-3.3000
Services for evangelism and W-3.5502
Services of acceptance and reconciliation and ... W-4.8003
Services of welcome and reception and W-4.2000
Services on the occasion of death and W-4.10004
Special occasions and recognitions and W-4.1000
Spirit and W-3.1002

Ordination for the Teaching Elder (See "Preparation for Ministry")

Ordination of Deacons and Ruling Elders:
Dissolution of relationship G-2.0405
Election provisions G-2.0401
Examination of G-2.0402
Nominations made by representative nominating committee G-2.0401
Period of study and preparation G-2.0402
Persons elected to be instructed and examined by session G-2.0402
Questions to be answered by congregation .... W-4.4004 a
Responsibility of session G-3.0201
Term of Ordered Ministry G-2.0404

Ordination Service W-4.4000

Ordination to the Ministry G-2.0102

Ordination to the Ordered Ministry:
Act of whole church G-2.0701
Definition of G-2.0102
General W-4.4000
Order of Worship and W-4.4000–.4005c
Recognition of teaching elders of denominations G-2.0505
Service for the Lord's Day and W-3.3101 (8)
                                                                        W-3.3503 (b)

Organic Union with Other bodies, How Effected G-5.03
Organizations Within a Church Under the Session G-3.0201c
Organizing of a Congregation:
By a commission G-3.0109
By the authority of a presbytery G-1.02
Organizing covenant G-1.0201

Original Jurisdiction in Judicial Process:
Of a presbytery .... D-3.0101 b
Of a session... D-3.0101 a
Of a synod.. D-3.0101 c
Over members... D-3.0101 a
Over teaching elders .... D-3.0101 b
Presbytery assumes, in church where session cannot act............. G-3.0303 e
Other Denominations, (See "Ecumenical Commitment")
Other Sunday Services.. W-3.5101
  W-3.5400
  W-3.5500
Parity of Ruling Elders in Councils G-2.0301
  G-3.0301
  G-3.0401
  G-3.0501
Participation, Full, of Persons................................. F-1.0403
  G-2.0401
  G-3.0103
Participation in Worship:
Children and W-3.1004
Cultural diversity and W-3.1003
Session's responsibility for encouraging W-1.4004
Who may lead in worship W-1.4003
Who may participate in worship................................ W-1.4003
Parties in Cases of Process:
Accused and Presbyterian Church (U.S.A.) are original parties.. D-10.0402 b
Copies of charges... D-10.0405
Counsel, right to.. D-7.0301
  D-10.0203 c
May challenge the right of any member to sit in trial D-11.0402
May cross-examine witnesses..................................... D-14.0302
Shall be required to withdraw during deliberation............ D-11.0403
Witnesses shall be examined in presence of accused............. D-14.0304
Parties in Remedial Cases.. D-6.0201
Pastor:
And the Directory for Worship:
Accountability to presbytery.................................. W-1.4008
And choir director.. W-1.4005 b
And session... W-1.4006
Baptism, responsibility for.................................... W-2.3011
Sacrament of.. W-3.3602–.3608
Death, service on occasion of W-4.10003
Alternatives and options W-4.10005
Committal, service of W-4.10006
Form and order of service.................................... W-4.10005
Ecumenical Eucharist, participation in W-3.6205
Elements of worship.. W-2.0000

Pastor: (*continued*)
   And the Directory for Worship: (*continued*)
      Lord's Supper:
         Administered by teaching elder .... W-2.4012 c
                                                      W-3.3612–.3618
         And the Word W-2.4008
         On special occasions...................................... W-2.4010
      Marriage:
         If considered unwise..................................... W-4.9002 b
         Preparation for... W-4.9002 a
         Service... W-4.9000
      Particular responsibilities................................ W-1.4005 a
      Proclaiming the Word...................................... W-3.3401
      Service for the Lord's Day W-3.3000
      Setting an order of worship.............................. W-2.0000
   Call G-2.0803
   Compensation G-3.0303
   Congregational meeting to call................................ G-1.0502
                                                           G-1.0503
                                                           G-2.0802
   Designated G-2.0805
   Designated term.. G-2.0504a
   Dissolution of relationship:
      After Dissolution G-2.0905
      Congregational Meeting G-2.0901
      Dissolved only by presbytery G-2.0901
      May be initiated by congregation G-2.0903
      May be initiated by pastor, co-pastor or associate pastor G-2.0902
      Presbytery Action G-2.0904
   Election of (See also under "Pastor, Election of")...................... G-2.0802
   Former pastor's pastoral services................................ G-2.0905
   Has power to convene session G-3.0203
   Installed Pastoral Relationships .... G-2.0504 a
   Moderator of congregational meeting......................... G-1.0504
   Must convene session when requested by two
      members of session G-3.0203
   Nominating Committee.. G-2.0802
Pastor, Counselor, and Advisor to Teaching Elders
   and Congregations... G-3.0307
   Responsibilities.. G-3.0307
Pastor, Election of:
   Installation service.. W-4.4006
   Nominating committee to be elected G-2.0802
   Presbytery must be consulted G-2.0803
   Public notice shall be given G-1.0502
   Terms of call... G-2.0504
Pastoral Care... W-6.1003
                                                                     W-6.3000
Pastoral Counseling W-6.3003

Pastoral Relationships:
    Installed Relationships:
        Associate Pastor.. G-2.0504 a
                                                                                     G-2.0805
        Co-Pastor .... G-2.0504 a
                                                                                     G-2.0805
        Pastor... G-2.0504 a
                                                                                     G-2.0805
        Temporary .... G-2.0504 b
Peace:
    Exchange of the Sign of Peace .... W-2.6001 b
                                                                                           W-3.3301 (e)
                                                                                       W-3.3507
                                                                                        W-3.3702
                                                                                        W-4.2007
    Making peace, ministry of... W-7.4003
Pentecost, Day of... W-3.2002 g
Per Capita Funds to Pay Operating Expenses G-3.0106
Permanent Judicial Commissions:
    Closed session.. D-11.0306
    Decision of General Assembly PJC to be authoritative.............. G-3.0501 c
    Election by each council above session D-5.0101
    Filling of vacancy on D-5.0104
    General Assembly, membership of................................. D-5.0101
    Ineligibility period D-5.0105
    Lack of quorum.. D-5.0206
    List of members of last six years to be kept................... D-5.0206 b
    Meetings of.. D-5.0203
    Member, as counsel D-7.0301
    Powers of... D-5.0202
    Presbytery, membership of D-5.0101
    Principles of church government F-3.02
    Quorum of.. D-5.0204
        When cannot be reached....................................... D-5.0206
        When lack of exists... D-5.0206
            Expenses paid by council .... D-5.0206 c
    Responsibilities of D-5.0202
    Synod, membership of.. D-5.0101
    Term of membership:
        In General Assembly D-5.0102
        In presbyteries and synods.................................... D-5.0103
Personal Worship, Daily Worship and................................ W-1.3012
                                                                                        W-5.2000
Petition for Review:
    Permanent Judicial Commission.................................... D-5.0204
    Petition for review if charges not filed D-10.0303
    Scope of Review... D-10.0204
                                                                                        D-10.0303 c
    Session may not conduct... D-10.0201
Place of Ordination G-2.0702

Plea in disciplinary cases .... D-11.0402 d

Polity, Church (See "Presbyterian Polity")

Power (See "Church Power")

Prayer:

    Adoration, prayers of W-2.1002
                                   W-3.3301 (c)

    Baptism and W-3.3604

    Centrality of W-2.1001

    Confession, prayers of W-2.1002
                                     W-3.3301 (d)
                                     W-3.3506

    Content of W-2.1002

    Councils' meetings G-3.0105
                                     W-3.6103

    Daily worship and W-1.3012
                                     W-5.2001
                                     W-5.4000

    Enacted .... W-1.1005 b
                                     W-2.1005
                                     W-3.5403
                                     W-6.3011

    Gatherings W-3.5301

    Intercession, prayers of W-2.1002
                                     W-3.3506 (a)–(c)

    Lord's Day and W-1.3011 (2)

    Lord's Prayer, place in service W-3.3506

    Marriage and W-4.9004

    Meetings W-3.5301

    Music and W-2.1003
                                     W-2.1004

    Ordination and .... W-4.4001 a
                                     W-4.4004 b
                                     W-4.4005 b
                                     W-4.4006 c

    Pastor's responsibility for .... W-1.4005 a(3)

    Preparation for .... W-2.6001 c

    Response to God's initiative W-1.2001

    Service for the Lord's Day and W-3.3101 (2)
                                     W-3.3301(a)(c)(d)
                                     W-3.3401 (a), (d)
                                     W-3.3506

    Service of Daily Prayer W-3.4000

    Services for evangelism and W-3.5502

    Services for wholeness and W-3.5403

    Services of acceptance and reconciliation and W-4.8003

    Services on the occasion of death and W-4.10004

    Session's responsibility for .... W-1.4004 c
                                     W-3.5301

Prayer: (*continued*)
    Supplication, prayers of W-2.1002
                                                                   W-3.3506 (d)–(i)
    Thanksgiving, prayers of W-2.1002
                                                                   W-3.3506
Preaching:
    Baptism and W-3.3602
    Centrality of W-2.2001
                                                                    W-2.2007
    Daily worship and W-1.3012
                                                                    W-3.4002
                                                                    W-3.6102
    In ordination or installation of teaching elder .... W-4.4001 b
    Lord's Day and W-1.3011 (2)
    Lord's Supper and W-2.4007
                                                                    W-2.4010
    Pastor's responsibility and .... W-1.4005 a
                                                                    W-2.2007
    Prayer gatherings and W-3.5302
    Presbytery authorization for W-2.2007
    Service for the Lord's Day and W-3.3101 (1)
                                                                    W-3.3401
    Service on the occasion of death and W-4.10004
    Services for evangelism and W-3.5502
    Services for wholeness and W-3.5404
    Session's responsibility for W-1.4004
    Space for worship and W-1.3024
    Word of God and W-2.2007
Prehearing Proceedings in Appeal of Disciplinary Case D-13.0300
Prehearing Proceedings in Appeal of Remedial Case D-8.0300
Preliminary Procedure, Initiation of D-10.0101
Preliminary Questions:
    Appeal in disciplinary case .... D-13.0302 a
    Appeal in remedial case .... D-8.0302 a
    Remedial case .... D-6.0306 a
Preparation for Ministry as a Ruling Elder and Deacon G-2.04
                                                                               G-2.0402
Preparation for Ministry as a Teaching Elder: G-2.06
    Call G-2.0803
        Readiness for G-2.0607
    Candidacy G-2.0604
    Certified ready for a call G-3.0301
                                                                        G-2.0607
        Requirements G-2.0607
    Covenant relationship with presbytery G-2.0601
        Minimum period G-2.0602
        Transfer of G-2.0608
        Withdrawal from G-2.0609
    Examination requirements G-2.0607
    Exceptions from examination requirements G-2.0610

Preparation for Ministry as a Teaching Elder: (*continued*)
    Inquiry G-2.0603
    Ordination:
        More inclusive of persons with disabling conditions............ W-4.4004 b
                                                                          W-4.4005 b
                                                                          W-4.4006 c

        Oversight G-2.0605
        Process.. G-2.06
        Purpose of.. G-2.0601
        Questions to be answered for ordination W-4.4003
                                                                          W-4.4005

        Welcome by presbytery.. W-4.4005 c
    Removal from G-2.0609
    Service in a Covenant Relationship G-2.0606
    Session responsibility G-2.0605
    Time requirements... G-2.0602
    Transfer.. G-2.0608
Presbyterian Government, Principles of .....:............................... F-3.02
    Decision by Majority Vote F-3.0205
    Gathered in Councils F-3.0203
    General Authority of Council F-3.0209
    Governed by Presbyters... F-3.0202
    One church... F-3.0201
    Ordination by Council F-3.0207
    Review and Control.. F-3.0206
    Shared Power... F-3.0208
    Will of Christ... F-3.0204
Presbyterian Polity:
    Basic principles of F-3.02
                                                                          F-3.03
    Christ's Authority F-1.0201
    Foundation of.. F-1.01
    What it consists of F-3.04
Presbyters, Government by.. F-3.0202
Presbytery:
    Annual audit required G-3.0113
    As a body for inquirers and candidates...................................... G-2.06
    As a body for teaching elders and congregations G-3.0307
    As a council G-3.0101
        Responsibilities... G-3.0301
    Authorize ruling elders to administer or preside
        at Lord's Supper... G-3.0301 b
    Budget of G-3.0113
    Committee on representation G-3.0103
    Composition... G-3.0301
    Council of original jurisdiction for teaching elder .... D-3.0101 b
    Covenant relationship with candidate and inquirer..................... G-2.0601
    Defined G-3.0301
    Directs session to meet G-3.0203

Presbytery: (*continued*)

Dissolves pastoral relation .... G-3.0301 a
Examines candidates for ordination G-2.0701
Executives and administrative staff G-3.0110
General mission budget of G-3.0113
Has jurisdiction over transferred teaching elder or
    candidate until received D-3.0104
Incorporated G-4.01
Lord's Supper and W-2.4010
                                                              W-2.4012
May assume original jurisdiction when session cannot
    exercise authority .... G-3.0303 e
May release from Ministry as a Teaching Elder G-2.0507
Meetings G-3.0105
                                                              G-3.0304
Membership, categories of G-2.0503
Membership of presbytery G-3.0306
Minimum Size of G-3.0301
Minutes and records G-3.0107
                                                              G-3.0305
Nominating Process G-3.0111
Ordains teaching elders .... G-3.0301 c
Original jurisdiction of session .... G-3.0303 e
Pastor, Counselor, and Advisor to Teaching Elders and
    Congregations G-3.0307
Principle of participation adhered to G-3.0103
Quorum of G-3.0304
Records of G-3.0305
Relations with sessions G-3.0303
Relations with synod and General Assembly G-3.0302
Representatives of churches G-3.0301
Responsibilities of G-3.0301
                                                              W-1.4009
                                                              W-2.4010
    with inquirers and candidates G-2.0605
Ruling elder commissioned to particular pastoral services G-2.10
Ruling elder representatives G-3.0301
Special meetings G-3.0304
Staff of G-3.0110
Teaching elders received from other denominations G-2.0505
Terms of call G-2.0804
Trustees G-4.0101
Validated ministries G-2.0503
Pretrial Challenges D-10.0204
Pretrial Conference, Purpose of D-6.0310
Pretrial Procedures D-6.0301–.0310
Principles of Administration:
Accountability to council G-3.0106
Definition of G-3.0106
Manual of operations G-3.0106

Principles of Administration: (*continued*)
    Mission determines form G-3.0106
    Structure of G-3.0106

Principles of Church Order:
    Church power F-3.0107
    Corporate judgment F-3.0102
    Ecclesiastical discipline F-3.0108
    Election by the people F-3.0106
    May Differ F-3.0105
    Ordered Ministries F-3.0103
    Rights of private judgment F-3.0101
    Truth and goodness F-3.0104

Principles of Inclusiveness F-1.0403
                                                 G-3.0103

Principles of Presbyterian Government F-3.02

Private Judgment Universal and Unalienable .... F-3.0101 b

Privilege:
    Ruling Elder Commissioned to Particular Pastoral Service s G-4.0301
    Teaching Elders G-4.0301

Procedure in Trials D-8.0000

Profession of Faith, to Membership in the Church G-1.0301
                                                 W-4.2003

Property (See "Church Property")

Prosecuting Committee:
    Designated by Investigating Committee .... D-10.0202 j
    Prosecutes case .... D-10.0202 j

Protest:
    Defined .... G-3.0105 b
    May be answered by council G-3.0105
    When it may be filed G-3.0105
    When it may be recorded G-3.0105

Psalms (See also "Music in Public Worship") W-2.1003

Public Profession of Faith (See also "Profession of Faith to
    Membership in Church") W-4.2003

Questions, Constitutional W-4.4003

Quorum of:
    Congregational meeting G-1.0501
    General Assembly G-3.0503
    Permanent judicial commissions D-5.0204
    Presbytery G-3.0304
    Session G-3.0203
    Synod G-3.0405

Racial Ethnic Congregations, Meeting Mission
    Needs of, and Non-geographic Presbyteries G-3.0403

Reaffirmation of Faith:
    Baptism and W-2.3009
                                      W-3.3701
    Member received on G-1.0303
                                       W-3.3502
                                       W-4.2004
                                       W-4.2005
    Service for the Lord's Day and W-3.3502
    Services for evangelism and W-3.5504
    Special times of renewal and W-4.2006
Rebuke:
    A church censure D-12.0102
    Rebuke with supervised rehabilitation D-12.0103
Receives Ecumenical Statements of Guidance G-5.0203
Reception of Members (See under "Members, Church, Received")
Reception of New Members, Services of (See "New Members")
Recognition, Acts of:
    Service for the Lord's Day and W-3.3502
                                         W-3.3504
    Service to the community and W-4.7000
Recognizing Civil Marriage W-4.9006
Reconciliation, Ministry of W-7.4004
Record of Proceedings, Defined D-13.0303
Records of a Council (See also "Minutes"):
    Of judicial proceedings D-11.0601
                                         D-14.0303
    Ownership of G-3.0107
    Preservation of G-3.0107
    Special Records kept by session G-3.0107
References:
    Defined D-4.0101
    Duty of higher council D-4.0201
    Duty of lower council D-4.0103
    Proper subject of D-4.0102
Reformed, Always Reforming F-2.02
Reformed Church F-1.0303
Registers to Be Kept by Session .... G-3.0204 b
Rehabilitation (Supervised) D-12.0103
Relations with Other Denominations:
    Churches in correspondence G-2.0503
                                         G-5.0201
    Recognition of ordination G-2.0505
Release from Exercise of Ordered Ministry:
    Deacon G-2.0406
    Ruling elder G-2.0406
    Teaching elder G-2.0507
Remedial Cases:
    Committee of counsel D-6.0302
    Complaint defined D-6.0102

Remedial Cases: (*continued*)
Counsel D-7.0301
Decisions .... D-7.0402 c
Defined D-2.0202
Initiation, method of D-6.0101
Parties involved D-6.0201
Procedure in trial.. D-7.0000
Stay of enforcement.. D-6.0103
Removal from Relationship G-2.0609
Removal from Ordered Ministry, as Censure D-12.0101
D-12.0105

Removed Teaching Elder:
Conditions necessary for restoration.................................. D-12.0200
How restored (early restoration)... D-12.0103 h
Pulpit declared vacant... D-12.0103 e
D-12.0104 e
Removal from Ordered Ministry D-12.0105
Renunciation of Jurisdiction (a Ruling Elder, Deacon) G-2.0407
Renunciation of Jurisdiction (a Teaching Elder)................................ G-2.0509
Report Child Abuse to Authorities....................................... G-4.0302
Representation G-3.0103
Representative Government of Church................................. G-2.0102
Represented by Counsel... D-7.0301
D-11.0301
Rescinding Action of Administrative Commission G-3.0109
Residence, Change of, by Member:
May subject teaching elder to jurisdiction .... D-3.0101 b(2)
Member's responsibility G-3.0204
Session's responsibility G-3.0204
Resignation of Ruling Elder or Deacon G-2.0405
Responsibilities of Each Council:
General Assembly.. G-3.0501
Presbytery... G-3.0301
Session G-3.0201
Synod G-3.0401
Restoration:
Application for restoration to be made D-12.0201
Authority of council to restore... D-12.0103 h
Council may act when fully satisfied................................. D-12.0103 g
To membership after removal... D-12.0105 d
To ordered ministry after removal .... D-12.0203 c
Restoration of Ordained Persons Released from Exercise
of Ordered Ministry.. G-2.0406
G-2.0507
Retirement.. G-2.0503 c

Retreats, Worship at... W-3.6200

Retroactive Prosecution .... D-10.0401 a

Review (see Administrative Review)

Right to Be Represented by Counsel D-11.0301

Rights of Accuser in Disciplinary Process......................... D-10.0202 b
                D-10.0203 a

Robert's Rules of Order, Newly Revised............................ G-3.0105

Roll of Members:
 Active.. G-3.0204
 Affiliate... G-3.0204
 Baptized G-3.0204

Rolls and Registers to be Kept by Session........................ G-3.0204

Ruling Elder:
 Defined G-2.0301
 Dissolution.. G-2.0405
 Election... G-2.0401
 Instruction and examination.. G-2.0402
 Limited term election.. G-2.0404
 Lord's Supper, authorization to administer.................. W-3.3616 e(3)
  When inquirer or candidate G-2.0606
 May resign with session's consent.............................. G-2.0405
 Ordination and Installation G-2.0403
 Preparation for Ministry.. G-2.0402
 Questions in ordination... W-4.4003
 Register of, to be kept... G-3.0204 b
 Release from exercise of the ordered ministry............. G-2.0406
 Renunciation of Jurisdiction G-2.0407
              D-12.0104
 Resignation of.. G-2.0405
 Responsibilities.. G-2.0301
 Same authority as teaching elders in councils G-2.0301
 Scriptural basis.. G-2.0301
 Terms of Service.. G-2.0404

Sacraments (See also "Baptism" and "Lord's Supper"):
 Acts of commitment and recognition and..................... W- 3.3701
 As signs and seals .... W- 1.3033 (2)
              W- 3.3601
 Lord's Day and .... W- 1.3011 (2)
 Matter and.. W- 1.3033 (1)
 Service for the Lord's Day and..................................... W- 3.3600
 Session's responsibility for.. W- 1.4004 b
 Space for worship and .... W- 1.3024
 Word of God and .... W- 1.1004

Scripture:
 Baptism and .... W- 3.3602
 Basis of Presbyterian Government............................... F-1.0401
 Christ's Will .... F- 1.0203

Scripture: (*continued*)

Centrality of	W- 2.2001
Congregational reading of	W- 2.2006
	W- 3.3401 (b)
Daily worship and	W- 1.3012 (2)
	W- 5.3000
Lectionaries and	W- 2.2003
Lord's Supper and	W- 2.4007
	W- 2.4010
Pastor's responsibility to select	W- 1.4005 a(1)
	W- 2.2002
	W- 2.2005
Personal worship and	W- 2.2004
	W- 5.3000
Prayer gathering and	W- 3.5302
Preaching and	W- 2.2007
Public reading and hearing of	W- 2.2006
Range of readings	W- 2.2002
Responsive readings of	W- 2.2006
Service for the Lord's Day and	W- 3.3101 (1)
	W- 3.3301 (b)
	W- 3.3401
Service of Daily Prayer and	W- 3.4002
Services for evangelism and	W- 3.5502
Services for wholeness and	W- 3.5404
Services on the occasion of death and	W- 4.10004
Study of	W- 5.3002 b
Versions of	W- 2.2005
Seasons (See also "Church Year")	W-3.2000
Self-Offering	W-2.5000
Sentence (Judicial): Forms of	D-12.0000
Sermon (See "Preaching")	
Service Books	W-1.4006
Service for the Lord's Day:	
Baptism in	W-3.3101 (4)
	W-3.3502
	W-3.3602
through	W-3.3608
Commissioning in	W-3.3101 (8)
	W-3.3503 (c)
	W-4.3003
	W-4.4000
Installation in	W-3.3101 (8)
	W-3.3503 (b)
	W-4.4000
Lord's Supper in	W-3.3101 (5)
	W-3.3609
through	W-3.3619

Service for the Lord's Day: (*continued*)
    Marriage in .... W-3.3503 (a)
    Mission concerns in W-3.3505
    Ordination in W-3.3101 (8)
                                            W-3.3503 (b)
                                            W-4.4000
    Services on the occasion of death and W-4.10003
    Special occasions and recognition and W-4.1001
    Suggested order for W-3.3200
                                  through   W-3.3700
    Transitions in life and ministry and W-3.3101 (8)
                                            W-3.3504
    What is included W-3.3101
Service of Daily Prayer:
    Leadership and W-3.4005
    Order of W-3.4004
    Prayer and W-3.4003
    Scripture and W-3.4002
    Who may lead W-3.4005
Service of Ordination W-4.4000
Services for Evangelism W-3.5500
                                              W-7.2002
Services for Mission Emphasis W-3.5601
Services for Wholeness W-3.5400
    Lord's Supper and W-3.5404
    Ordering of W-3.5602
Services of Acceptance and Reconciliation W-4.8000
Services of Welcome and Reception:
    Baptism W-4.2001
    Enacting welcome and recognition W-4.2007
    Of other members W-4.2004
    Reaffirmation by all W-4.2005
    Renewal and fresh commitment W-4.2006
    To the Lord's Table W-4.2001
Services on the Occasion of Death:
    Committal, service of W-4.10006
    Former teaching elder officiating at G-2.0905
    General W-4.10000
    Lord's Supper and W-4.10003
    Music and W-4.10004
    Ordering of W-4.10004
    Planning for W-4.10002
    Prayer and W-4.10004
    Preaching and W-4.10004
    Rites by civic, fraternal, or military W-4.10005
    Scripture and W-4.10004
    Teaching Elder and W-4.10003
    Where should a funeral be held? W-4.10003
                                               W-4.10005

Session:

Accountability to presbytery.. W-1.4008

And the Directory for Worship:
  Accountability to presbytery.. W-1.4008
  And extraordinary baptisms... W-2.3011 a
  Approving resources for nurture.................................... W-6.2006
  Arranging for preaching W-2.2007
  Arranging for reading and preaching of the Word.............. W-2.2001
  Authorizing other Sunday services................................ W-3.5101
  Authorizing service of Daily Prayer W-3.4005
  Authorizing services for mission interpretation................. W-3.5601
  Authorizing the Lord's Supper W-2.4012
    At retreats, etc.. W-3.6204
    On certain occasions.. W-2.4010
  Baptism:
    Requests from parents not members........................... W-2.3011
                                                              W-2.3014
    Responsibilities for... W-2.3012
  Children and Worship... W-3.1004
  Counsel about manifestations of the Spirit....................... W-3.1002 b
  Counsel teaching elder on decision not to marry couple ...... W-4.9002 b
  Encouraging disciplines of personal worship W-5.1004
  Joint responsibility with pastor..................................... W-1.4006
  Lord's Supper:
    And funeral.. W-4.10003
    Disposal of elements.. W-3.3619
    Manner of distribution.. W-3.3616
    Responsibility.. W-2.4012 a
    Special Occasions... W-2.4010
    Use of wine.. W-3.3611
  Marriage W-4.9003
  Ordering worship on the Lord's Day................................ W-3.3201
  Pastor's responsibility for worship W-1.4004
                                                             W-1.4005 a
  Prayer meetings .... W-3.5301 p
  Preaching and W-2.2007
  Reception of new members W-4.2003
                                                             W-4.2004
  Responsibility for education in worship W-1.4007
  Responsibility for program of nurture W-6.2005
  Responsibility for worship... W-1.4004
  Services for evangelism.. W-3.5501
  Services for wholeness W-3.5402
  Services on the occasion of death.................................. W-4.10002

Session (*continued*)
    And the Directory for Worship: (*continued*)
        Sharing people's sense of renewal W-4.2006
        Sign of Peace:
            General .... W-2.6001 b(2)
            Sacraments and W-3.3702
            Service for the Lord's Day and .... W-3.3301 (e)
                                                W-3.3507
        Sin and Forgiveness, Care in W-6.3009
        Space for Worship:
            Arrangement of W-1.3024
            Early Church and W-1.3023
            Jesus and W-1.3022
            Old Testament and W-1.3021
            Session's responsibility for .... W-1.4004 g
        Terms in Directory .... Preface
        Welcomes new persons in ordered ministry .... W-4.4004 d
        Welcoming children to the Lord's Table W-4.2002
        Worship in councils W-3.6101
    Annual audit required G-3.0113
    Clerk of G-1.0505
    Composition of G-3.0201
    Co-pastors moderator G-3.0104
    Council of original jurisdiction for members .... D-3.0101 a
    Finance G-3.0113
                                        G-3.0205
    Joint meeting with deacons G-3.0204
    Keeps records of G-3.0204
    Lord's Supper, authority in observing .... G-3.0201 b
    May delete names from the church rolls G-3.0204
    Meeting in absence of pastor G-3.0104
    Meetings:
        General principles G-3.0105
        Special and stated G-3.0203
    Meets when called to do so by the moderator G-3.0203
    Meets when directed by presbytery G-3.0203
    Meets when requested by two ruling elders G-3.0203
    Membership roll .... G-3.0204 a
    Minutes G-3.0204
    Moderator of G-3.0104
        When church is without an installed pastor G-3.0201
        When the installed pastor is unable G-3.0201
    Pastor and associate may vote G-3.0201
    Pastor is moderator of G-3.0201
    Quorum of G-3.0203
    Reasonable notice of meetings G-3.0203
    Records G-3.0107
                                        G-3.0204

Session: (*continued*)
    Registers .... G-3.0204 b
    Relations with other councils.......................... G-3.0202
    Responsibilities of G-3.0201
        Regarding worship (See above, "Session, And
        the Directory for Worship")
        To assist those preparing for ministry................. G-2.0605
    Rolls and registers which must be kept.......................... G-3.0204
    Stated meetings at least quarterly G-3.0203
Sexual Abuse:
    Administrative leave when alleged.................... D-10.0106
    Definition.. D-10.0401 c
    Pastoral inquiry.. G-3.0109
    Time limit for charges .... D-10.0401 b
Sexual Misconduct Policy.................................... G-3.0106
Sign of Peace:
    General... W-2.6001 b(2)
    Sacraments and W-3.3702
    Service for the Lord's Day and........................ W-3.3301 (e)
                                          W-3.3507
Sin and Forgiveness, Care in W-6.3009
Space for Worship:
    Arrangements of W-1.3024
    Early Church and W-1.3023
    Jesus and... W-1.3022
    Old Testament and... W-1.3021
    Session's responsibility for .... W-1.4004 g
Special Groups, Worship of................................. W-3.5700
Special Meetings:
    Congregation G-1.0501
    General Assembly... G-3.0503
    Presbytery G-3.0304
    Session.. G-3.0203
    Synod.. G-3.0405
Special Occasions and Recognitions.................... W-4.1000
Special Services of:
    Acceptance and reconciliation W-4.8000
    Censure and restoration W-4.6000
    Commissioning for specific acts of discipleship.......... W-4.3000
    Death, on the occasion of................................ W-4.10000
    Evangelism W-3.5500
    Marriage.. W-4.9000
    Mission interpretation W-3.5600
    Ordination and installation............................. W-4.4000
    Program interpretation W-3.5600
    Recognition of service to the community W-4.7000
    Transitions in ministry................................... W-4.5000
    Welcome and reception W-4.2000
    Wholeness.. W-3.5400
Spirit (See "Holy Spirit")

Sponsors, baptismal W-2.3013
Staff:
    Fair employment practice G-3.0106
                                                         G-3.0110
    Termination of G-3.0110
Stated Clerk (See also "Clerk") G-3.0305
Stated Meetings:
    Of General Assembly G-3.0503
    Of presbytery G-3.0304
    Of session G-3.0203
    Of synod G-3.0405
Statute of Limitations (See "Time Limit for")
Stay of Enforcement D-6.0103
    Filed within forty-five days after decision or action .... D-6.0103 a, d
    How obtained .... D-6.1300 a
                                                         D-11.0801
    Temporary .... D-6.0103 c
Stewardship W-5.5004
                                                         W-5.5005
                                                         W-7.5000
Stewardship of Resources G-3.0106
    Session to challenge people regarding G-3.0201
Supervised Rehabilitation D-12.0103
Symbol:
    Baptism as W-2.3004
    New Testament and W-1.2004
    Old Testament and W-1.2003
    Use in worship W-1.2002
Symbolic language in worship W-1.2002
Synod:
    Annual audit required G-3.0113
    Committee on representation G-3.0103
    Composition G-3.0401
    Creating non-geographic presbyteries G-3.0403
    Equitable compensation G-3.0106
    Executives and administrative staff G-3.0110
    Fair employment practices G-3.0106
    General mission budget of G-3.0113
    Incorporated G-4.0101
    Meetings G-3.0405
    Meets when directed by General Assembly G-3.0405
    Membership of G-3.0401
    Minutes and records G-3.0107
                                                         G-3.0406
    No fewer than three presbyteries G-3.0401
    Nominating process G-3.0111
    Presbytery participation G-3.0401
    Quorum of G-3.0405
    Relationship with General Assembly G-3.0402
    Relationship with presbyteries G-3.0403

Synod: (*continued*)

Reduced Function G-3.0404

Responsibilities G-3.0401

Special meetings G-3.0405

Trustees... G-4.0101

Teachers to Be Sound in the Faith F-3.0105

Teaching Elder, Censured:

Membership placed in church when removed from ordered

ministry .... D-12.0105 d

Procedure when two citations disregarded................................. D-11.0202

Restoration after censure of temporary exclusion...................... D-12.0200

Teaching Elder of Other Denominations, Transfer of......................... G-2.0505

Teaching Elders:

Administers the Lord's Supper .... W-2.4012 c

As associate pastor.. G-1.0503

G-2.0504

As chaplain G-3.0306

As co-pastor.. G-2.0805

As designated pastor G-2.0504

As pastor G-2.0504

G-2.08

As teacher G-3.0306

Baptism administered by W-2.3011

Categories G-2.0503

Calling and installing of.. G-2.08

Choir Director and .... W-1.4005 b

Confidentiality.. G-4.0301

Defined G-2.0501

Engaged in a Validated Ministry .... G-2.0503 a

Failure to Engage in.. G-2.0508

Honorably retired.. G-2.0503 c

How received from another denomination................................. G-2.0505

Installed pastoral relationships.. G-2.0504 a

Lord's Supper administered by... W-2.4012 c

Manner of life G-2.0104

Marriages and W-4.9002

W-4.9003

May be removed from ordered ministry against will

in certain circumstances D-12.0104

Member-at-large .... G-2.0503 b

Member of presbytery.. G-2.0501

G-3.0301

Membership placed in church if deposed or divested.................. D-12.0105 d

New Immigrant Teaching Elders, recognize ordination of.......... G-2.0505 a

Of another Church G-2.0505

Ordinarily required to hold membership in presbytery

where work located G-3.0306

Exceptions G-3.0306

Ordination and W-4.4000

Teaching Elders: (*continued*)
Pastoral relationship.. G-2.0504
Participation in Ecumenical Lord's Supper W-3.6205
Possesses suitable gifts G-2.0104
Preaching and W-2.2007
Presbytery and G-2.0502
Presbytery council of original jurisdiction............................. D-3.0101 b
Procedure for restoration after release from ordered ministries... G-2.0507
Qualifications of G-2.0104
Release from Ministry as a Teaching Elder.............................. G-2.0507
Renunciation of Jurisdiction G-2.0509
Required to report child abuse.. G-4.0302
Responsibilities of, in worship... W-1.4005
                                                                                                                           W-1.4006
Restoration after censure of temporary exclusion....................... D-12.0103 g,h
Restoration after release from exercise of ordered ministries...... G-2.0507
Retired, honorably .... G-2.0503 c
Transitions in ministry and W-4.5000
Under jurisdiction of dismissing presbytery until received D-3.0104
Validated ministry:
    Criteria for .... G-2.0503 a
    Description .... G-2.0503 a
When serving Church outside the U.S. G-3.0306

Temperature of Records... G-3.0107

Temporary Exclusion:
A Church censure D-12.0104
Cannot vote or hold ordered ministry .... D-12.0104 e
Refrain from exercise of ordered ministry................................ D-12.0104 d

Temporary Membership in Presbytery... G-2.0506

Temporary Pastoral Relationships .... G-2.0504 b
Ordinarily not eligible to serve as the next installed positions .... G-2.0504 b

Temporary Stay of Enforcement.. D-6.0103
How obtained.. D-6.0103 a

Term of Ordered Ministry:
Advisory Committee on the Constitution G-6.02
Clerks.. G-3.0104
General Assembly Permanent Judicial Commission D-5.0102
Moderators.. G-3.0104
Ruling elders and deacons G-2.0404
Termination of:
Executive and staff G-3.0110
Stated Clerk G-3.0104
Termination of Censure and Restoration:
Application for restoration to be made D-12.0201
Authority of council to restore.. D-12.0103 h
Council may act when fully satisfied....................................... D-12.0201
When censure is rebuke.. D-12.0102
When censure is temporary exclusion .... D-12.0103 b

Terms of Call:
    Annually Reviewed G-2.0804
    Minimum requirements G-2.0804
Testimony in Remedial or Disciplinary Cases (See also "Evidence
    in Remedial or Disciplinary Cases"):
    by deposition... D-14.0304
    Defined D-14.0101
    Husband not compelled to testify against wife D-14.0202
    Kinds of D-14.0101
                                         through D-14.0402
    New, accused may ask for new trial D-14.0501
    Newly discovered D-14.0501
    One council may take testimony for another .... D-14.0304 a
    Record of D-14.0303
    Records, admissibility of, of a council
        or judicial commission D-14.0401
    Refusal to give may bring censure.. D-11.0203
    Taken by one council valid in every other council D-14.0402
    Wife not compelled to testify against husband D-14.0202
Three-Fourths Vote Required:
    Associate Pastor to be eligible to serve as the next
        installed pastor G-2.0504
    In presbytery for exceptions for extraordinary candidate G-2.0610
Time Limit for:
    Amendments to *Book of Order* received prior to meeting of
        General Assembly (120 days) .... G-6.04 a
    Challenge to findings of PJC moderator and clerk
        Appeal in disciplinary case.. D-13.0302 a
        Appeal in remedial case... D-8.0302 a
        Remedial case... D-6.0306 a
    Filing of allegations in disciplinary case.............................. D-10.0401
    Inquirer's membership in particular church (six months)............ G-2.0602
    Notice of appeal (30 days).. D-13.0201
    Notice of complaint (30 days) .... D-6.0202 a
    Special meeting of General Assembly (60 days)....................... G-3.0503
    Special meeting of session (reasonable) G-3.0203
    Stay of enforcement.. D-6.0103 a, d
    Where civil proceedings have commenced............................ D-10.0401 a
Time of Worship:
    Daily Worship... W-1.3012
                                                      W-3.2001
    General.. W-1.3010
    Lord's Day... W-1.3011
                                                      W-3.2001
                                                      W-5.5001 b
    Session's responsibility for... W-1.4004 f
Time Requirement for Inquiries and Candidates G-2.0602
Tithes (See also "Offering") W-2.5003
Transcript (See also "Verbatim Transcript") D-7.0601
                                                      D-13.0700 b

Transfer of Covenant Relationships G-2.0608
Transitions in Life and Ministry:
    Care in W-6.3010
    General W-4.5000
    Service for the Lord's Day and W-3.3101 (8)
                                      W-3.3504
                                        W-4.5002

Treasurer G-3.0205
Trials:
    Announcement of decision in disciplinary case .... D-11.0403 d
    Citation of parties and witnesses D-11.0201
                                          D-11.0202
    Conduct of D-7.0303
    Conducted by whom when remedial or disciplinary cases D-7.0101
                                          D-11.0101
    Counsel D-11.0301
    Decision in remedial case .... D-7.0402 c
    Disqualification and challenges .... D-7.0401 (b)(1)
    Enforcement D-11.0801
    Materials, circulation of, ordinarily not permitted D-11.0303
    Questions of procedure decided by moderator .... D-7.0303 a
    Record of proceedings D-11.0601
    Stated clerk, duty of D-11.0701
    Voting .... D-11.0403 a, b
    When decision becomes final judgment .... D-11.0403 a
    Witnesses, citation of D-11.0201
                                          D-11.0202 a, b
    Witnesses, refusal of to testify D-11.0203
Trust and Love G-1.0102
Trustees:
    Of General Assembly G-4.0101
    Of incorporated church G-4.0101
    Of local congregation G-1.0503
                                          G-4.0101
        Supervised by session G-3.0201
    Of presbytery G-4.0101
    Of synod G-4.0101
    Of unincorporated church G-4.0101
Truth:
    And duty F-3.0104
    And goodness F-3.0104

Two-Thirds Vote Required:
    Exemption of the examinations required of candidates G-2.0505
    Of presbyteries on amending confessional documents .... G-6.03 d
    Union presbytery G-5.0402
Types of Cases (See also "Cases") D-2.0200
Union Churches:(See "Joint Congregational Witness")

Union, Full Organic G-5.03
Union Presbyteries G-5.04
   Constitutional Authority G-5.0401
   Plan of union.. G-5.0402
Unity in Diversity F-1.0403
Unity of Church:
   Defined F-1.0302
   Ecumenical statements..................................... G-5.0101
Validated Ministries.. G-2.0503 a
                                                      G-3.0306
   Of Ruling Elder Commissioned to Particular Pastoral Service.... G-2.1001
Verbatim Recording... D-11.0601 a
   Required in trial unless waived by parties D-14.0303
Verbatim Transcript.. D-11.0601 a
   At expense of requesting party .... D-11.0601 f
Victim Impact Statement .... D-11.0403 e
Vindication, Request for... D-9.0101
   and preliminary procedure D-9.0101
Visitation of the Sick:
   General.. W-6.3005
   Lord's Supper and... W-2.4010
Visitors, Welcome of... W-2.6001 a(2)
Vocation, Christian W-5.6000
                                                       W-6.2003
Voluntary Acts of Repentance .... D-12.0103 d
                                                       D-12.0104 c
Voters, Qualifications in Judicial cases D-7.0402
                                                       D-11.0403
Voting, Special Provision (See "One-Third Vote,"
   "Two-Thirds Vote," "Three-Fourths Vote")
Waivers G-2.0610
Weddings (See also "Marriage") W-4.9000
Welcoming (See also "Services of Welcome and Reception").......... W-4.2000
Wholeness, Services (See also "Services for Wholeness").......... W-3.5400
Wife Not Compelled to Testify Against Husband D-14.0202
Witness to the Resurrection, Service of (See also
   "Services on the Occasion of Death") W-4.10000
Witnesses:
   Citation of.. D-11.0202
   Credibility of... D-14.0205
   Disclosed D-10.0406
   Examination of... D-14.0301
   Member of session or permanent judicial commission as D-14.0305
   Oath or affirmation to be administered..................... D-14.0302
   Refusal to testify... D-7.0204
                                                       D-11.0203

Women, Eligible to Hold Ordered Ministry G-2.0101
Word of God:
    Forms of proclamation of W-2.2008
    Jesus Christ as... W-1.1003 c
                                                W-1.2002 c
                                                  W-1.2004 b
    Lord's Day and W-1.3011 (2)
                                          through W-3.3700
    People's responsibility to hear....................................... W-2.2010
    Preaching as.. W-1.1004
                                                  W-2.2007
    Sacraments as W-1.1004
                                                  W-3.3601
    Scripture as W-1.1004
                                                  W-2.2001
Work, Worship and.. W-5.6003
Worship:
    And ministry of the Church in the world W-7.0000
    And ministry within the community of faith W-6.0000
    And personal discipleship... W-5.0000
    And work.. W-5.6003
    Artistic expressions in.. W-1.3034 (2)
    As praise W-7.7000
    Description.. W-1.1001
    Elements of... W-2.0000
    God's initiative .... W-1.1002 a
                                                  W-1.2001
    Holy Spirit and... W-1.1002 a
    Jesus Christ and W-1.1003
                                                  W-1.1004
    Language of... W-1.2000
    Ordering of W-3.0000
    Pastor's responsibilities W-1.4005
    Responsibility for, in session... W-1.4000
    Selection of hymns .... W-1.4005 a, b
    Session's responsibilities... W-1.4004
Written Decision of Permanent Judicial Commission:
    Disciplinary .... D-11.0403 c
                                                  D-13.0405 c
    Remedial.. D-7.0402 c
                                                  D-8.0404 c